IMAGES
of America

WOOD COUNTY

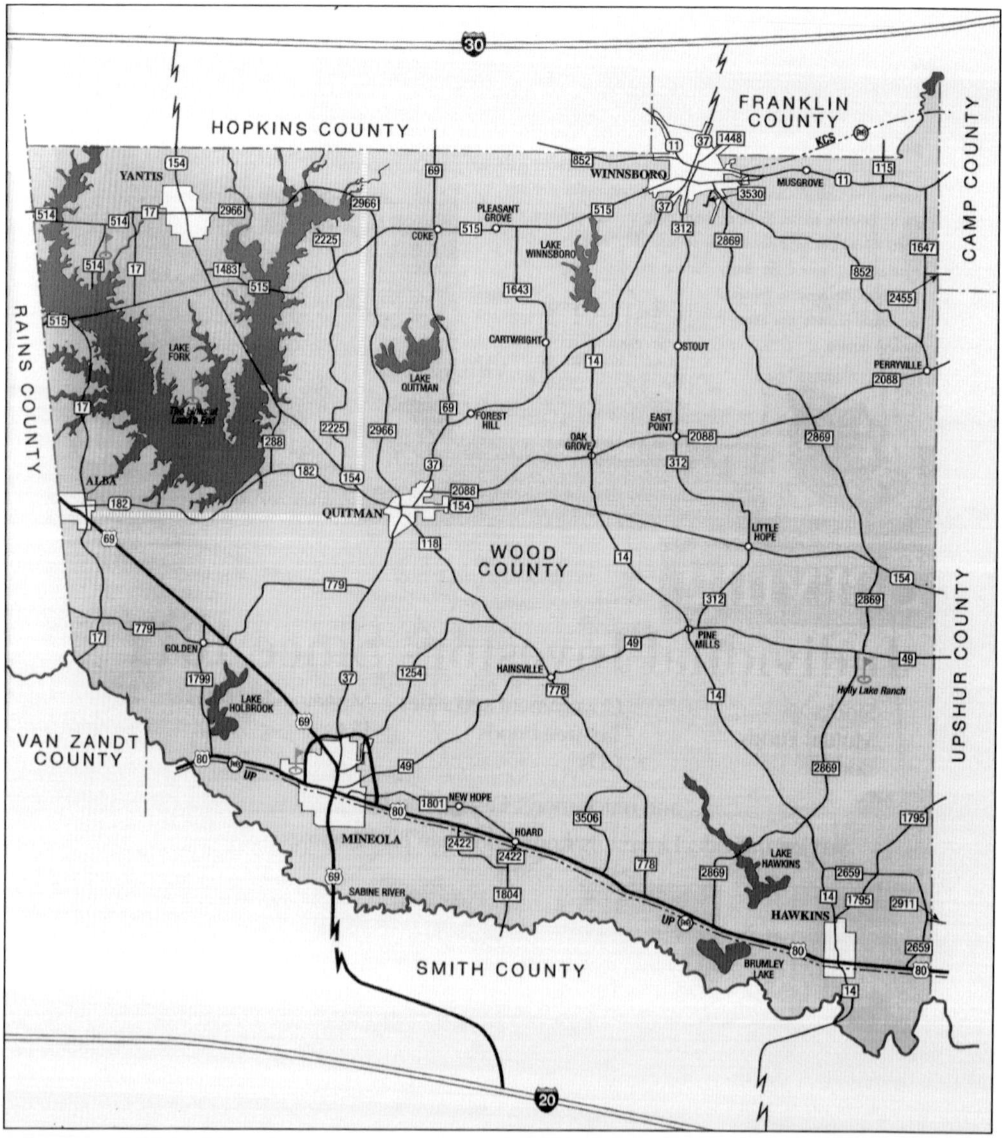

HOPKINS COUNTY
FRANKLIN COUNTY
CAMP COUNTY
RAINS COUNTY
WOOD COUNTY
UPSHUR COUNTY
VAN ZANDT COUNTY
SMITH COUNTY
YANTIS
WINNSBORO
MUSGROVE
PLEASANT GROVE
COKE
LAKE WINNSBORO
LAKE FORK
CARTWRIGHT
STOUT
PERRYVILLE
LAKE QUITMAN
FOREST HILL
OAK GROVE
EAST POINT
ALBA
QUITMAN
LITTLE HOPE
GOLDEN
PINE MILLS
HAINSVILLE
LAKE HOLBROOK
Holly Lake Ranch
NEW HOPE
MINEOLA
HOARD
LAKE HAWKINS
SABINE RIVER
HAWKINS
BRUMLEY LAKE
KCS
UP

IMAGES
of America

WOOD COUNTY

Wood County Historical Commission

ARCADIA
PUBLISHING

ISBN 978-0-7385-2936-3

Published by Arcadia Publishing
Charleston, South Carolina

Printed in the United States of America

Library of Congress Catalog Card Number: 2004110476

For all general information contact Arcadia Publishing at:
Telephone 843-853-2070
Fax 843-853-0044
E-mail sales@arcadiapublishing.com
For customer service and orders:
Toll-Free 1-888-313-2665

Visit us on the Internet at www.arcadiapublishing.com

Contents

ACKNOWLEDGMENTS

The book committee and all members of the Wood County Historical Commission extend their heartfelt gratitude and appreciation to all who lent their assistance, expertise, and resources to this project.

The two people we must thank first are Dr. Steve Davis and Rosemary Bell. Without their encouragement, expertise, and willingness to give so unselfishly of their time and talents, this book would not have become a reality. Rosemary Bell used her tremendous talent and knowledge to scan all of the images for the book. Also, we must thank Lee Shafer of the Mineola Memorial Library for all of her help and for suggesting the idea to do this book.

For the pictures and images we must thank the following: the East Texas Genealogical Society; the Mineola Historical Museum; the *Wood County Democrat*; the Sesquicentennial Committee of the City of Winnsboro; the Alba Ladies Club; Harold Simmons; the Mineola Centennial Corporation; Mrs. David H. Lott; Ulna McWhorter; Patrick Bogan; the Tom Pegues family; the Tom Flournoy family; Susan Merritt; Norma Wilkinson; Accurate Quick Printing of Longview; the Wisener family; M-Prints; REA Cooperative; Peoples Telephone Cooperative; the Sabine River Authority; the Links Country Club; Don and Linda Rhodes; Larry Barlow; Peggy Bray Mallory; Gene Bright; Lillian Pegues Speights; the Quitman Public Library; Texas Department of Parks and Wildlife; Diane Brown; Marlin C. Ingram; Gayle Ingram; Cargie Lyons; Imogene Glenn; Betty Miller Bozeman; Lessie Powell; Nell Freeman; Lynd Melvin; Joseph Spaits; Sam Curry; Gary Yamamoto; Virginia McCalla; Carroll R. Dawson; Saundra Burge; Gene Mallory; the City of Mineola; Gwendolyn Boyd Hill; Jewel McCalla; and Stanley Richard.

INTRODUCTION

Wood County, located in northeastern Texas, approximately 90 miles east of Dallas and 100 miles west of Shreveport, Louisiana, sits between Interstates 20 and 30. The area was not extensively settled until after the end of the Texas Revolution in 1836. This East Texas timbered area was originally part of the large Nacogdoches County that was later divided by the Texas legislature. Present-day Wood County was a part of Van Zandt County until the state legislature demarked and created Wood County on February 5, 1850. Quitman, located in the central part of the county, was chosen as the county seat. Wood County is named for Georgia native George T. Wood, who was the second governor of Texas, elected in 1847, and who also served as a member of the Congress of the Republic in 1841–1842. In 1870, Rains County was created and the new county took a section of what was then western Wood County.

Wood County is comprised of 689 square miles of timberland with an elevation of 250 to 600 feet above sea level. The county has many good water sources—the Sabine River drains the southern part and forms its southern boundary; a tributary of the Sabine River, Lake Fork Creek, drains the central portion of the county. The Sabine River Authority built Lake Fork Lake near Yantis in the northwest part of the county in the 1980s and water rights are now sold to Dallas and other nearby cities. Lake Fork currently attracts thousands of people each year who are eager to fish at the "Bass Capital of the World." Many of these visitors have bought homes and become residents. Coffee Creek drains the northwestern part of the county before it empties into Lake Fork Creek. Big Sandy Creek drains the eastern part of the county and one of its tributaries, Indian Creek, drains the northeastern part.

Excavations have determined that Wood County was the home of the industrious Caddo Indians and related tribes who were peace-loving agriculturists. They planted corn, beans, and sunflowers, as well as fruit orchards. Through the years, archaeologists and farmers plowing their fields have found arrowheads, grinding stones, and pottery articles, as well as burial sites. While traveling between Natchitoches, Louisiana and San Antonio, Texas, Pedro Vial initially explored the area in 1788. Martin Varner, the first white settler, visited this area in 1824. After the Texas Revolution, in which Varner served with Sam Houston's Army, he received land grants for his service. He and his family moved to a homestead in 1841, which later became a part of Wood County. Webster, in north Wood County, was the county's first real community; it was established in 1845.

From its beginning, Wood County has been a rural area inhabited primarily by people who originated in the southern part of the United States. These settlers brought slaves with them and reestablished the cotton plantation society they had enjoyed previously. Wood County remained agricultural and rural from 1870 to 1920, with an increase in the number of farms that had corn and cotton as their main crops.

Jay Gould's Texas & Pacific Railway line was responsible for much of the initial growth and development in Wood County. In 1873, a small rural community called Sodom, later renamed Mineola, sprang to life and began to prosper with the arrival of this railway line, which ran through southern Wood County. The town of Hawkins also flourished on this rail line spanning from the East Coast to the West Coast. The East Line & Red River Railroad came through the small community of Winnsboro, located in northeastern Wood County, when the tracks were laid from Jefferson to Greenville in 1876.

Unfortunately, the Great Depression produced setbacks for Wood County. The population fell, the number of farms declined, and between 1935 and 1940 unemployment reached 13 percent of the workforce. However, in 1941 with the discovery of oil in the Hawkins area, an influx of people arrived and a brighter future emerged. The area was producing 25 million barrels of oil a year by 1948 and produced a total of nearly one billion barrels by 1984.

As with the railroad, the automobile also transformed Wood County. Paved roads increased from 49 miles in 1922 to 1,155 miles in 1982, and there were 24,719 registered vehicles. These figures have all risen significantly in the last 5 to 10 years. Much of this rapid increase in Wood County's population is attributable to two factors: more people wanting a relaxed and small-town atmosphere for their retirement, and many people moving to the county to provide their children with a more stable school environment.

With the decline of agriculture, Wood County has moved away from its dependence on timber and agricultural products to beef and dairy cattle. Currently, manufacturing, retail trade, and service-connected businesses, in conjunction with such industries as the Ozarka Water Plant built in 2003, have expanded the workforce appreciably. At the beginning of the 21st century, Wood County is home not only to Ozarka, but also such industries as Keller's Creamery, Team Worldwide, Texas Wall Systems, oilfields, the Exxon Gas Plant in Hawkins, Trinidad-Benham, Danaplex, and Southeastern Lumber (Georgia Pacific).

Currently, Wood County offers an exceptionally high quality of life for its residents. It features many lakes for fishing and boating, beautiful natural areas such as the Mineola Nature Preserve, numerous golf courses, and private fishing and hunting clubs. A wealth of cultural activities are also available, including art leagues, quilting groups, and two working theater groups. The Select Theater in Mineola is reputed to be the oldest continuously operated movie theater in Texas. The relaxed small-town ambiance and comfortable lifestyle enjoyed by Wood County residents and visitors points to a bright and promising future for this vibrant northeast Texas area.

One

COMMUNITIES
STYLE AND ARCHITECTURE

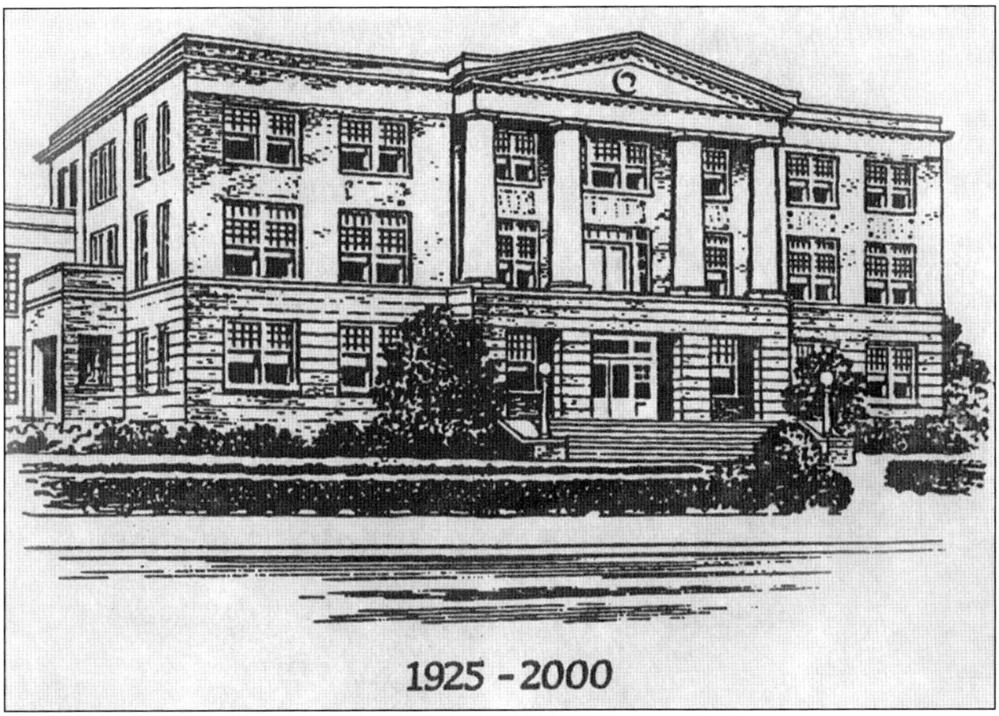

Wood County, created February 5, 1850 by an act of the Texas legislature, had been the home of the Caddo tribe for centuries. In 1841, Martin Varner was the first Anglo to reside in Wood County. Today, the courthouse, which houses the county government in Quitman, serves as the "hub" of the county. The first courthouse at this location was a two-story frame building destroyed by fire in 1878. A brick courthouse was built in 1883–1884 as a replacement but it was also destroyed by fire, in December 1924. The courthouse shown above was built in 1925 and has served the county ever since.

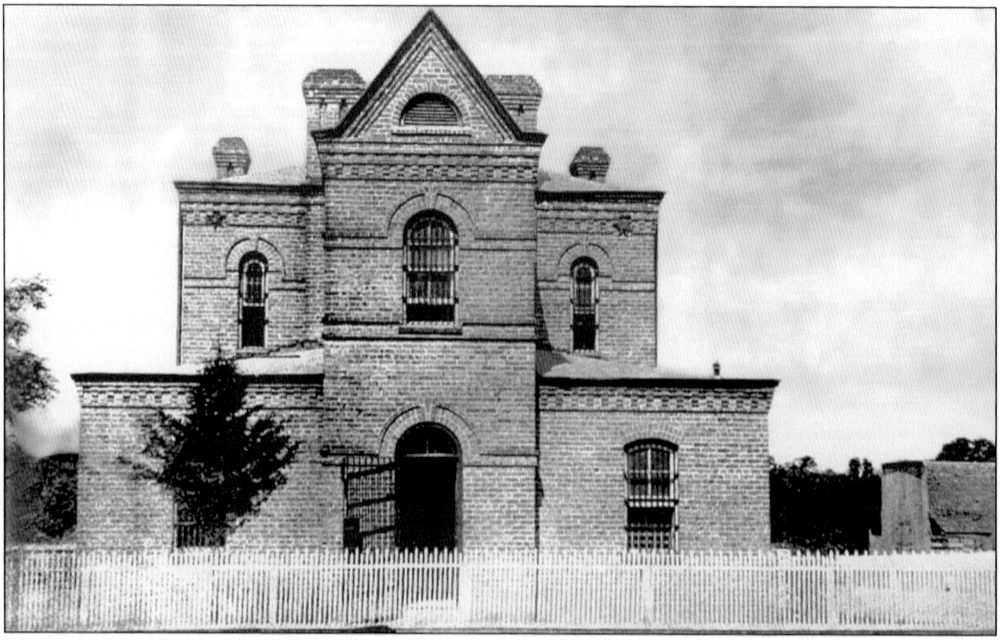

This building, located in Quitman in 1884, served as the Wood County Jail.

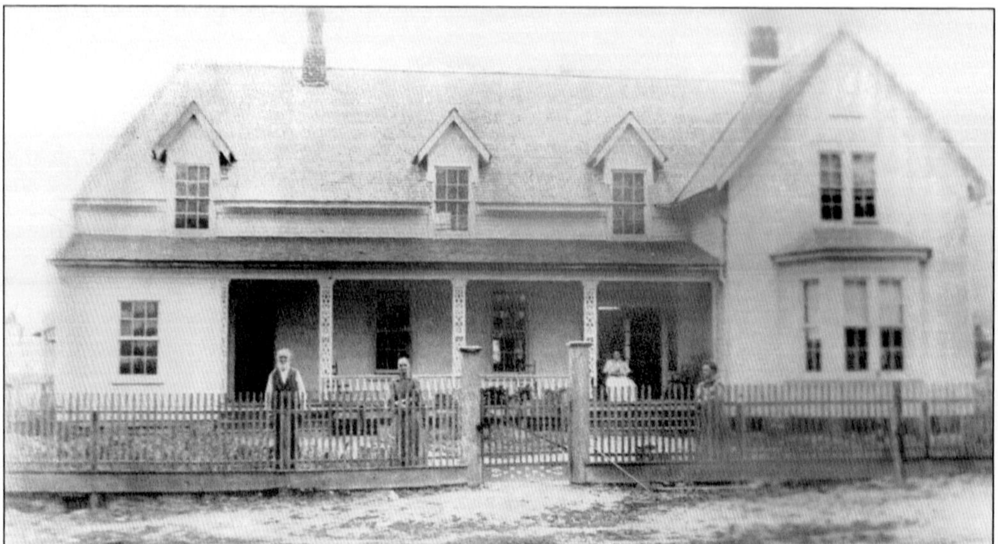

Sallie Stinson married Jim Hogg (who later became governor) in the Stinson family home pictured here. The house was in the Speer community near Pine Mills but was moved to the Governor Hogg Park in Quitman and restored.

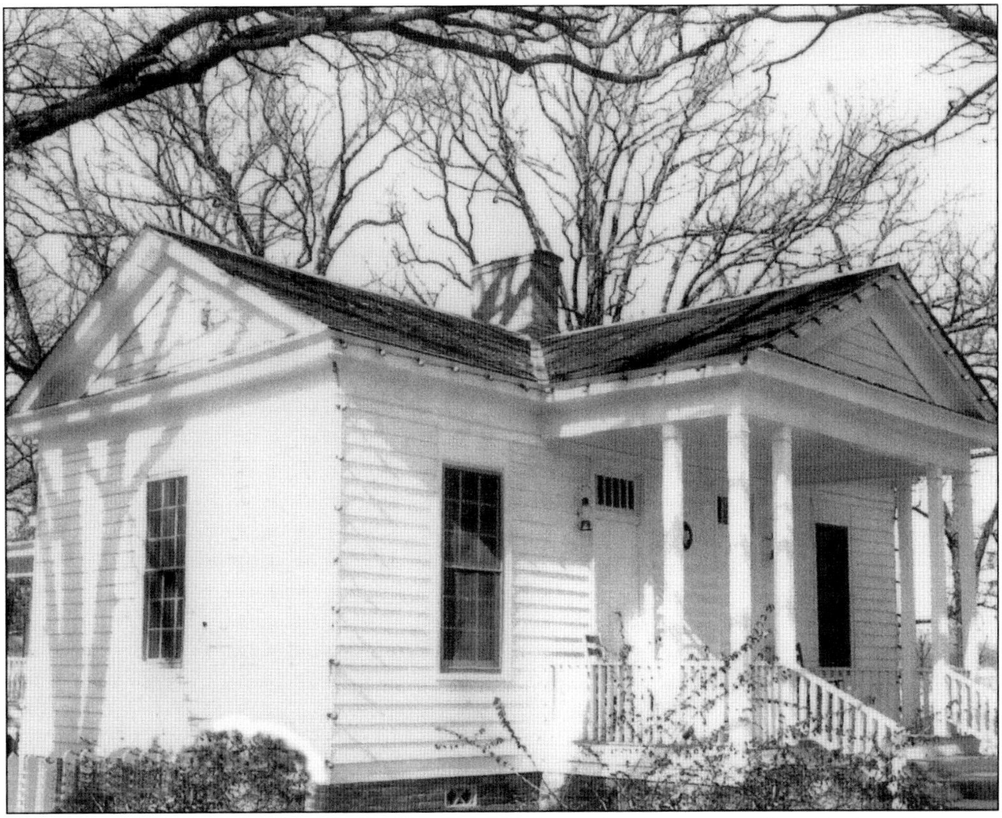

This replica of Jim and Sallie Hogg's first home is located at Governor Hogg Park in Quitman. The house was constructed of heart pine. Miss Ima Hogg, the daughter of Gov. Jim and Sallie Hogg, had the home moved to the Park in Quitman and completely restored.

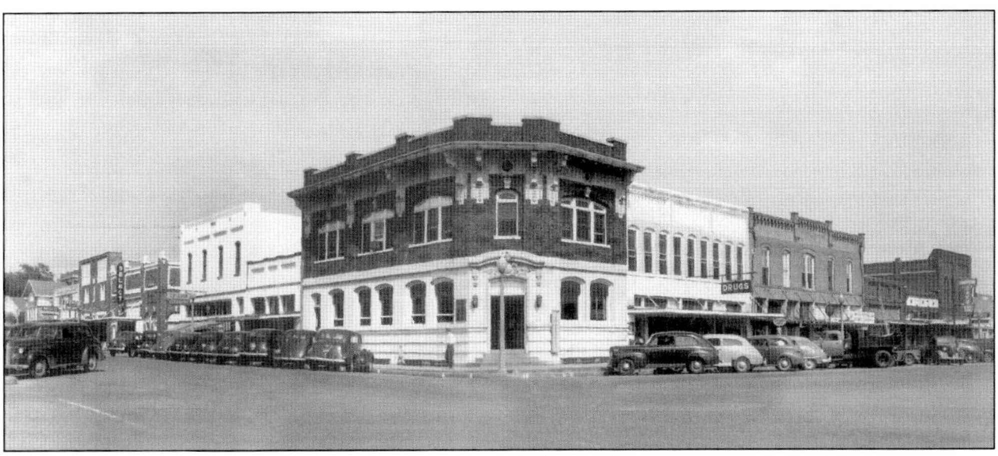

The First National Bank of Mineola constructed this Sullivanesque-style building in 1912 at the corner of Broad and North Johnson Streets. It is by far the most ornate building in Mineola. When the bank built and moved to its new location in 1965 it gave the building to the Mineola Chamber of Commerce for their offices.

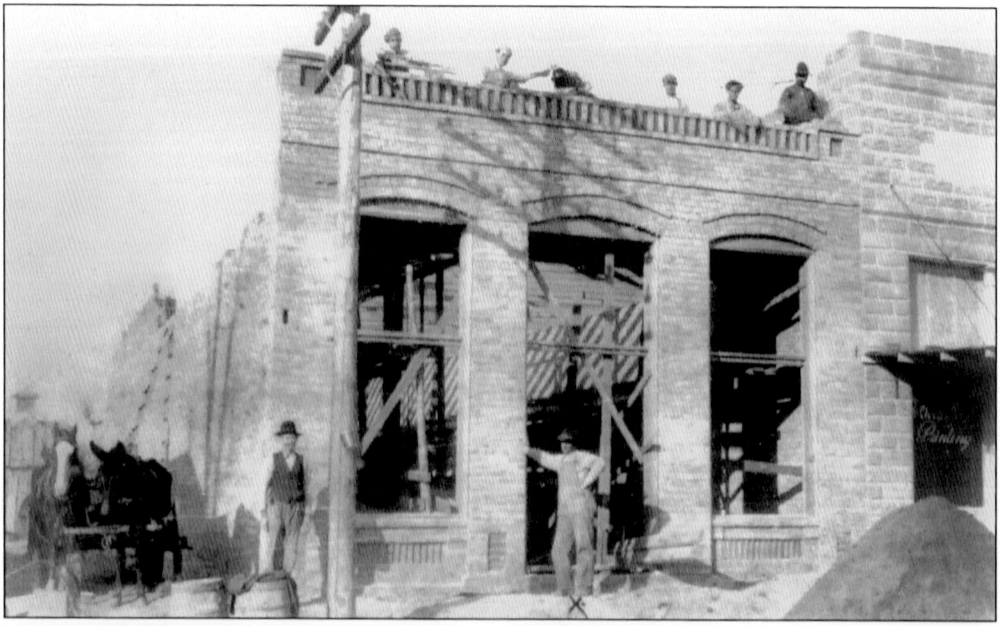

This brick building, shown under construction, is the Cathey Building in Quitman on the north side of the square. The building was the home of Cathey Grocery for many years and today is the location of Ramsey's, a clothing store.

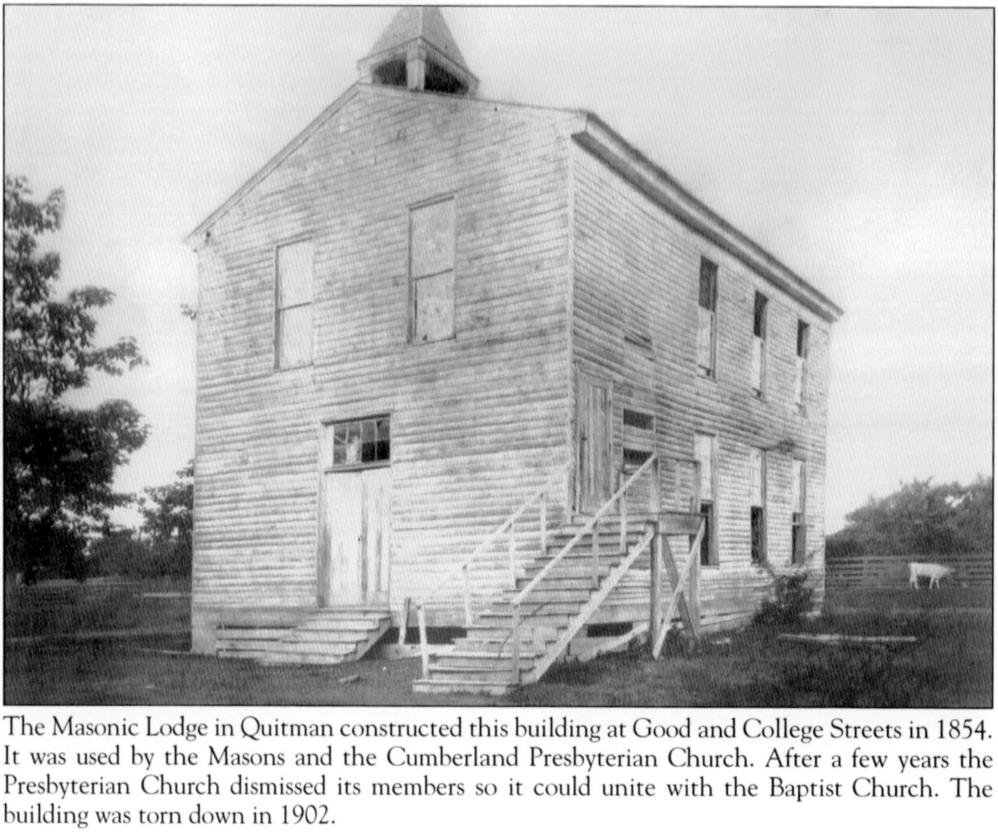

The Masonic Lodge in Quitman constructed this building at Good and College Streets in 1854. It was used by the Masons and the Cumberland Presbyterian Church. After a few years the Presbyterian Church dismissed its members so it could unite with the Baptist Church. The building was torn down in 1902.

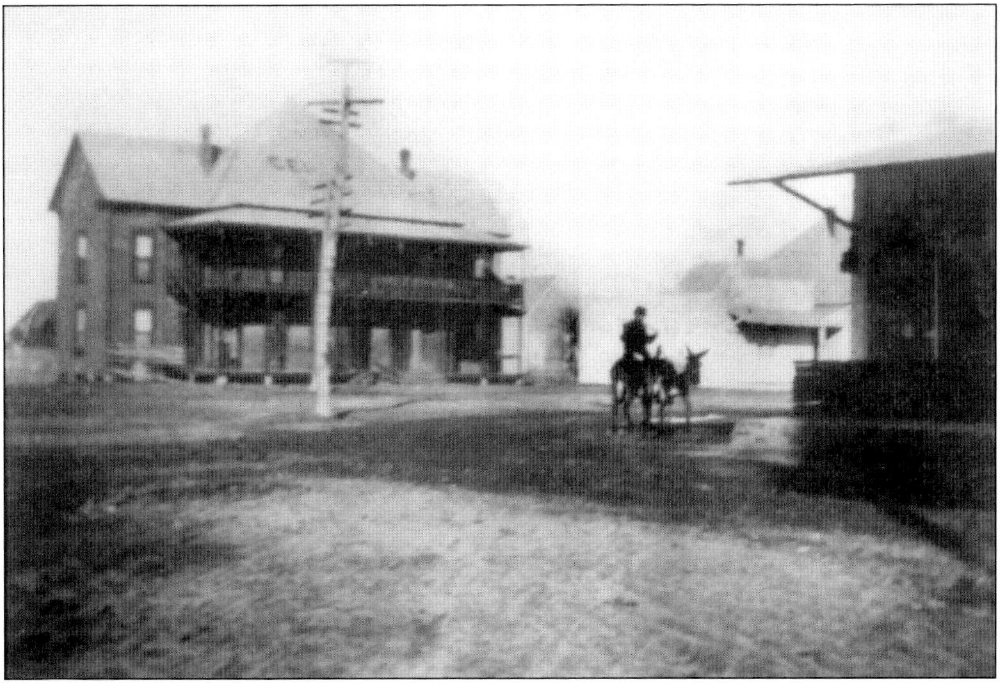

The Central Hotel in Alba was built around 1915 and later became known as the Graham Hotel. The hotel was the scene of many community events such as school banquets.

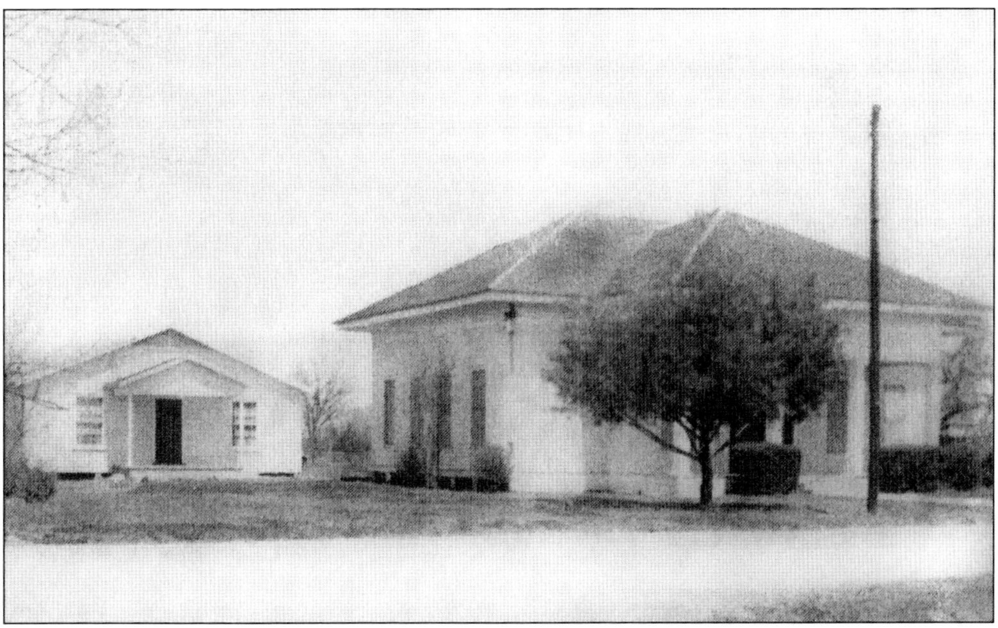

The Methodist Church in Alba was built in 1914 and is still used by the congregation today.

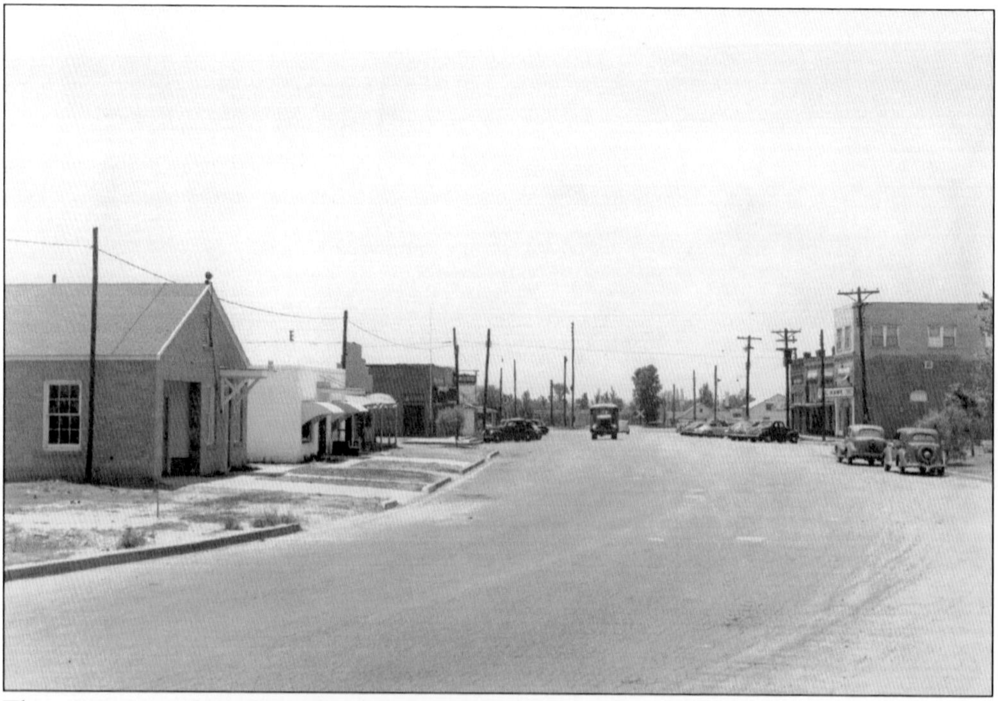

This 1941 scene of Hawkins reflects the changes brought about after the discovery of oil—new homes and business structures were being built. The two-story building on the right housed a well-equipped theater on the first floor and offices on the second floor.

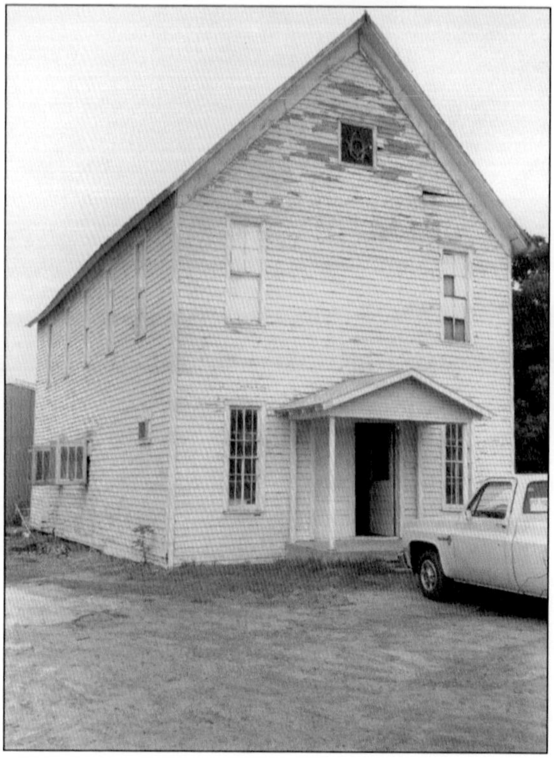

This old Lodge Building in Yantis is on Highway 154, but the builder and date of construction are unknown. In recent times, the building has been used for commercial purposes but now sits empty and is an endangered historic property.

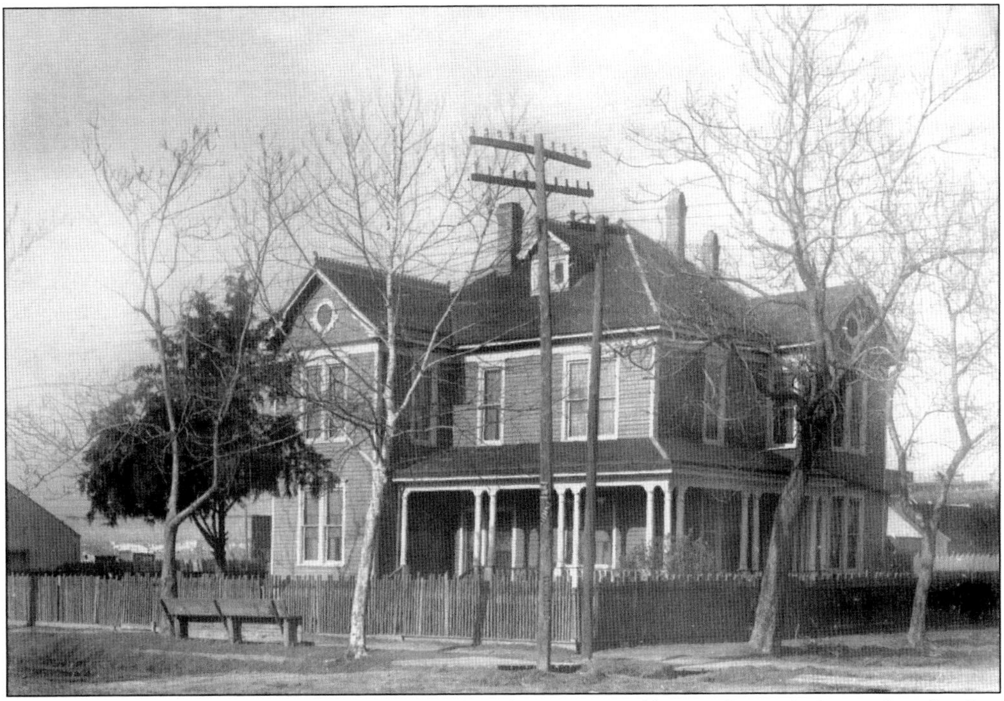

Thomas Breen came to Mineola with the railroad in 1873, and he met his wife, Lucy, shortly after his arrival. They had 12 children and lived in this turn-of-the-century house. The Breens were the first Catholic family in the area and they held services in their home. The house was located on North Pacific Street across from the U.S. Post Office Building, but is no longer standing.

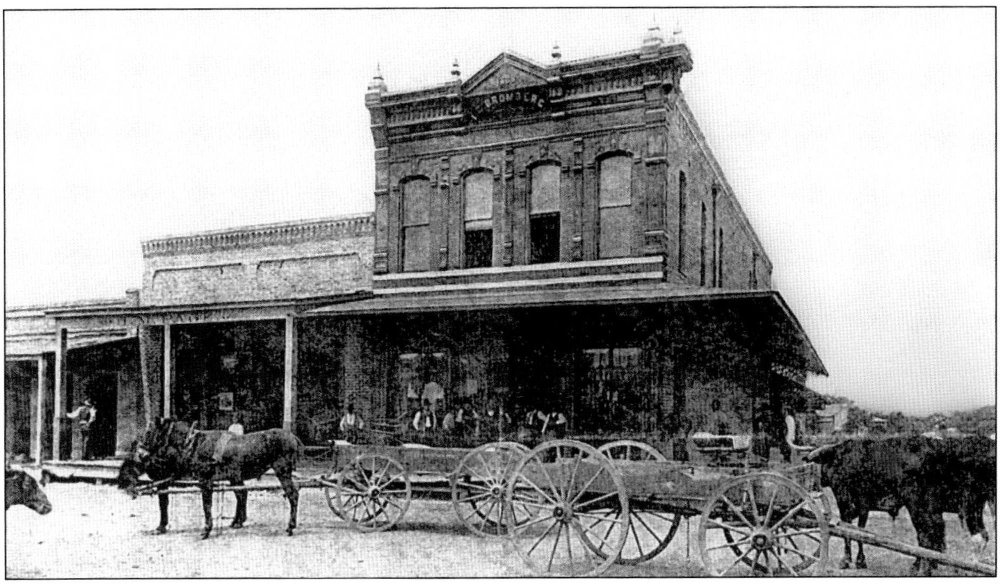

The Bromberg Building was erected in 1888 at the corner of South Johnson and West Broad Streets in downtown Mineola. Mr. Bromberg moved to this building in order to secure larger quarters for his general merchandise business. The structure has been home to numerous businesses through the years and is still occupied today.

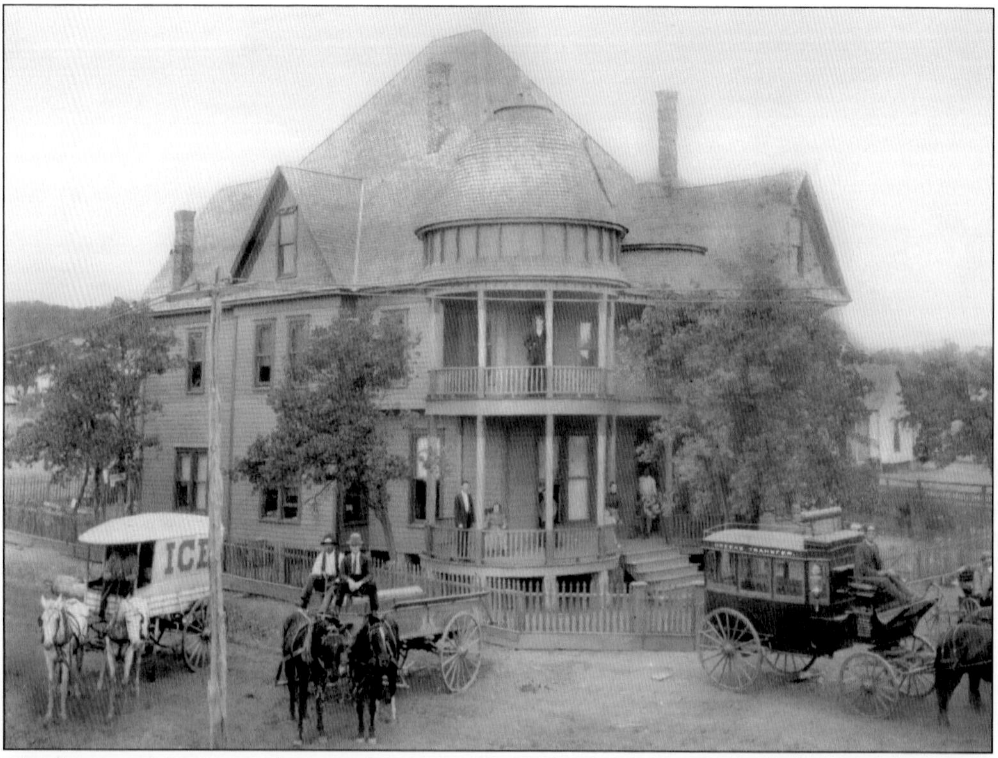

The Ferguson Hotel, seen here in the very early 1900s, was later renamed The Abney and was situated on the southwest corner of Commerce and South Johnson Streets in Mineola across from the railroad tracks.

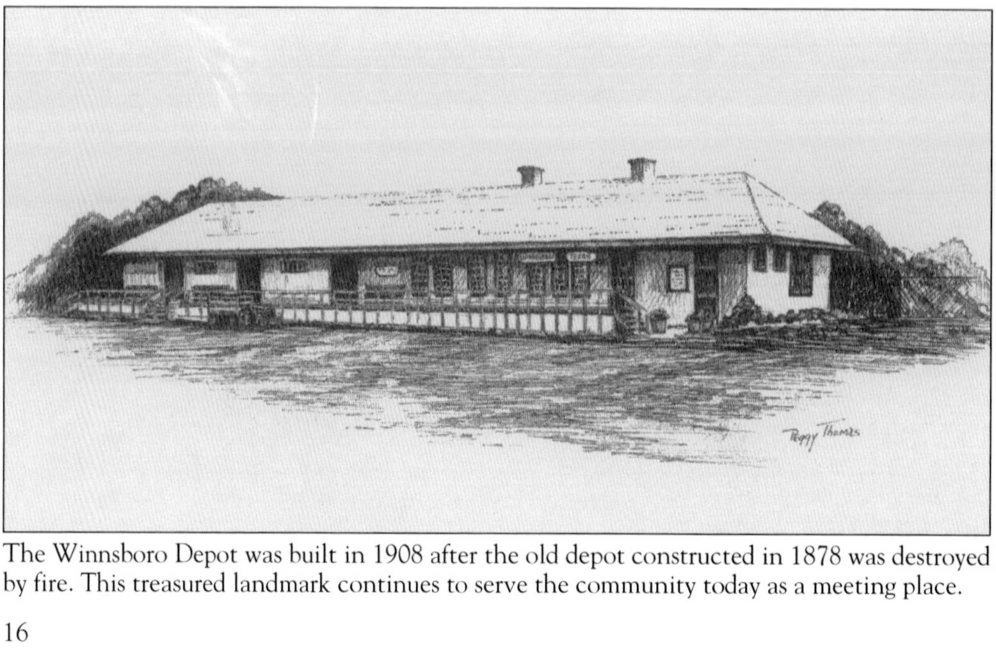

The Winnsboro Depot was built in 1908 after the old depot constructed in 1878 was destroyed by fire. This treasured landmark continues to serve the community today as a meeting place.

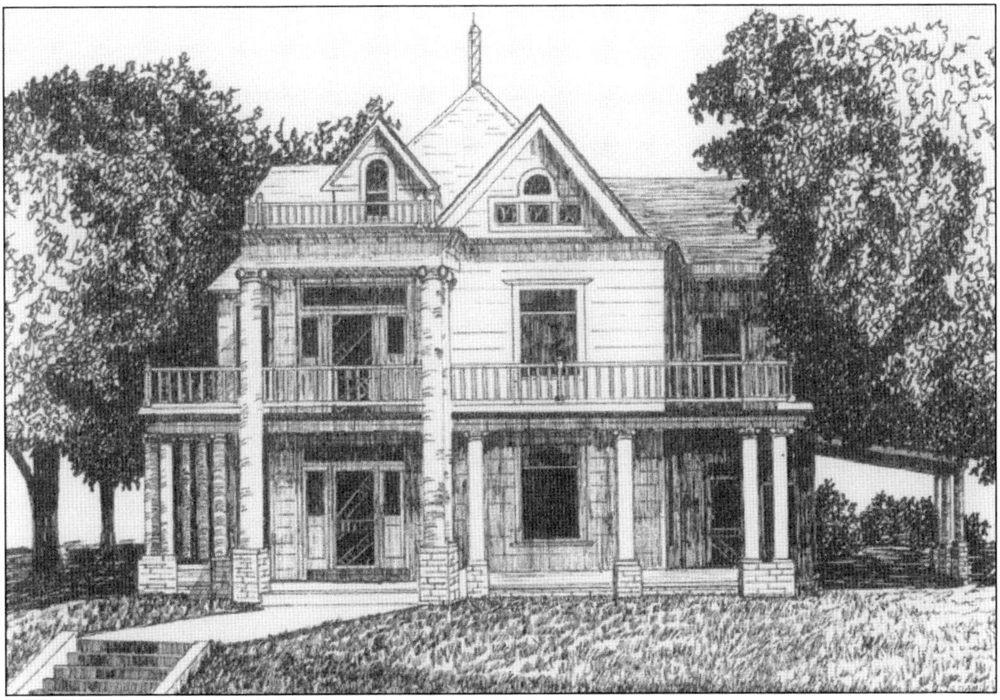

The Cain home was built in 1904 by Charlie Morris, a local banker, as one of his residences. The house still stands at the corner of West Broadway and Peach Streets in Winnsboro.

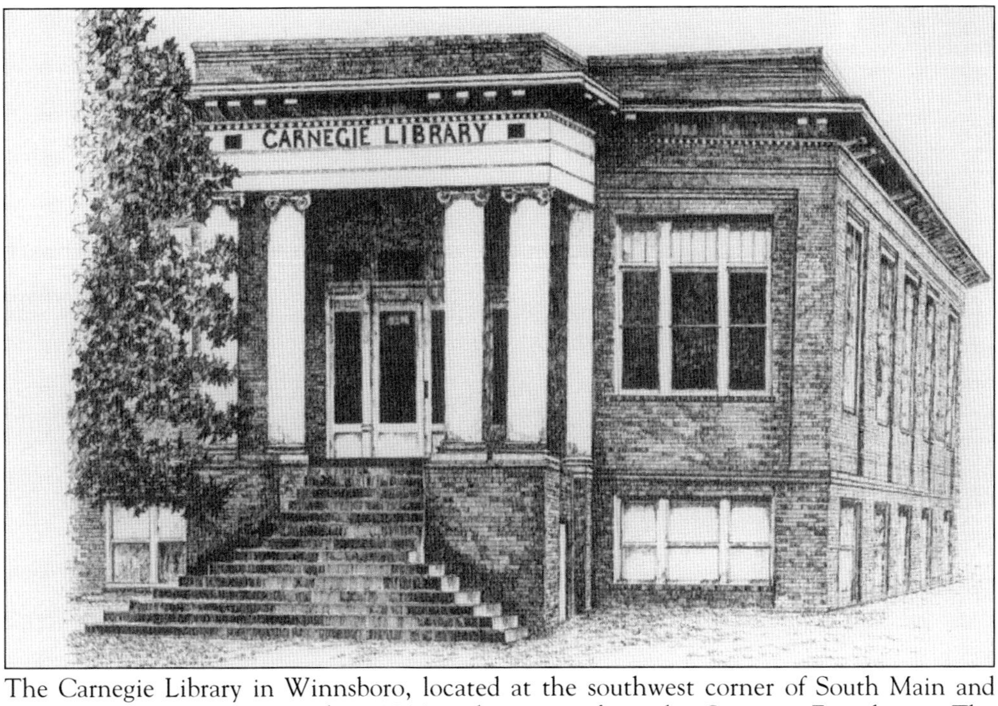

The Carnegie Library in Winnsboro, located at the southwest corner of South Main and Carnegie Streets, was erected in 1909 with a grant from the Carnegie Foundation. The basement was used as a community center for local groups. The space was also used as an opera house. The building was finally torn down in 1967.

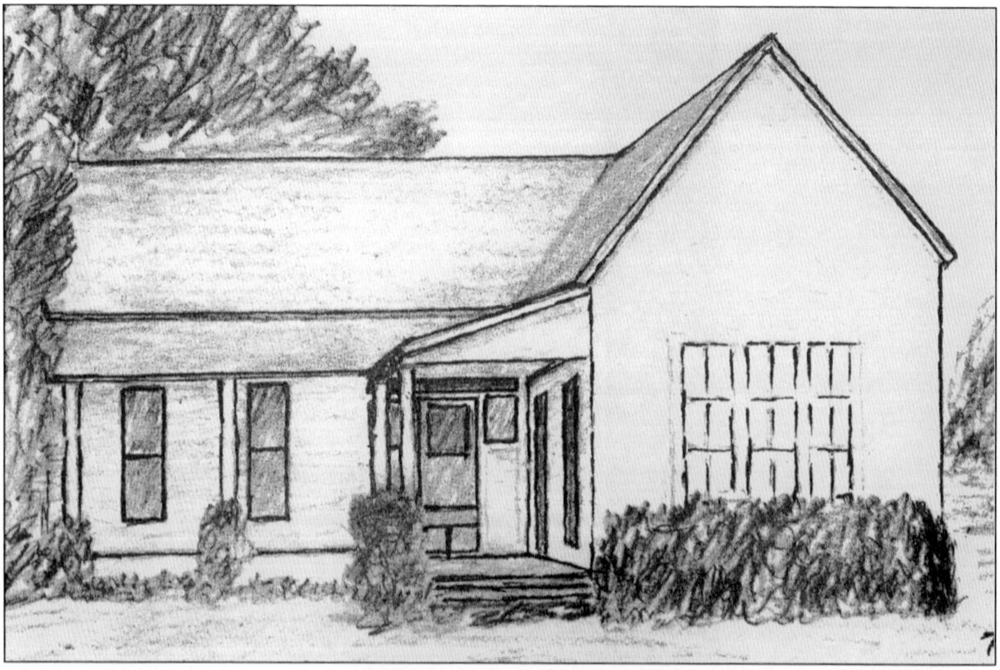

The Lindley home was constructed about 1902 in Hainesville by the George Lindley family. Later it became the home of Dick and Mary Lindley and their eight children. The home is no longer standing.

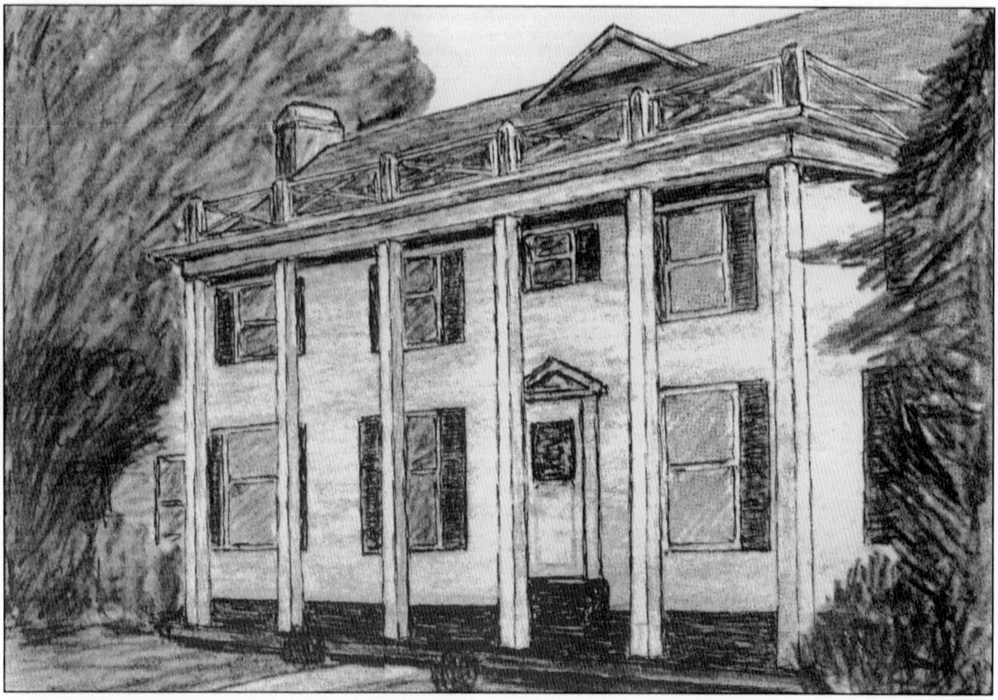

Originally the home of Dr. J.M. Puckett, this structure was remodeled by his son James Julius into a lovely Southern colonial home. After the death of Sue, James's widow, the family sold the home. The house is located at the intersection of FM 49 and FM 778 in Hainesville.

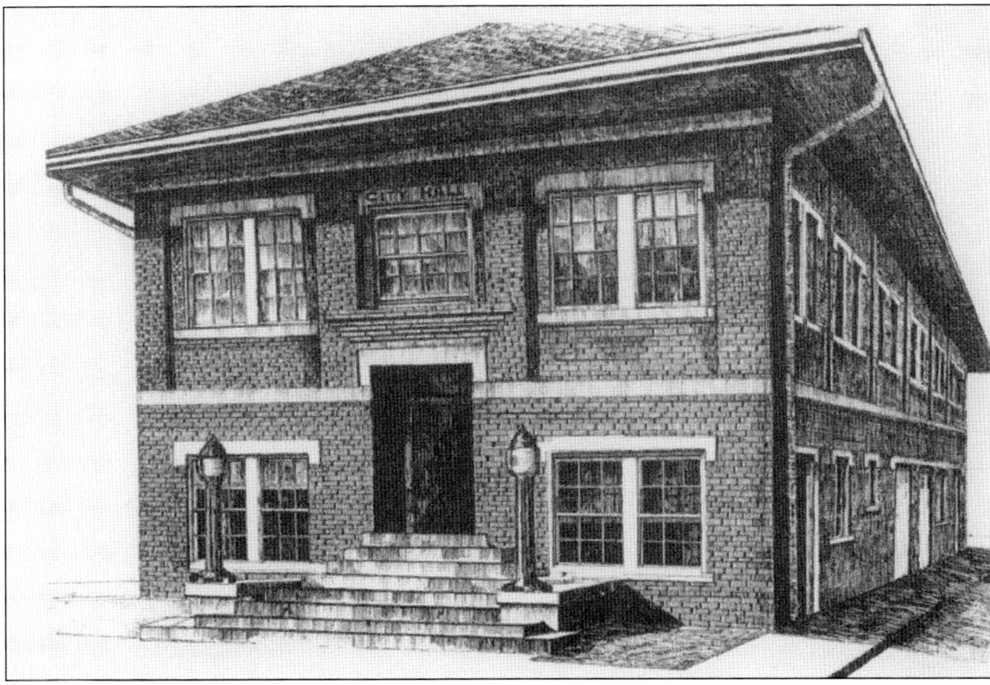

Winnsboro City Hall was constructed in 1923 to house the city offices, the fire department, and the jail. Elections were also held on the second floor of the building. The city now has a new city hall, and this building is home to the Winnsboro branch of the Franklin National Bank.

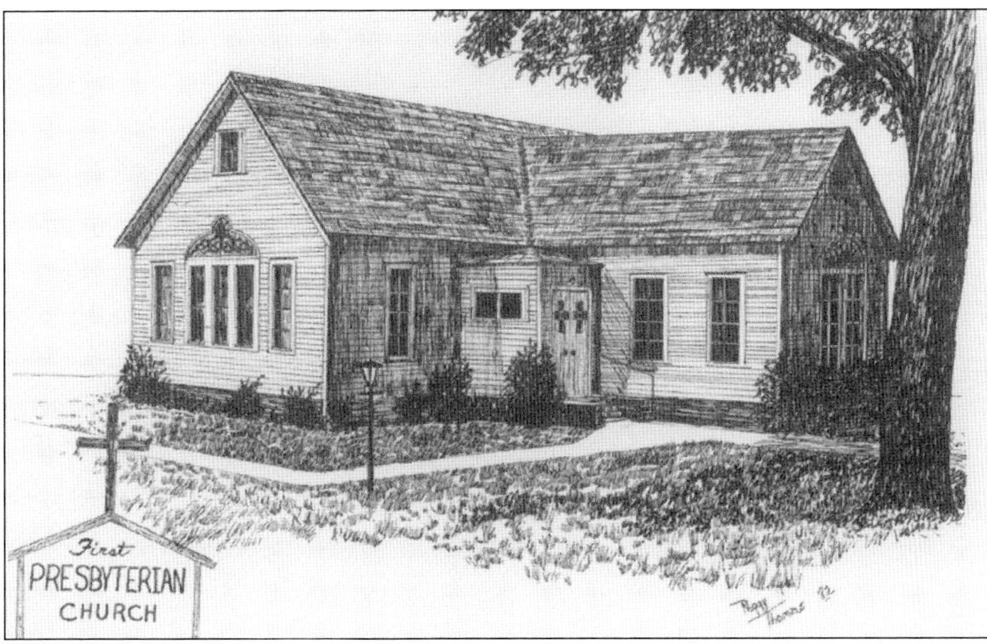

The First Presbyterian Church was organized in 187; however, in 1907 the church relocated to a frame schoolhouse they had moved to the corner of Myrtle and South Chestnut Streets in Winnsboro. That building, pictured here after being remodeled, is still used by the congregation today.

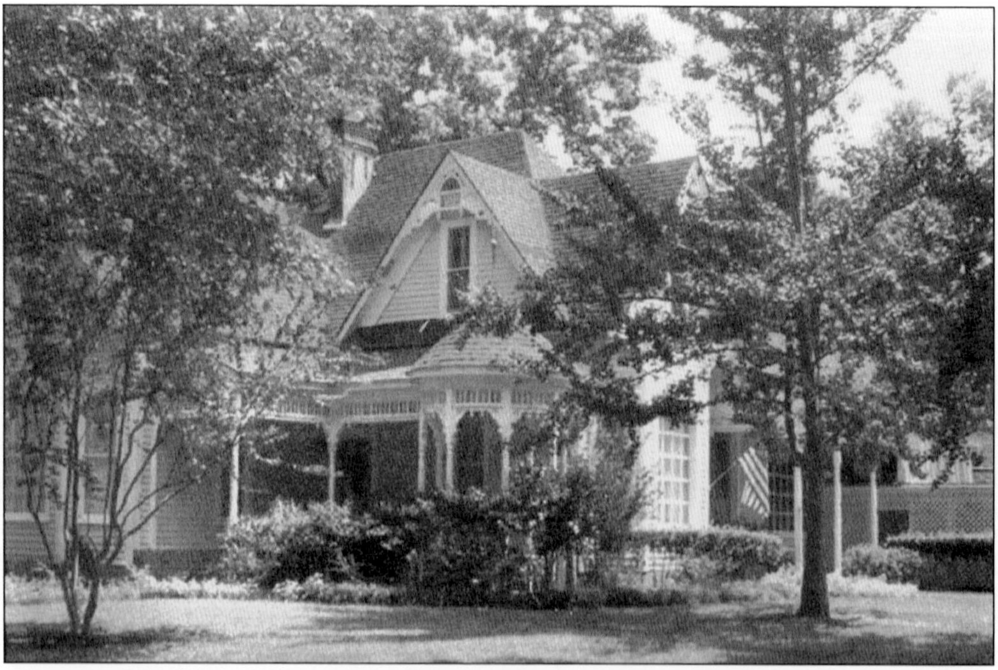

This gingerbread-trimmed Victorian home was built by Bynum and Florence Moore at the corner of Cedar and Beech Streets in Winnsboro in 1898. The home is still standing and is now used as a bed and breakfast.

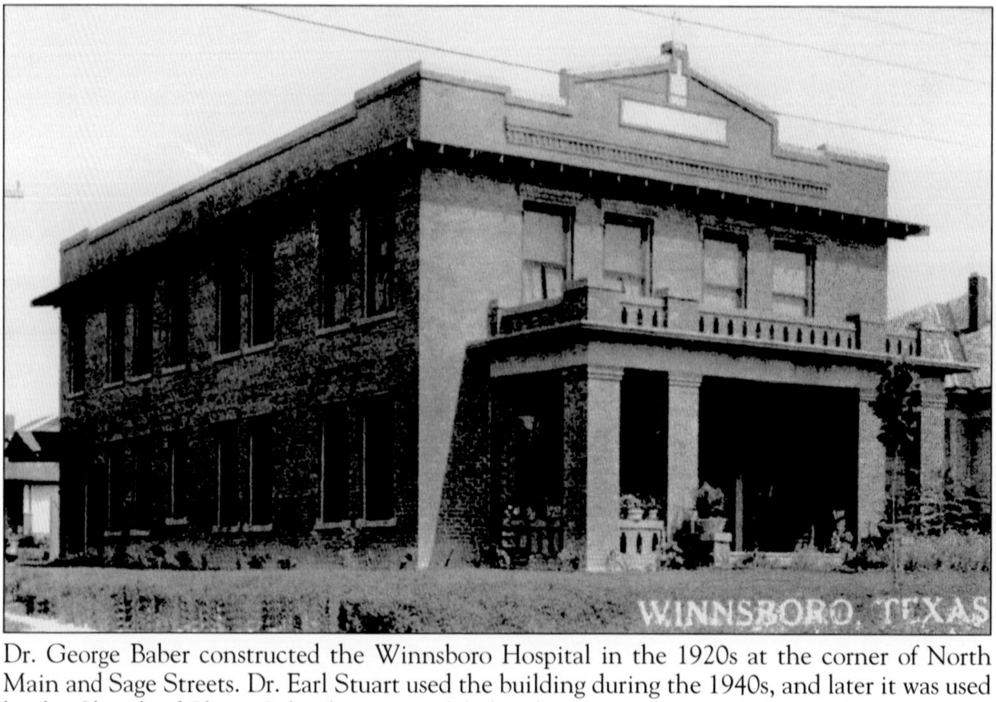

Dr. George Baber constructed the Winnsboro Hospital in the 1920s at the corner of North Main and Sage Streets. Dr. Earl Stuart used the building during the 1940s, and later it was used by the Church of Christ. It has been remodeled and now serves as an apartment house.

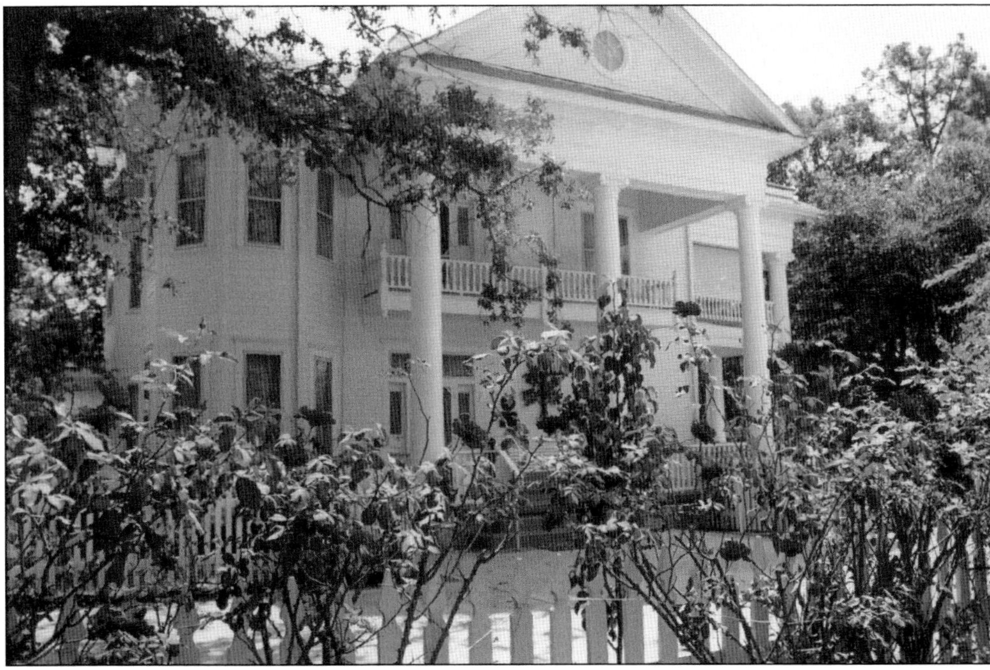

M.D. Carlock, an early prominent attorney in Winnsboro, built this 22-room colonial mansion. Carlock was a friend of Gov. Jim Hogg and was very active in politics. The Carlocks entertained many important officials in this home, which sits on a four-acre estate on South Main Street. Today it is a bed and breakfast.

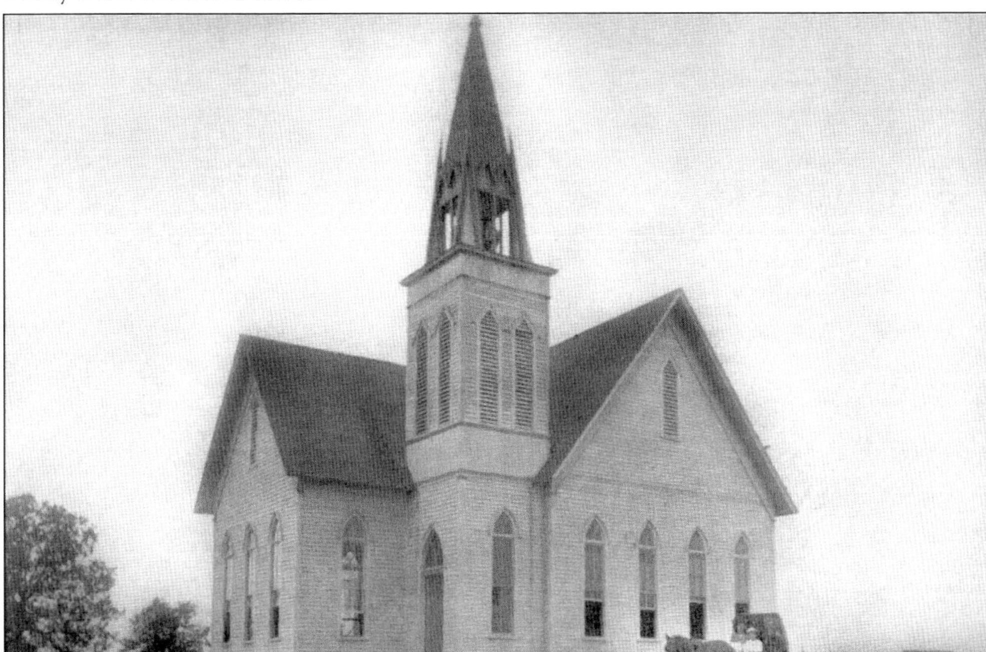

The Christian Church in Winnsboro was built in 1894, but the following year a tornado destroyed the original steeples, which were never replaced. The church building, which sits at the corner of Sage and Mill Streets, continues to serve as the sanctuary for the church.

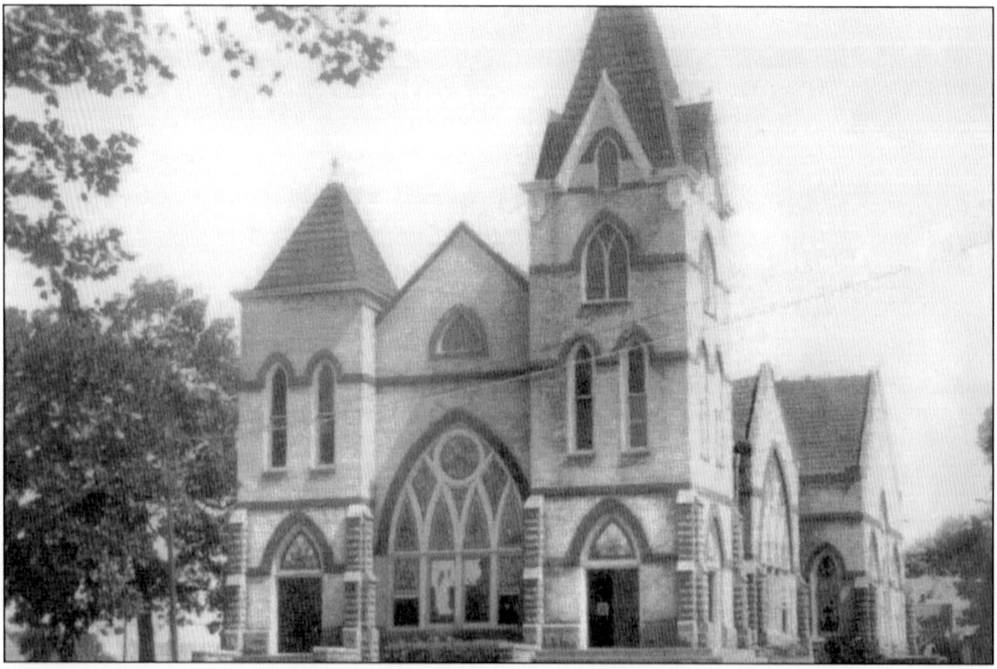

The Methodist church, shown here, was built in 1904 at the corner of Church and Elm Streets in Winnsboro at a cost of $12,000. In 1961, the church needed additional space, and this structure was torn down to make room for a new sanctuary.

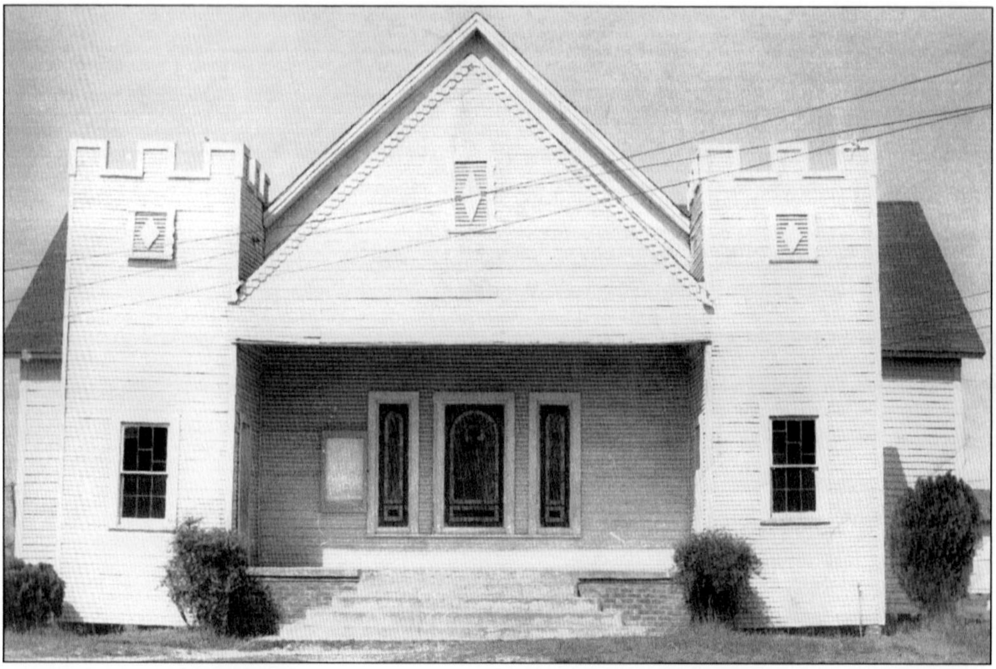

St. Paul Baptist Church in Mineola was organized in 1871 under the leadership of Rev. John Branham. This first church building was located about three blocks south of the present location at the corner of Stone and Front Streets. Charter members included Mandy Hall, Marian Lee, Mary Garrett, Ellis Lee, Willis Oliver, and Betty Brooks.

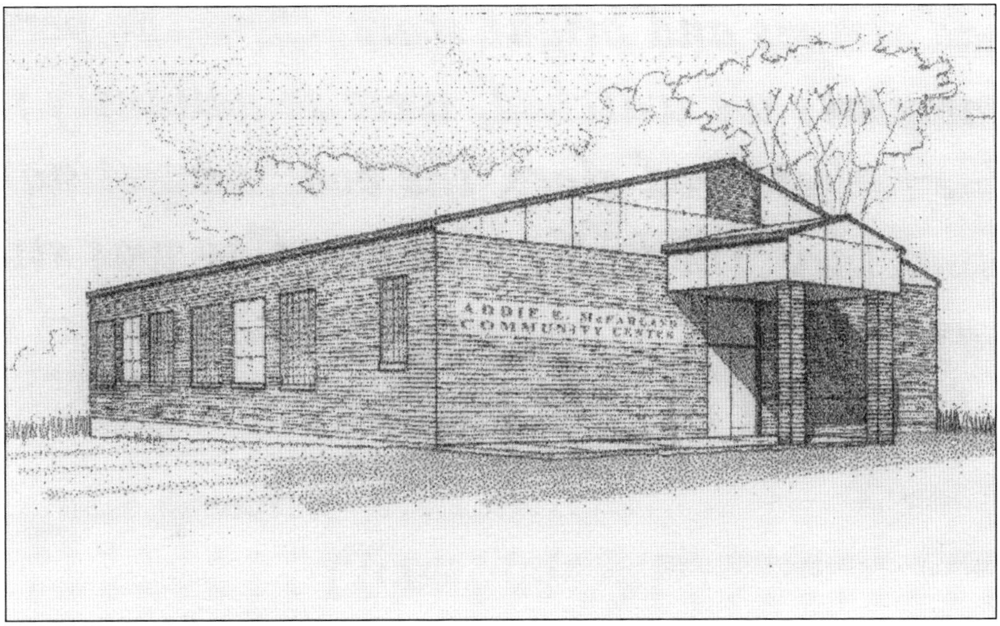

This school building in Mineola was named for Miss Addie McFarland, an African-American educator in Mineola. The school was built between 1937 and 1939, and the last class graduated in 1966. The building has been extensively remodeled, and now serves as a civic center for the community.

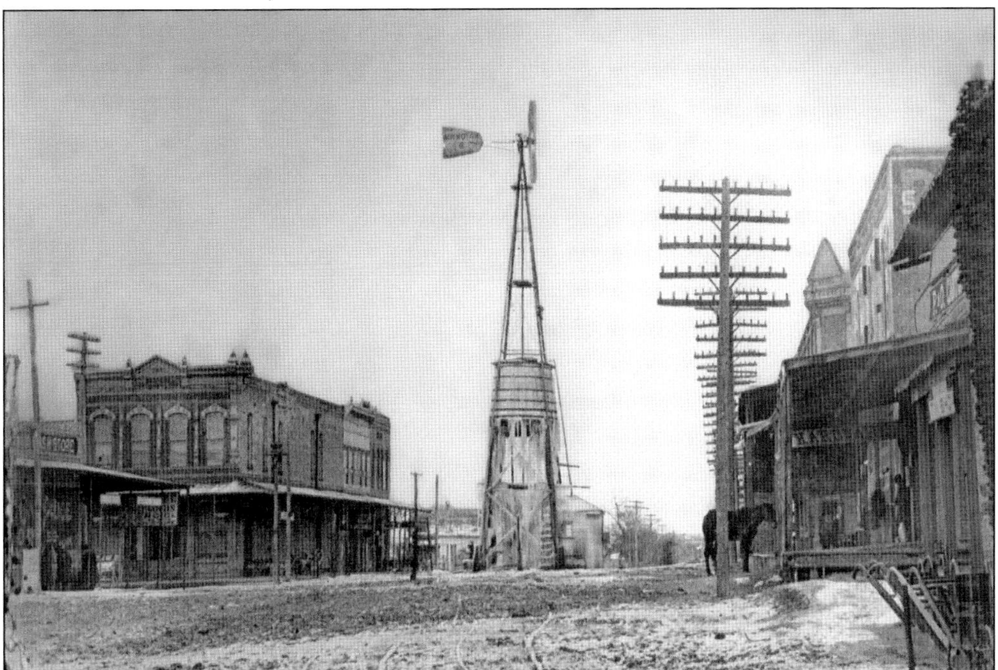

This "winter day scene" of downtown Mineola was taken looking west on Broad Street. Numerous businesses, including W.E. Lott's Blacksmith Shop, are featured. The water well situated in the middle of the intersection of Johnson and Broad Streets furnished artesian mineral water for the community and was a popular gathering spot.

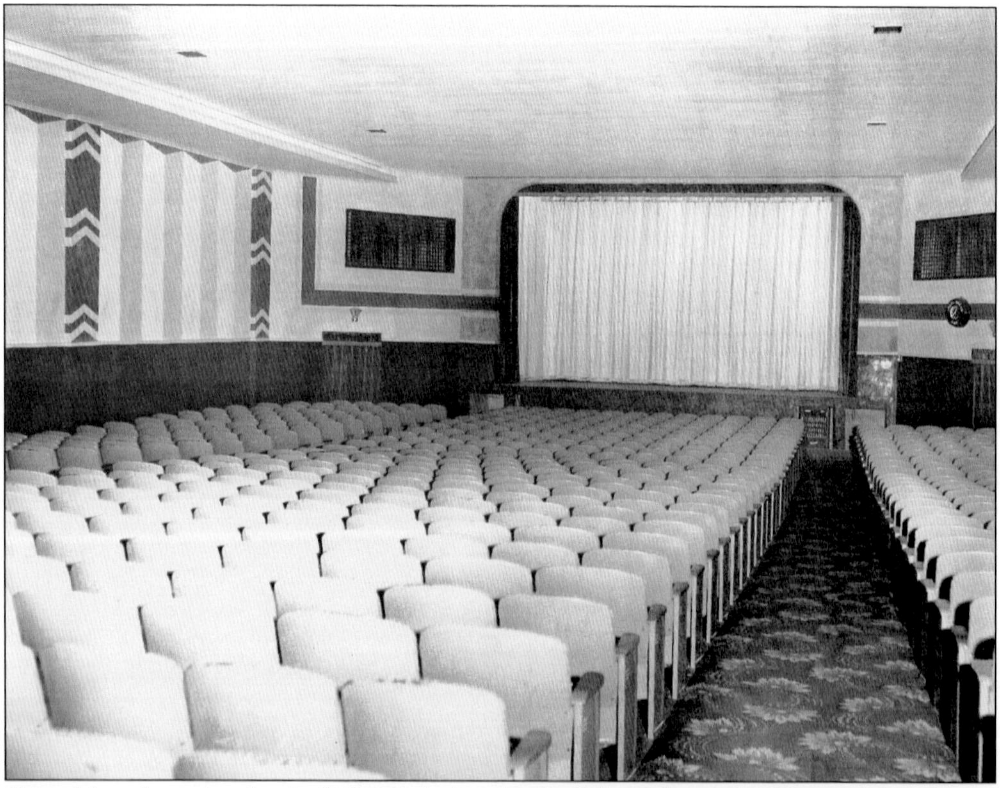

Owned for a long time by the R.T. Hooks family, the Select Theater Building in Mineola was built in 1920 and remodeled in 1948 and 2001. This Art Deco–style building had a distinct architectural feature—a revolving neon tower that could be seen for miles. The 2001 remodeling restored the theater to its 1948 appearance.

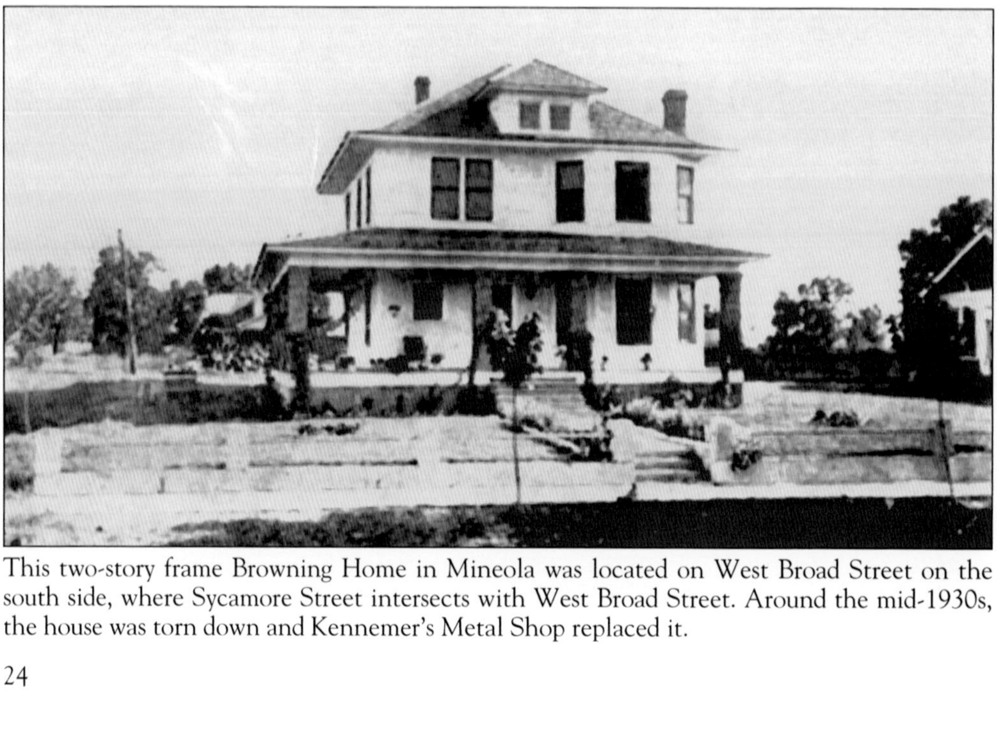

This two-story frame Browning Home in Mineola was located on West Broad Street on the south side, where Sycamore Street intersects with West Broad Street. Around the mid-1930s, the house was torn down and Kennemer's Metal Shop replaced it.

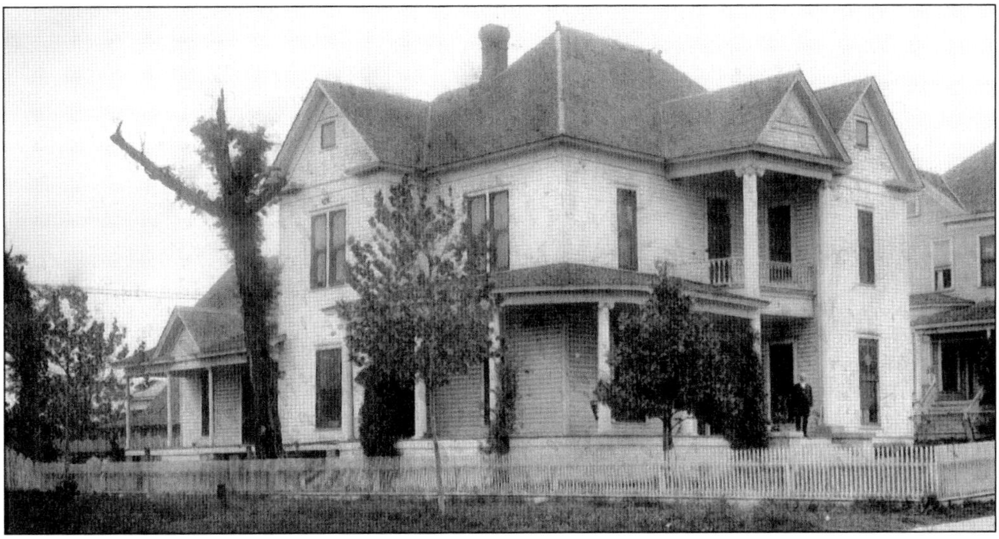

J.J. McLeod built the Hart Home at the corner of North Johnson and West Kilpatrick Street, one block north of downtown Mineola, in 1906. Mr. Hart practiced law in Mineola and was a partner of later Gov. Jim Hogg while Mr. Hogg resided in Mineola. The home was occupied by members of the Hart family until the death of Polly Hart Peterson and her husband, Dr. "Pete" Peterson. After their deaths, the home was sold.

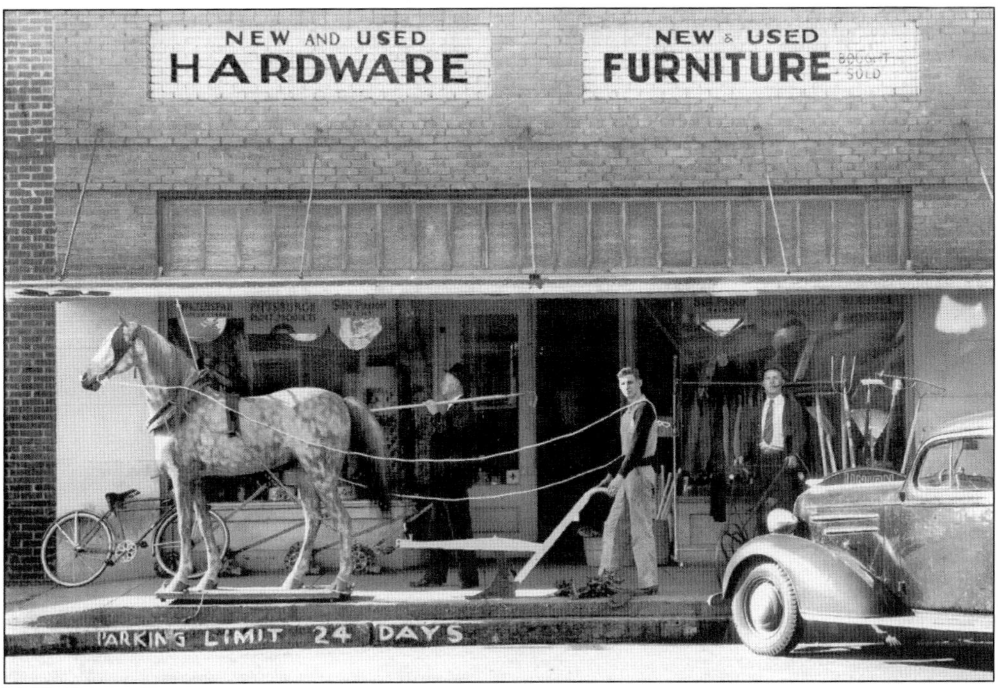

This photograph was taken in front of Kitchen's Hardware and Furniture Store, which was on West Broad Street in downtown Mineola, in 1936. The Stuffed Horse at the curb was a local attraction that was later sold to a Dallas tourist. The sign in front of the horse read "Parking Limit 24 days." David Kitchens said it was to imply that Mineola was unhurried and restful. Kitchen's Hardware remains open today with a restaurant in front and hardware store in the rear of the building.

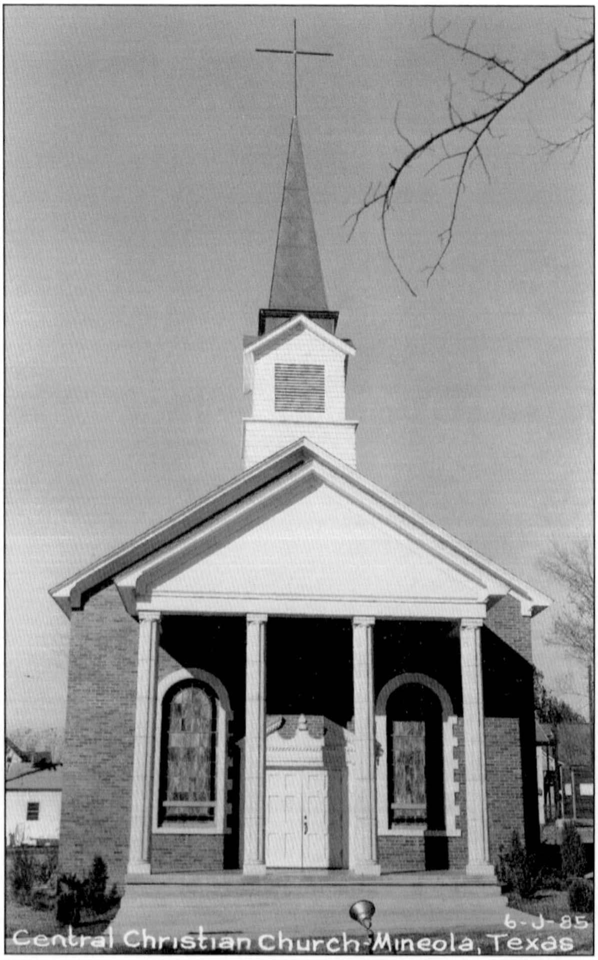

Central Christian Church (left) in Mineola had its birth in 1895 but the congregation met in various locations. The church was finally chartered with 103 members in 1902. The church bought the lot at Kilpatrick and North Pacific Streets in 1911 and erected a frame building the following year. The church decided to change its name in 1965 to First Christian Church. Mineola was hit with a devastating tornado in 1908 and the Christian Church was demolished (below).

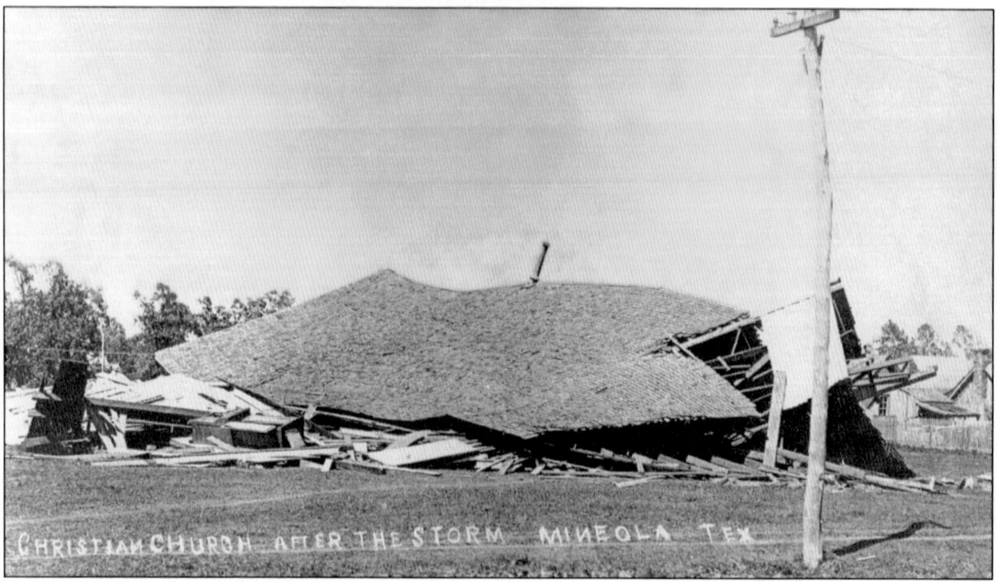

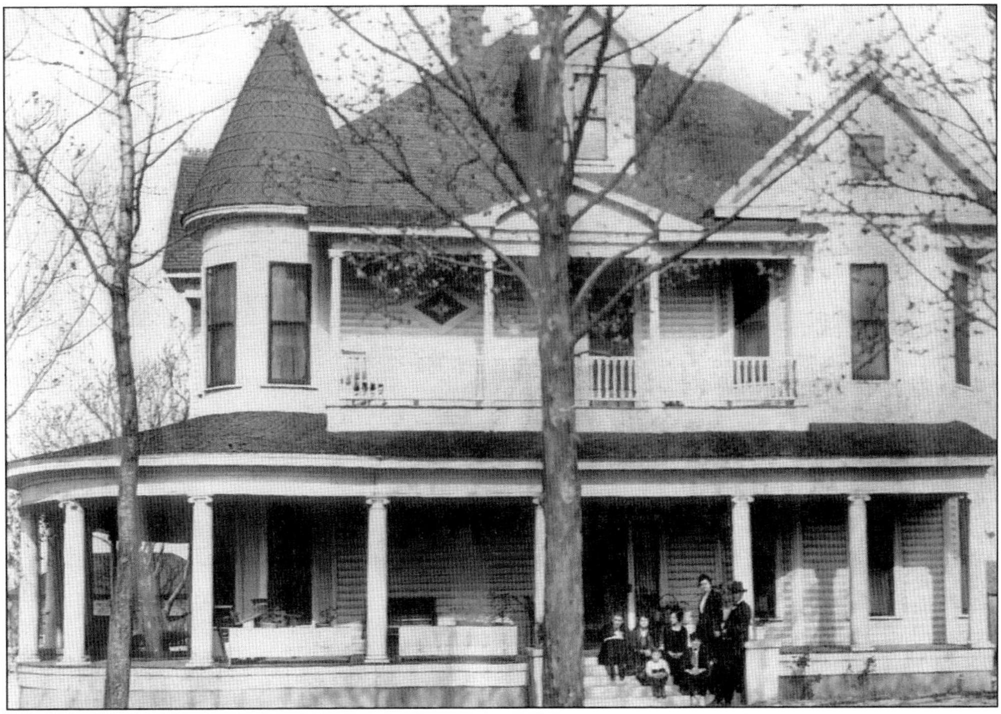

This beautiful Victorian two-story home was built by Mr. Pyle at the intersection of West Kilpatrick and North Line Streets in Mineola. It sits on the site of the home where Gov. Jim and Sallie Hogg lived and where their daughter Ima was born in 1882. This building has also been the residence of several other prominent Mineola families, including the Kitchens and the Tharps. The home is still used today as a private residence.

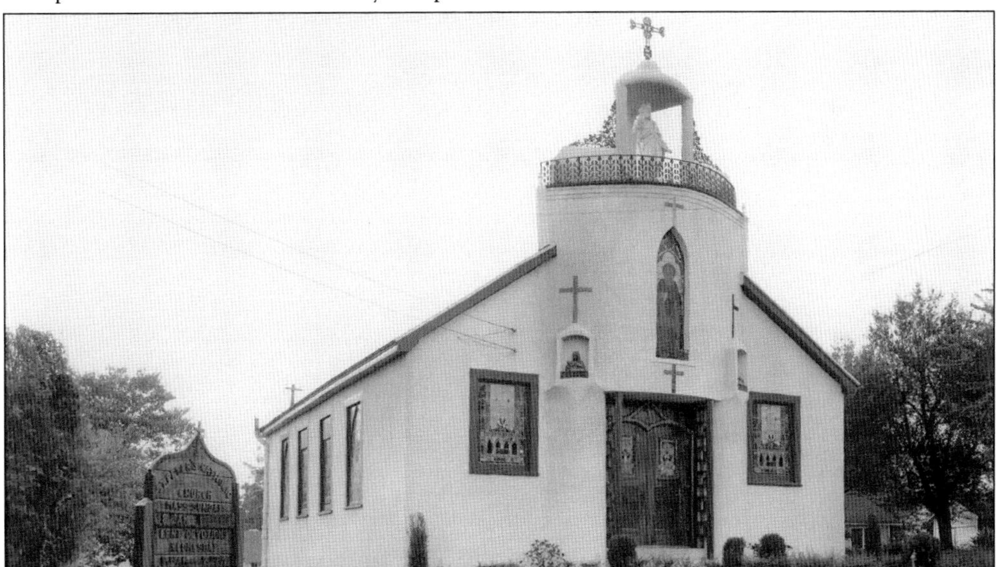

St. Peter's Catholic Church has been a part of Mineola since 1873 and the coming of the railroad. The church used the building depicted here for more than 30 years but moved to Meadowbrook Drive in 1965 and erected a modified Spanish-style building. The church shown here was later torn down.

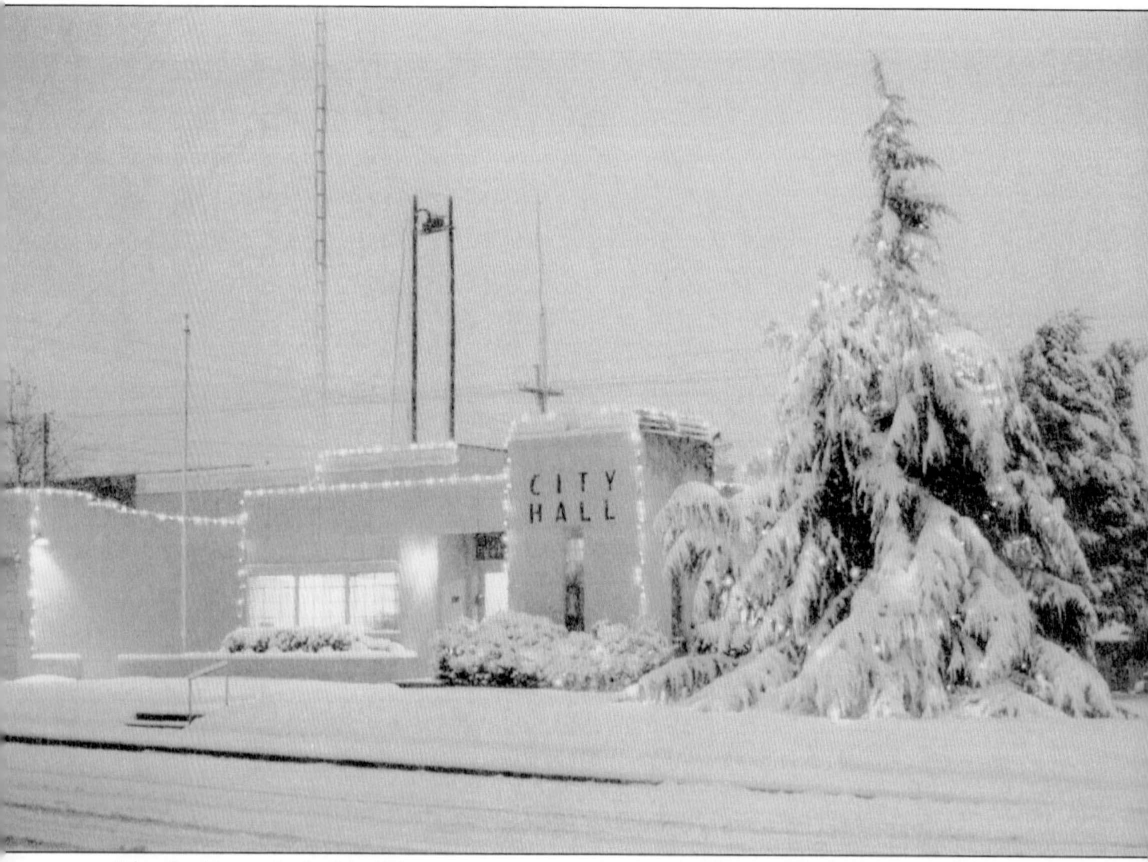

The Art Deco city hall building was constructed in the 1930s as a Works Progress Administration (WPA) project. The building served for many years as the city hall for Mineola until a new facility was constructed. Snow is not a common occurrence in East Texas, and so seeing Mineola wrapped in a white blanket of snow was a beautiful sight, especially during the holiday season.

Two

TRANSPORTATION

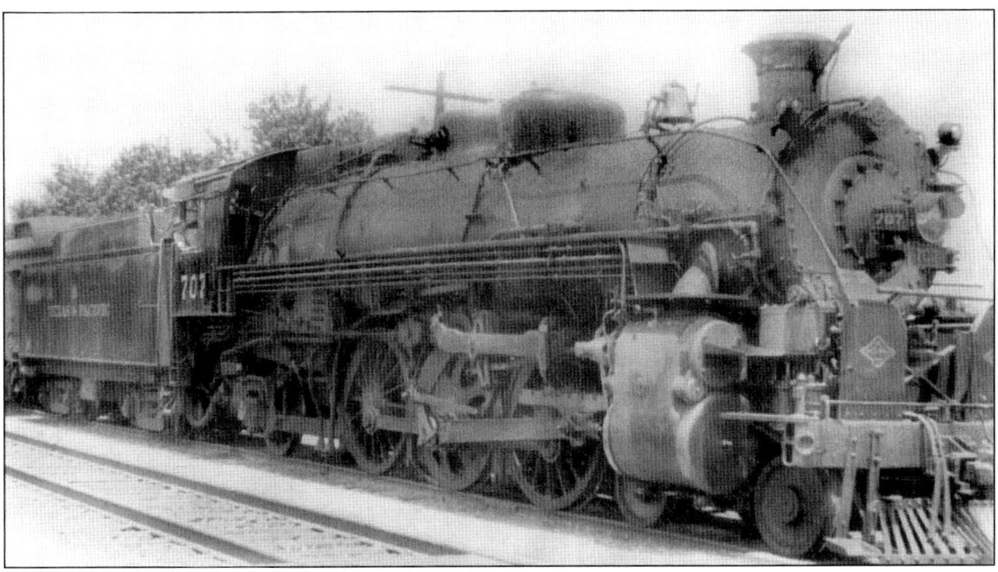

Early travelers and people searching for a place to live found Wood County a very difficult place through which to travel. Horses and wagons were the main mode of transportation; later came the automobile and the construction of better roads. Trains arrived in Wood County in late 1873 and airplanes c. 1917. Shown here is a locomotive on the Texas & Pacific Railroad.

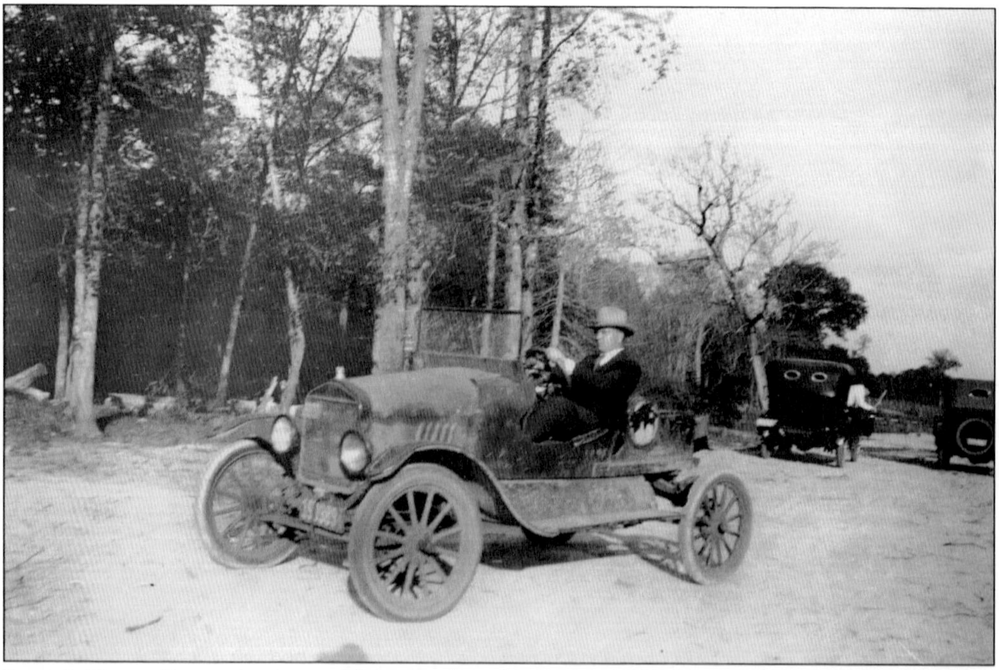

Patrick Henry Bogan is pictured here at the wheel of a 1920s automobile. Mr. Bogan was a rural mailman on Route 1 and, later, a clerk in the Mineola Post Office until his retirement in the early 1950s.

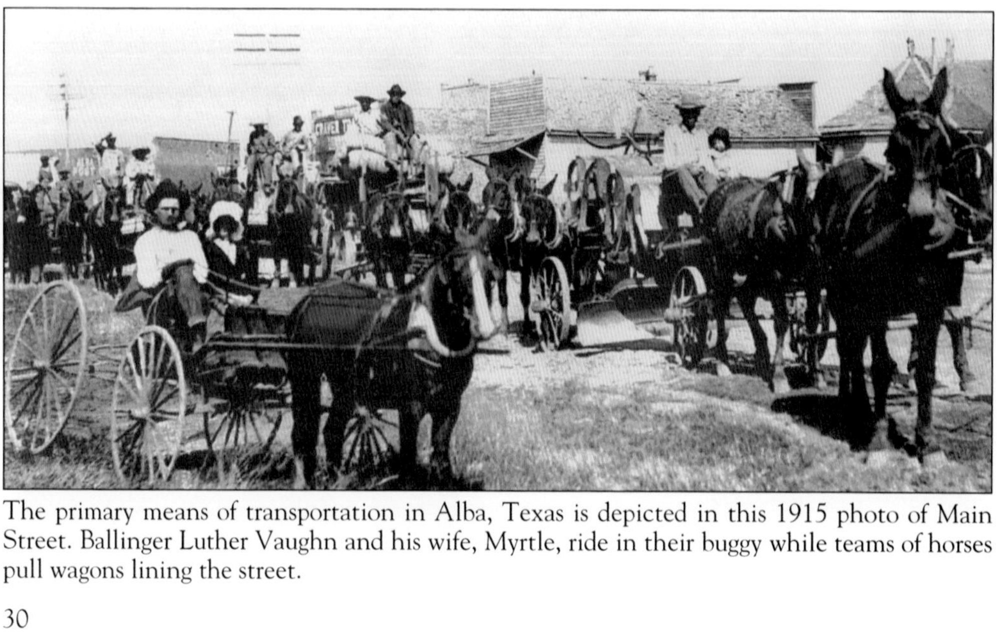

The primary means of transportation in Alba, Texas is depicted in this 1915 photo of Main Street. Ballinger Luther Vaughn and his wife, Myrtle, ride in their buggy while teams of horses pull wagons lining the street.

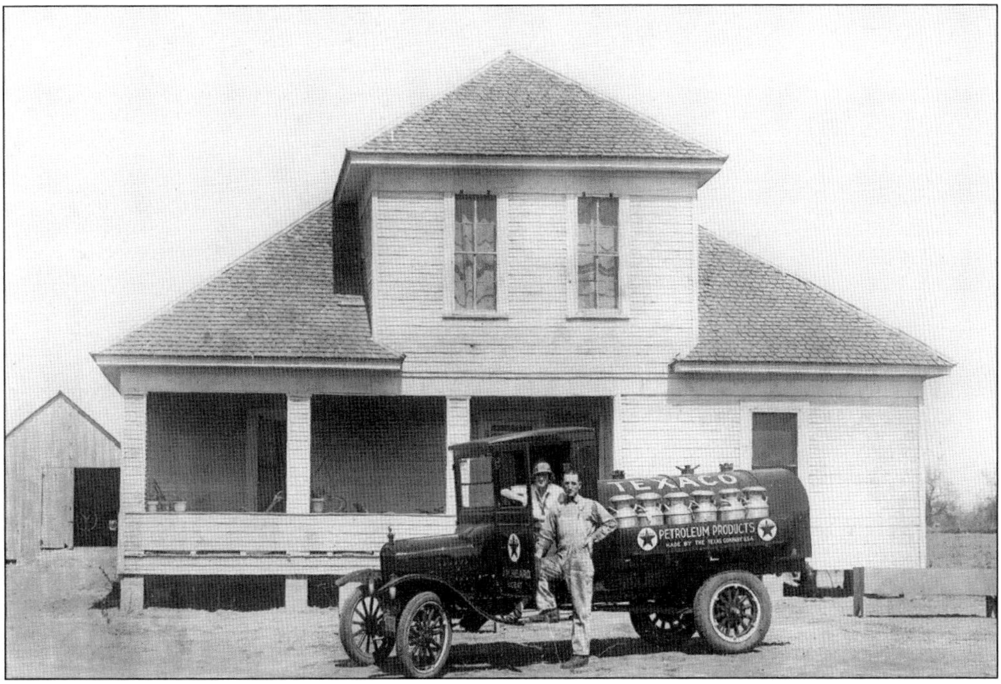

J.P. (Jake) English and his wife, Bessie, are pictured here with their Texaco gasoline truck at their home in Mineola, *c.* 1925.

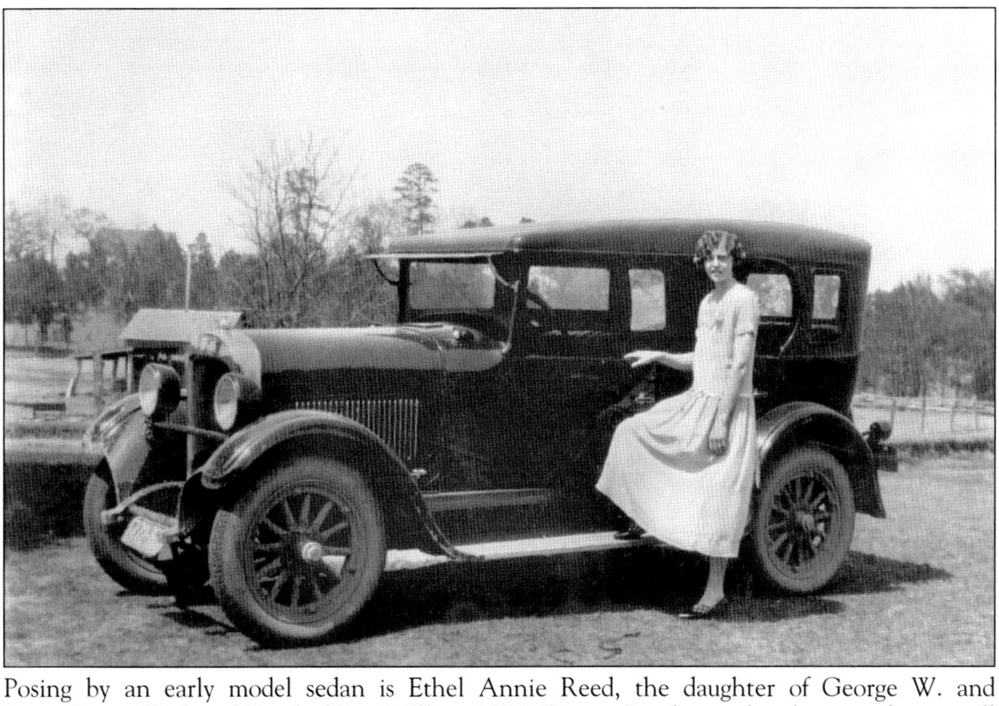

Posing by an early model sedan is Ethel Annie Reed, the daughter of George W. and Lizzie Annie (Jackson) Reed of Pine Mills, *c.* 1927. George Reed owned and operated a sawmill and a cotton gin in Pine Mills that was named by his father, Richard Reed, when he was the first postmaster in Pine Mills.

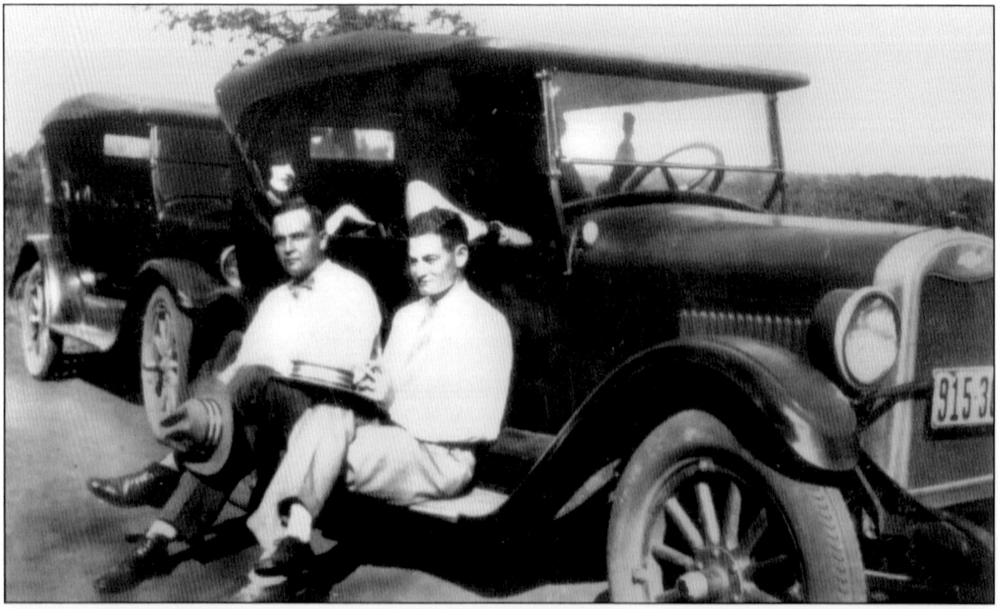

Two late 1920s Chevrolet vehicles are shown here; Henry Bogan appears on the left with some friends. The driver appears to have a guitar. Mr. Bogan was a musician with the East Texas Serenaders from 1927 to 1937.

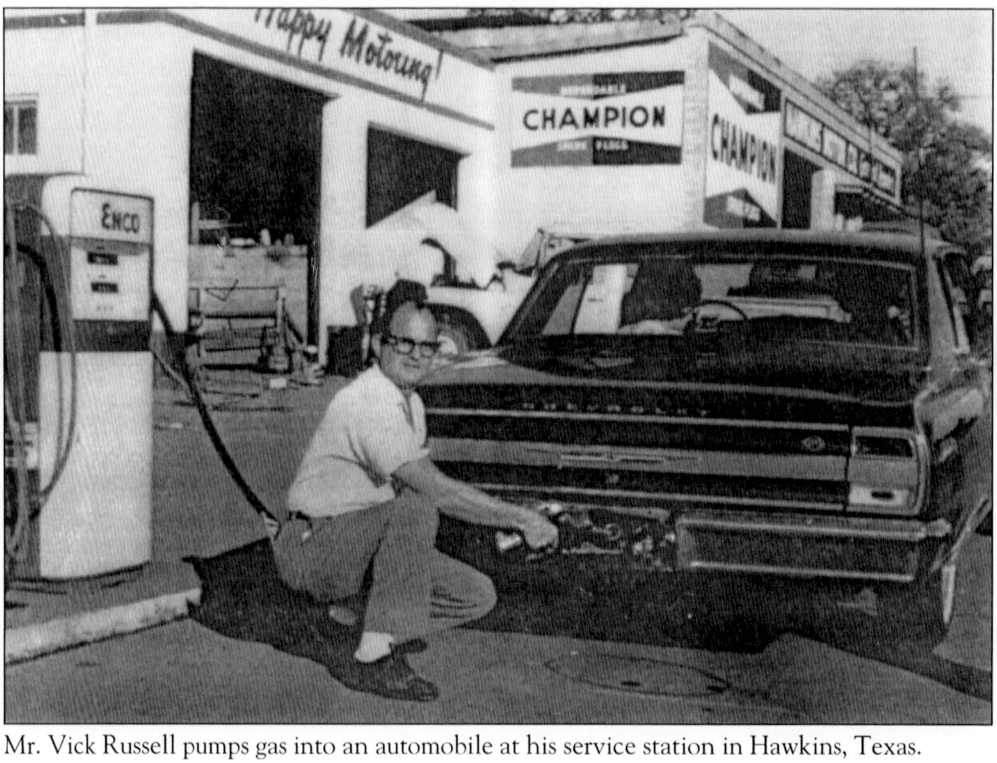

Mr. Vick Russell pumps gas into an automobile at his service station in Hawkins, Texas.

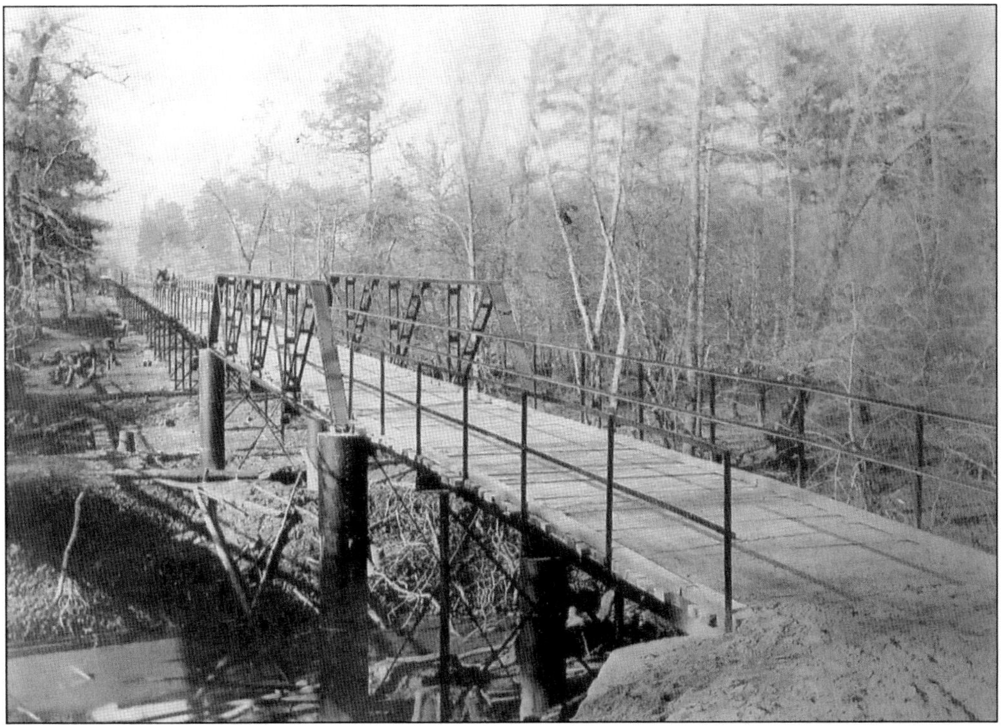

This is the iron bridge that crossed Lake Fork Creek between Mineola and Quitman, one of several similar bridges that spanned Lake Fork Creek across Wood County.

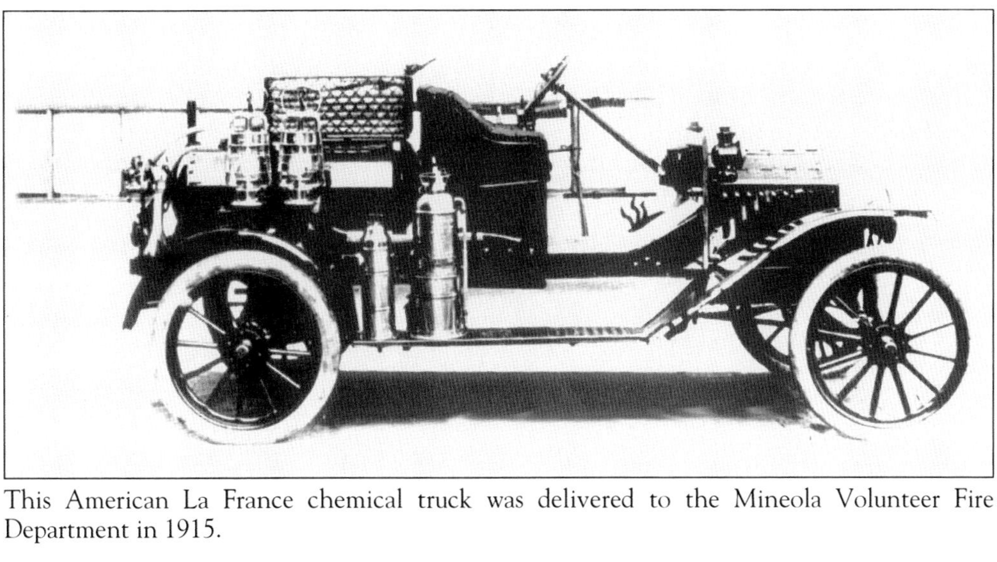

This American La France chemical truck was delivered to the Mineola Volunteer Fire Department in 1915.

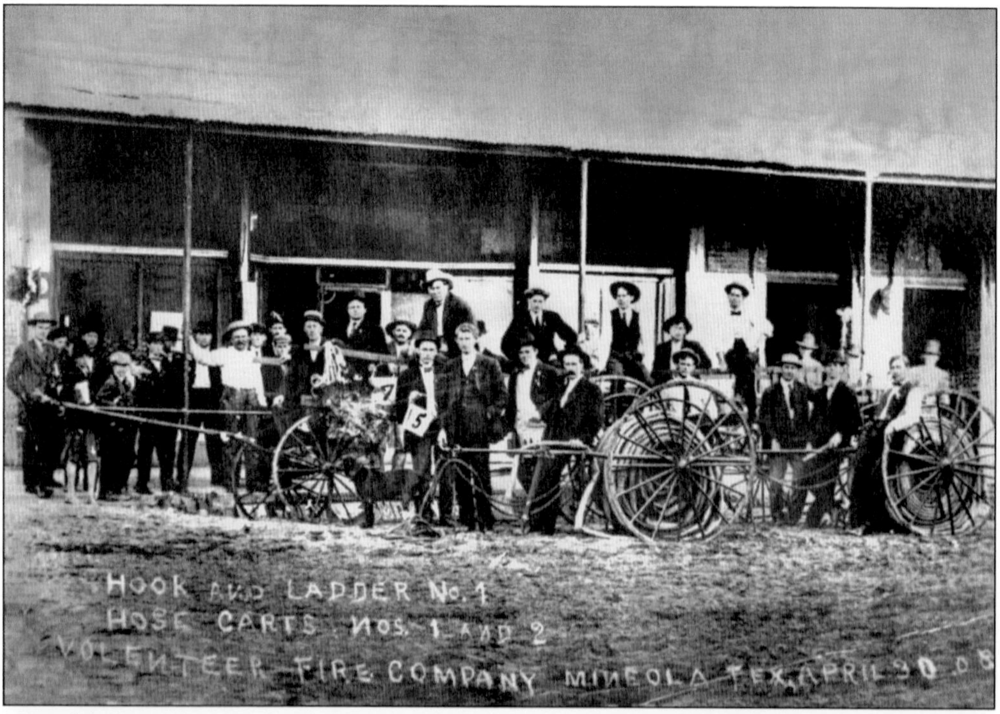

Mineola's first volunteer fire department, known as the Hook and Ladder Company, is pictured in 1908 with hose carts.

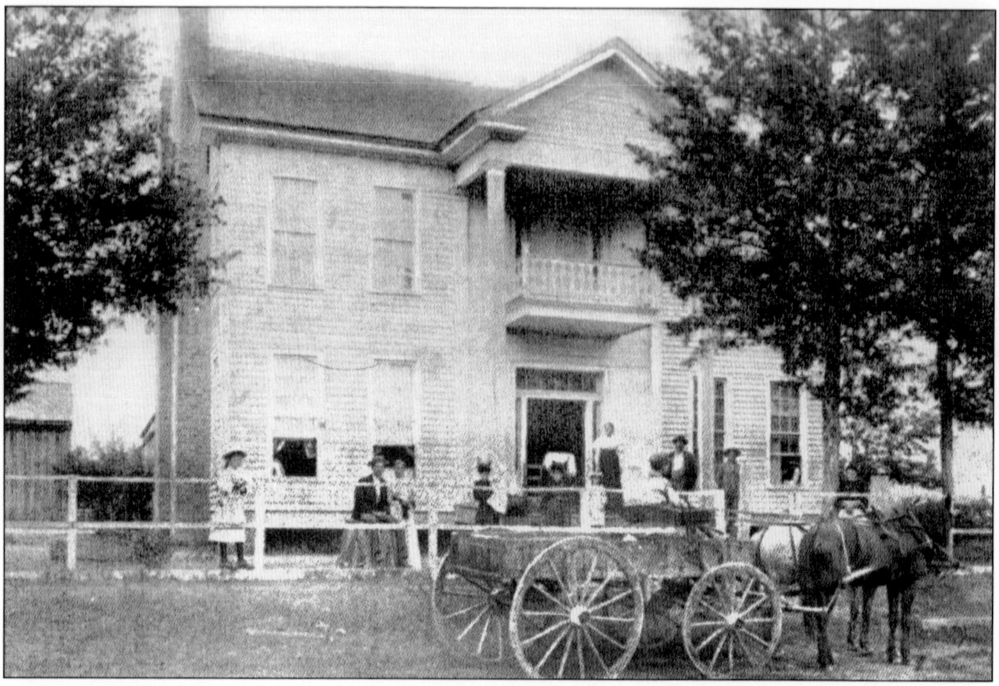

The Grogan Hotel in Quitman was built about 1870 as a residence for Dr. A.L. Patten by his brother-in-law Wesley Trout. The wagon and team shown are typical of that era.

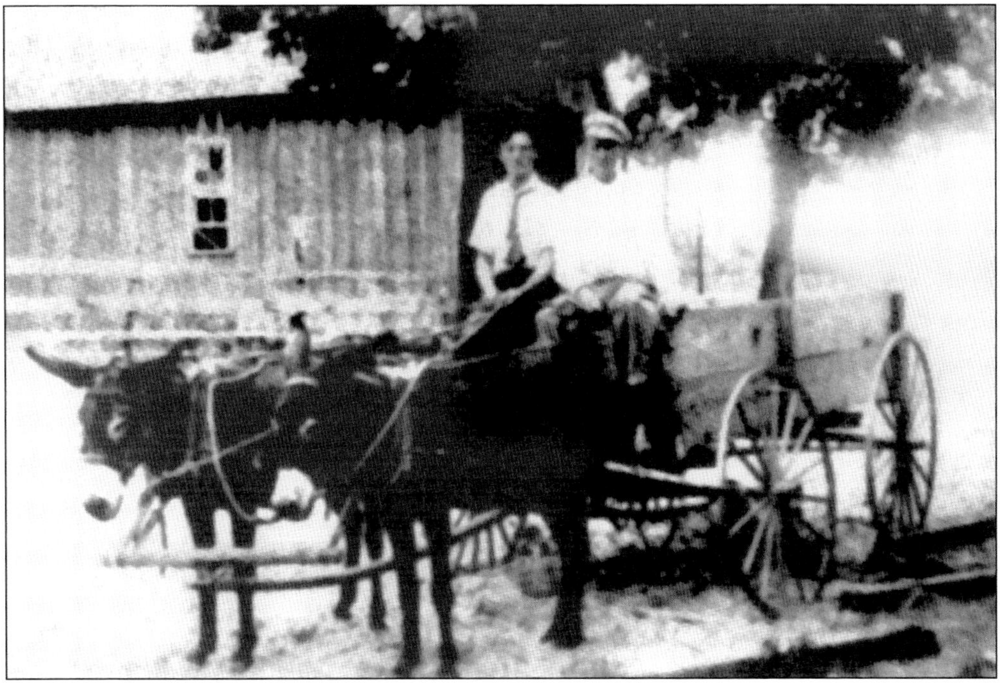

Pictured here is the post office in Peach along with Carl Cowles, Jessica Bogue, and their mule-drawn wagon.

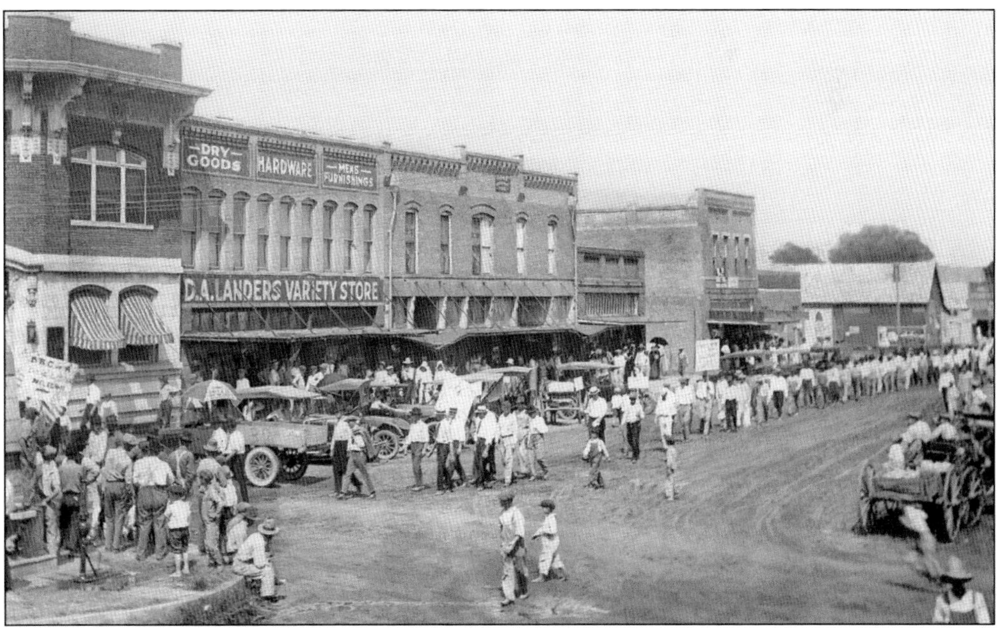

This Farmer's Labor Rally took place in the early 1900s.

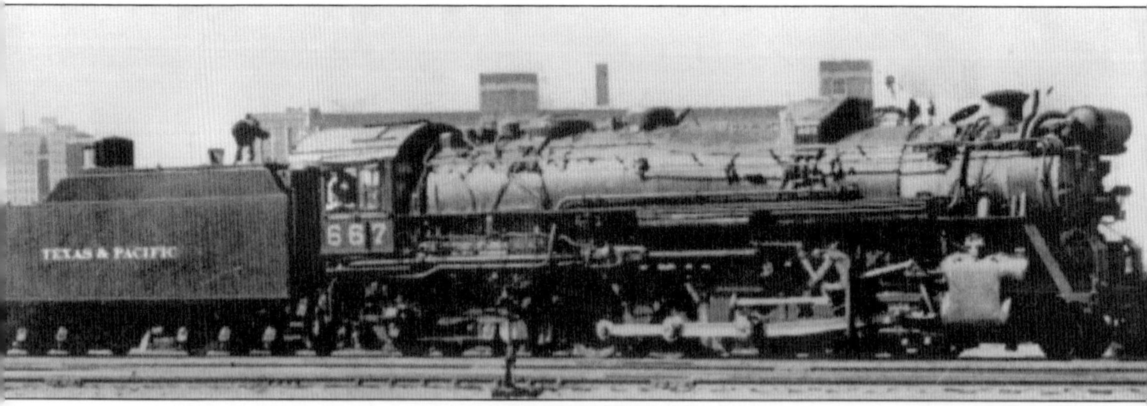

Pictured here is the Texas and Pacific engine #667.

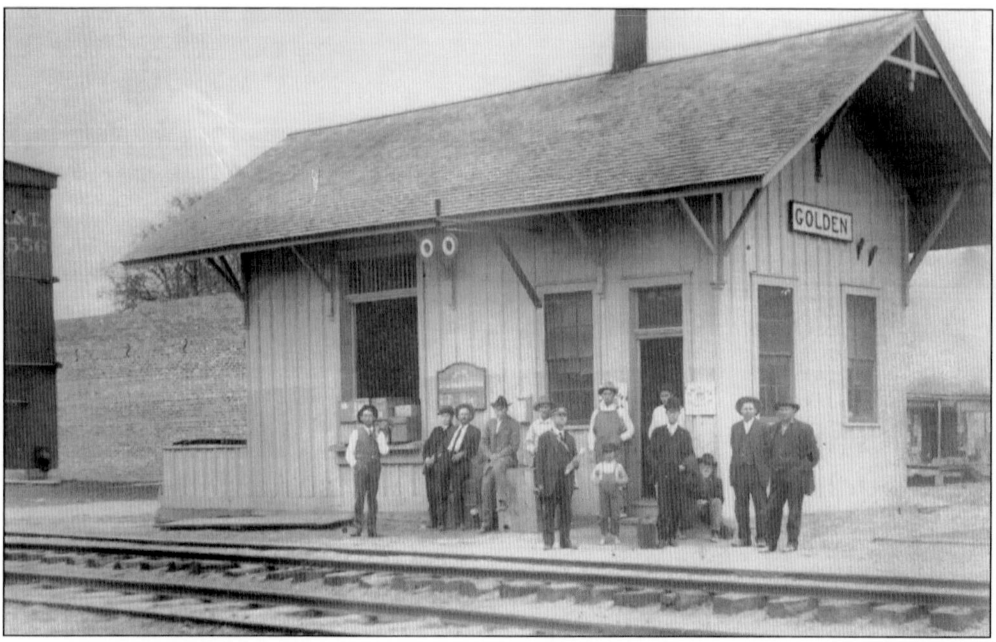

Pictured here is the Katy railroad station in Golden, Texas.

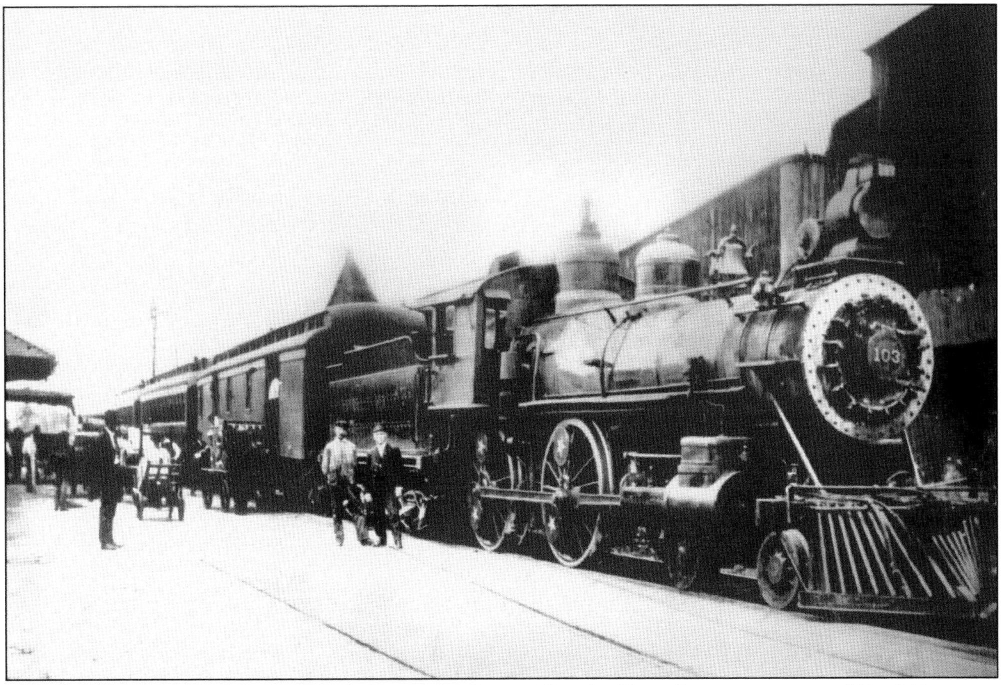

This photo, taken c. 1918 in Tyler, Texas, shows Charles Reitch, engineer, and Fred Reneau, conductor, of the International & Great Northern Railroad passenger train that ran from Mineola to Troup.

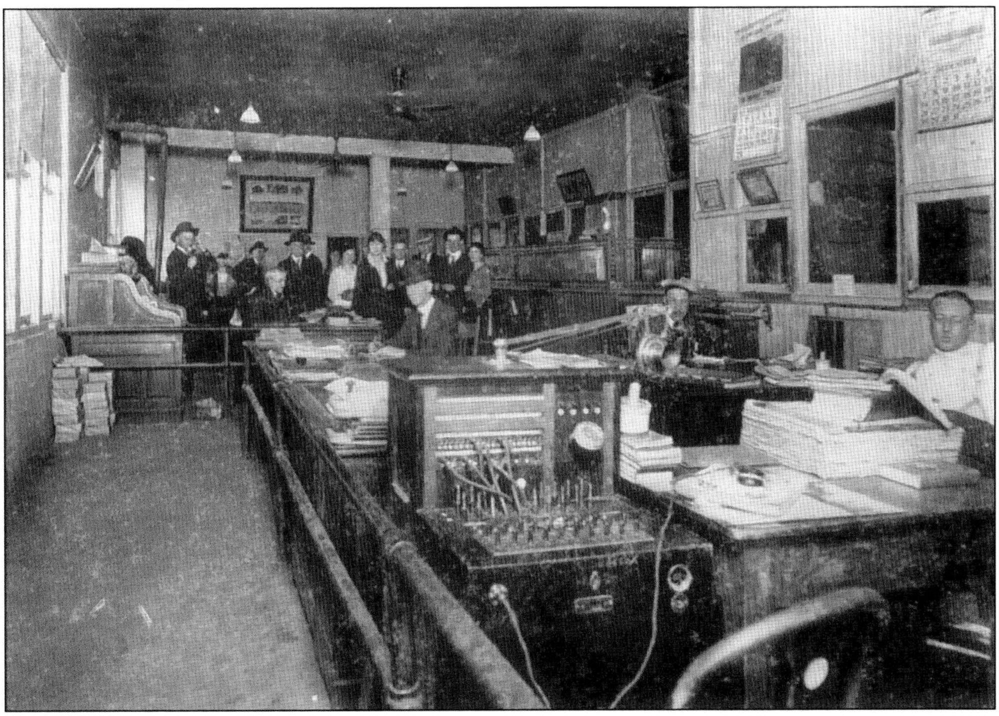

This was a busy day at the train depot in Alba, which served the Missouri, Kansas & Texas (Katy) Railroad.

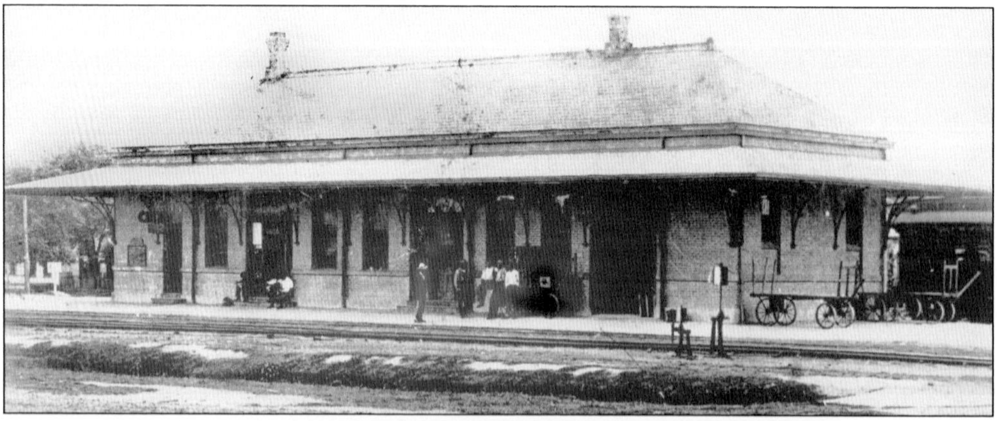

The Mineola Depot is pictured above in 1906. Below, on the throttle of #473, is engineer W.E. (Gene) McCreary of Mineola, in the 1940s.

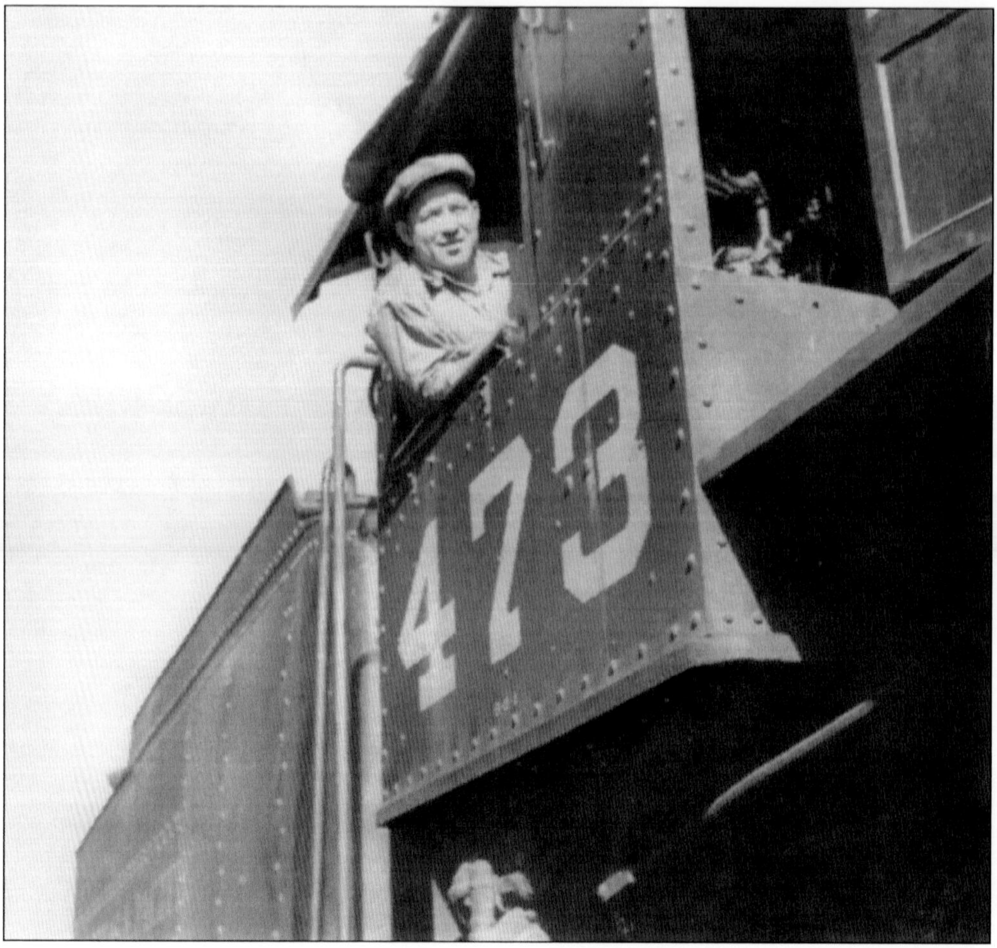

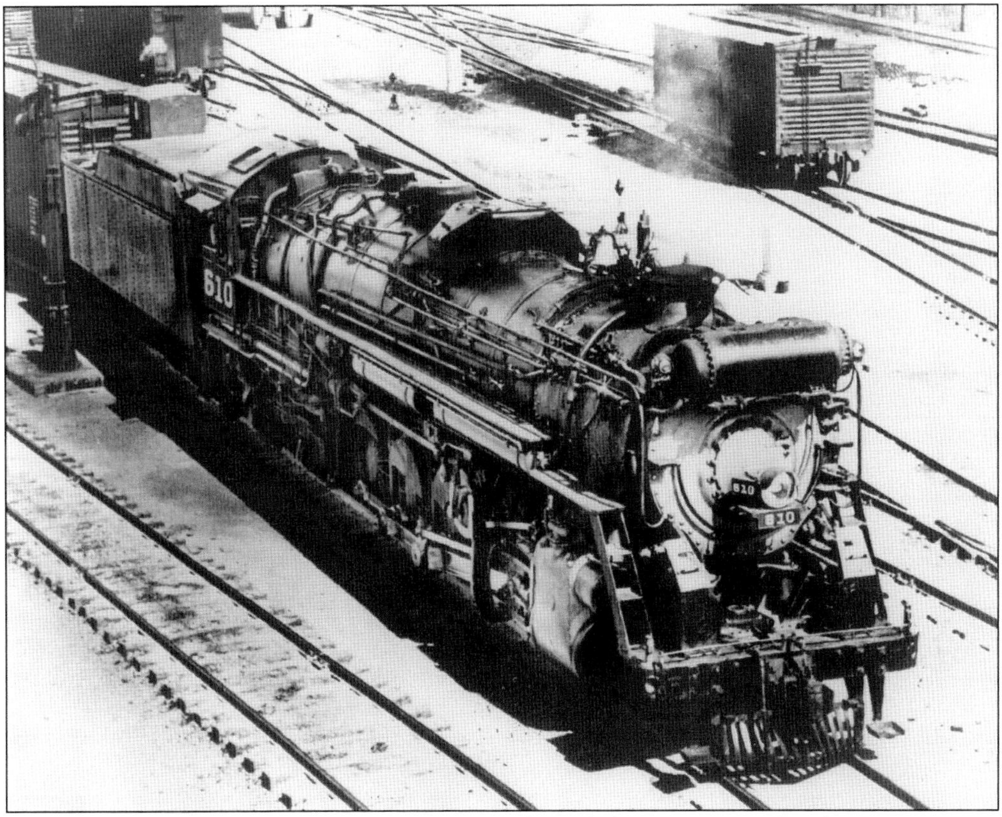

Engine #610 is steamed up and ready. It is believed that Eugene L. Bright was engineer on this engine.

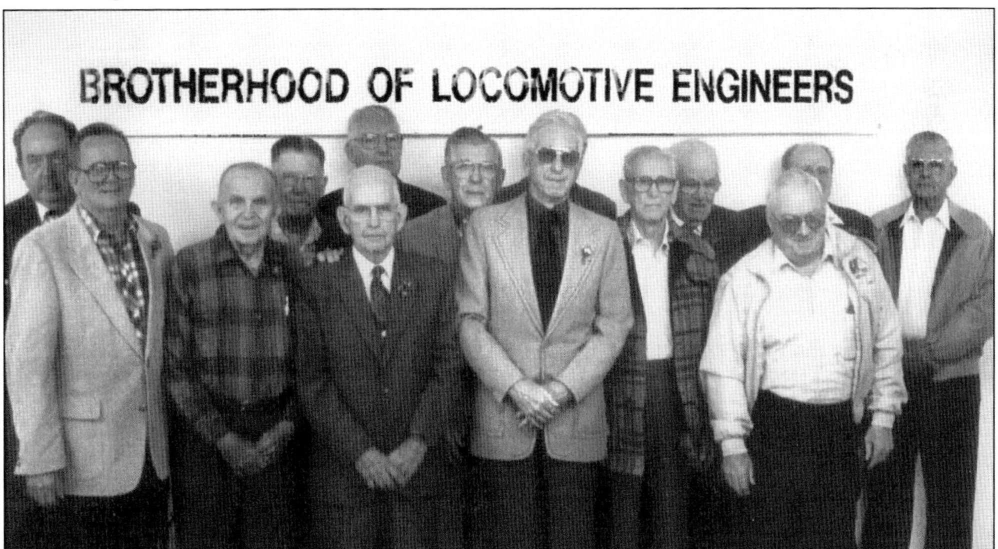

The "Brotherhood of Locomotive Engineers," from left to right, includes the following: (front row) unidentified, W.J. "Billy" Bray, C.O. Richardson, unidentified, Ben Board, and unidentified; (back row) unidentified, Red Findley, five unidentified men, and Basil Couch.

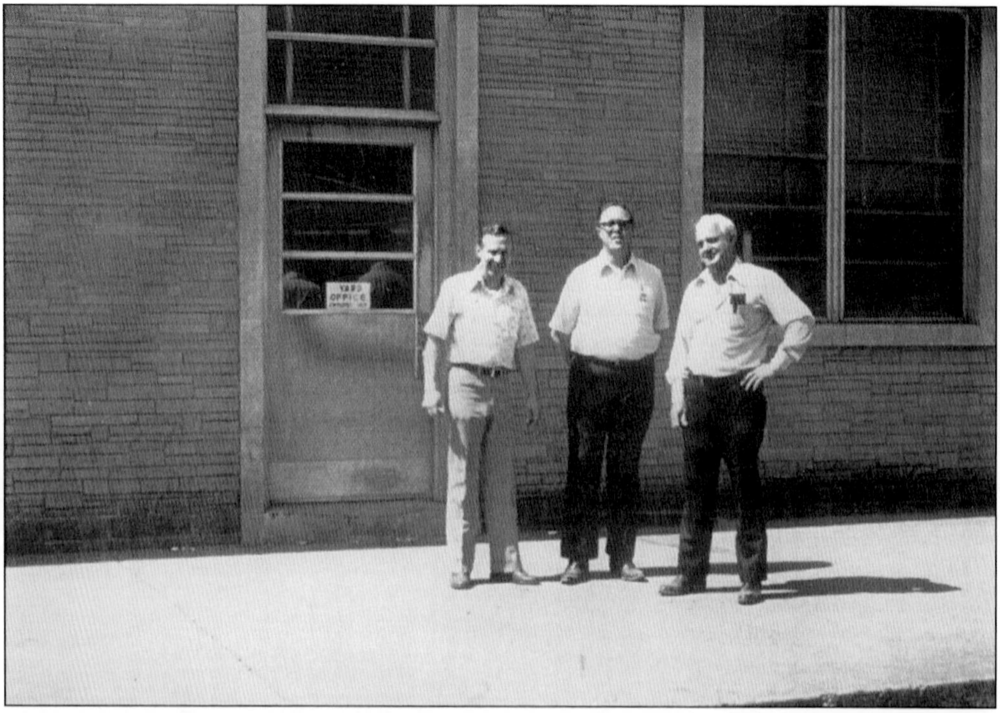

In this August 1977 view of the train depot in Mineola are, from left to right, Agent Ray Blakeney, operator; James Bue; and Jack Airhart, crew dispatcher and caller.

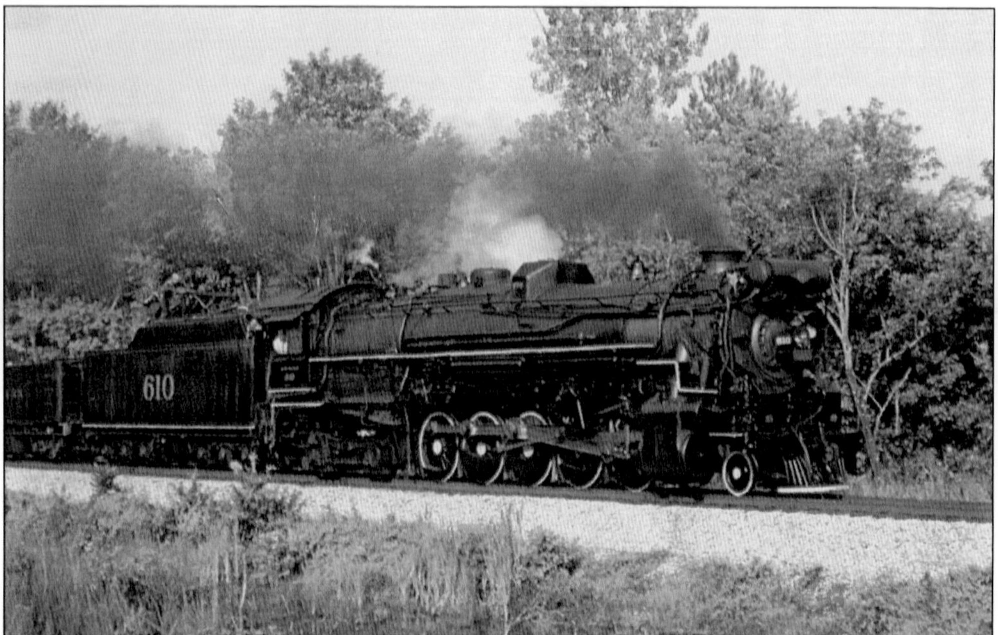

Engine #610, seen here under full steam, was later used to power "The Freedom Train" all around Texas.

Retired engineer William Jefferson "Billy" Bray reviews the controls on "The Freedom Train."

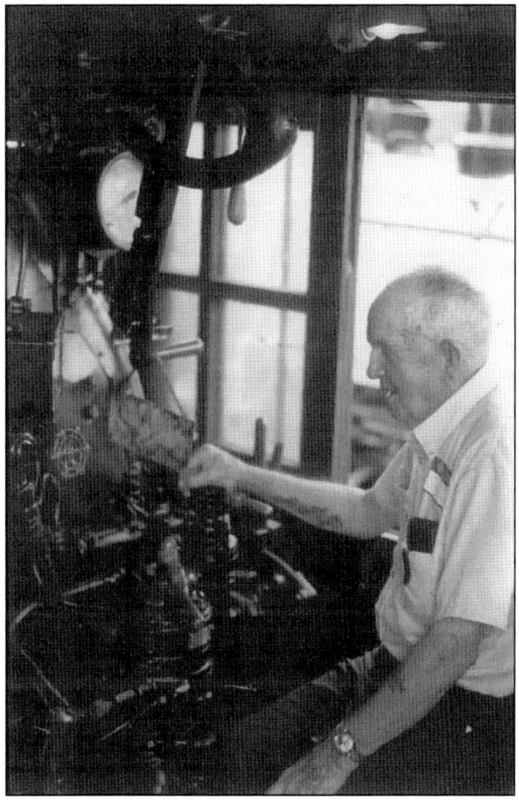

In July 1971 (below), a more modern Engine #739 approaches the Hoard Crossing with Engineer W.J. Bray at the controls and conductor L.M. Bostick also on board.

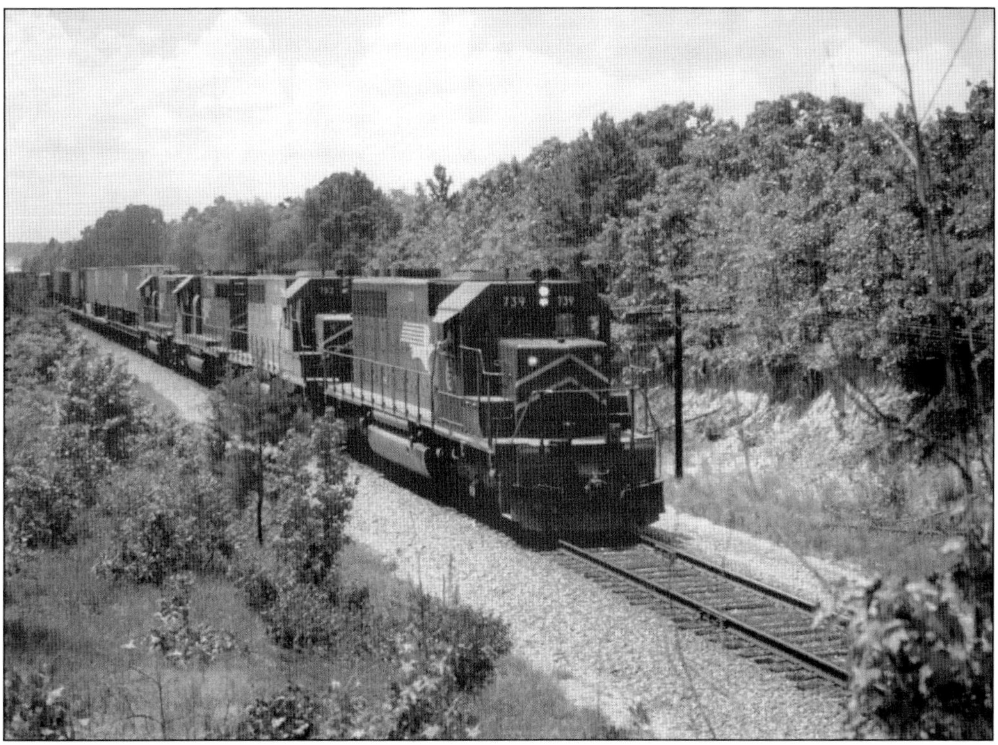

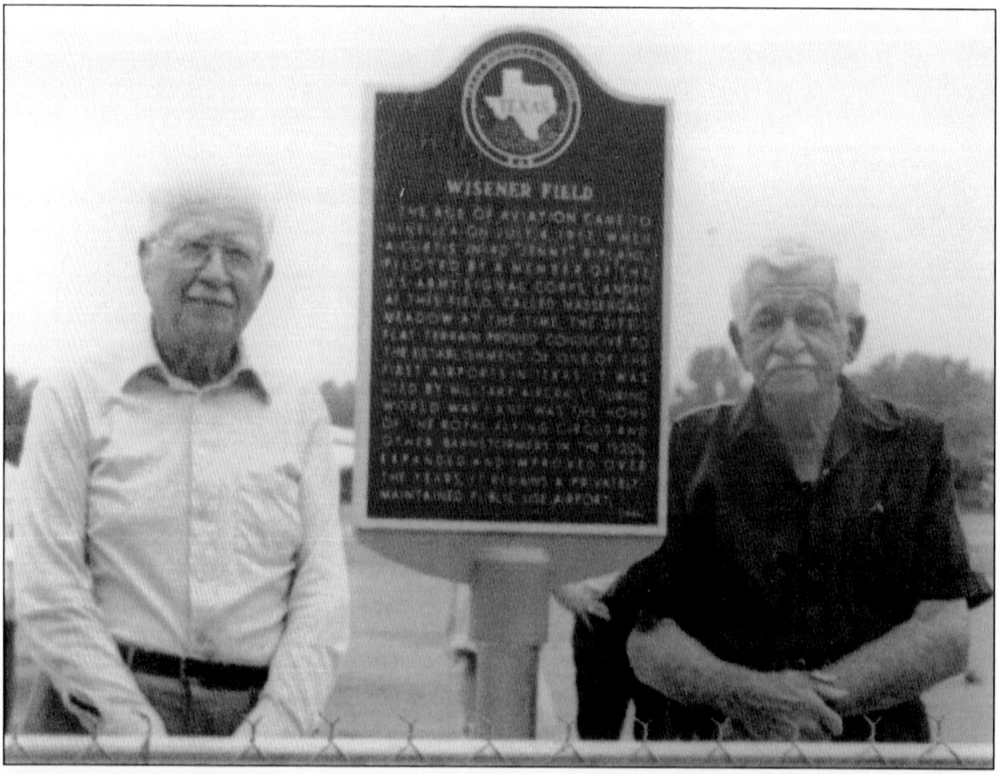

Henry and Bruce Wisener pose next to the state historical marker commemorating Wisener Field. On July 4, 1917, a Curtiss JN-4C Jenny piloted by a member of the U.S. Army Signal Corp landed here and officially began the age of aviation in Wood County.

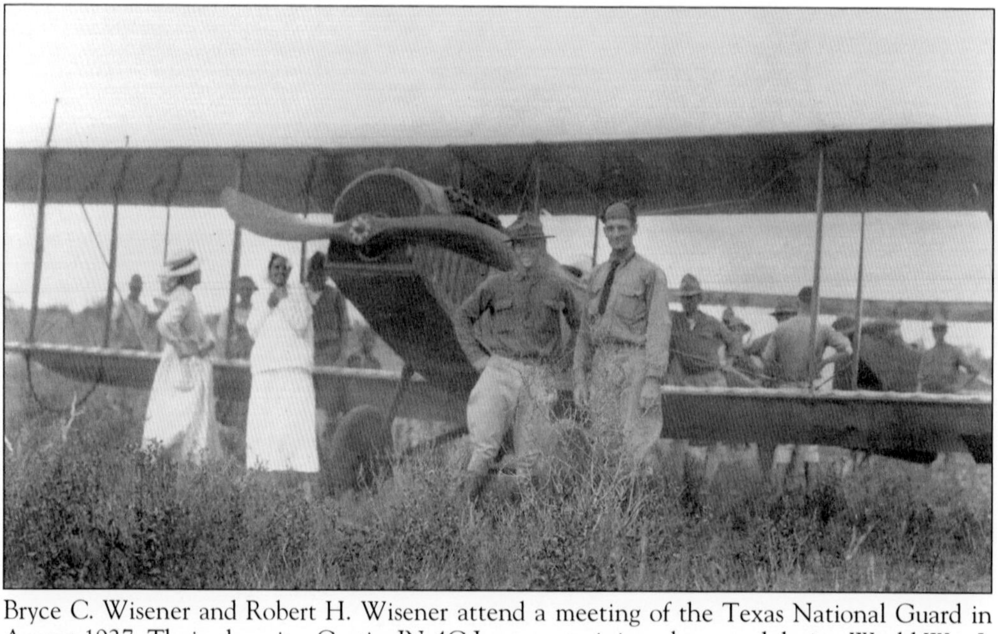

Bryce C. Wisener and Robert H. Wisener attend a meeting of the Texas National Guard in August 1927. Their plane is a Curtiss JN-4C Jenny, a training plane used during World War I. Henry Wisener was the first licensed pilot and Bryce was the second from Mineola, Texas.

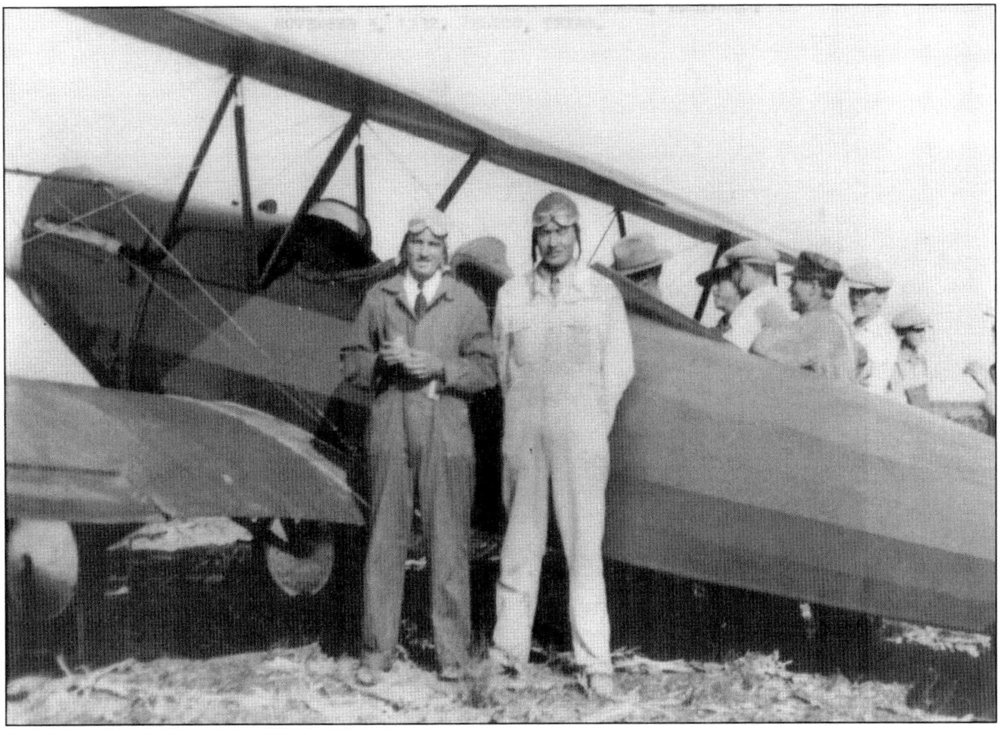

The Wisener brothers, Bryce on the left and Henry on the right, are shown with their "Air King" airplane in November 1931. Henry's original pilot's license #1424 was issued by the Federation Aeronautique International and signed by Orville Wright.

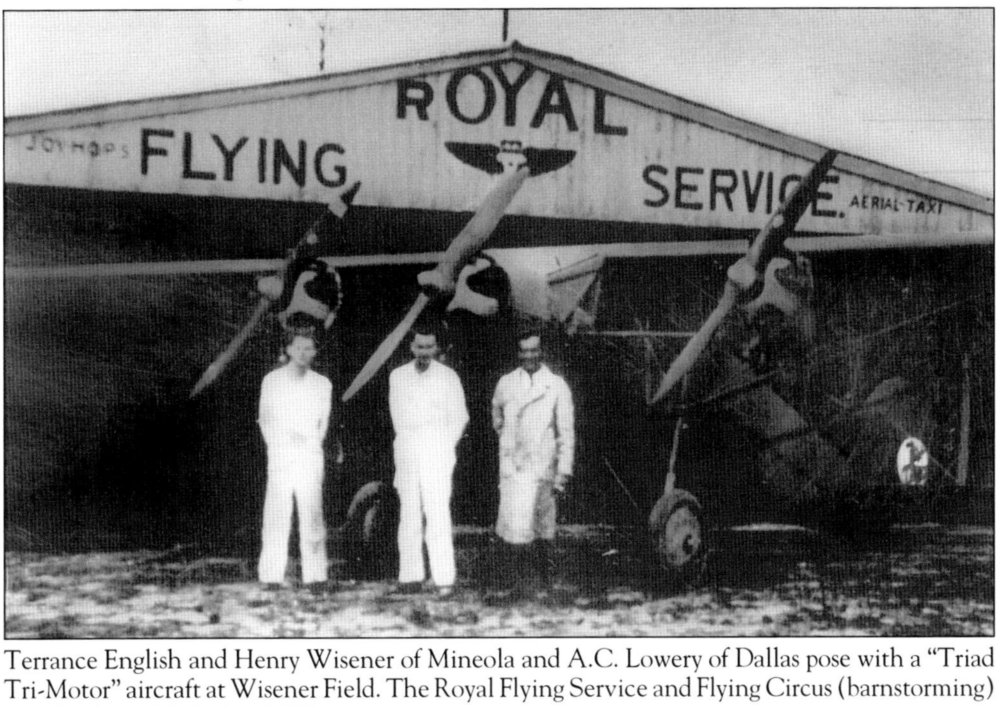

Terrance English and Henry Wisener of Mineola and A.C. Lowery of Dallas pose with a "Triad Tri-Motor" aircraft at Wisener Field. The Royal Flying Service and Flying Circus (barnstorming) were both established in 1926.

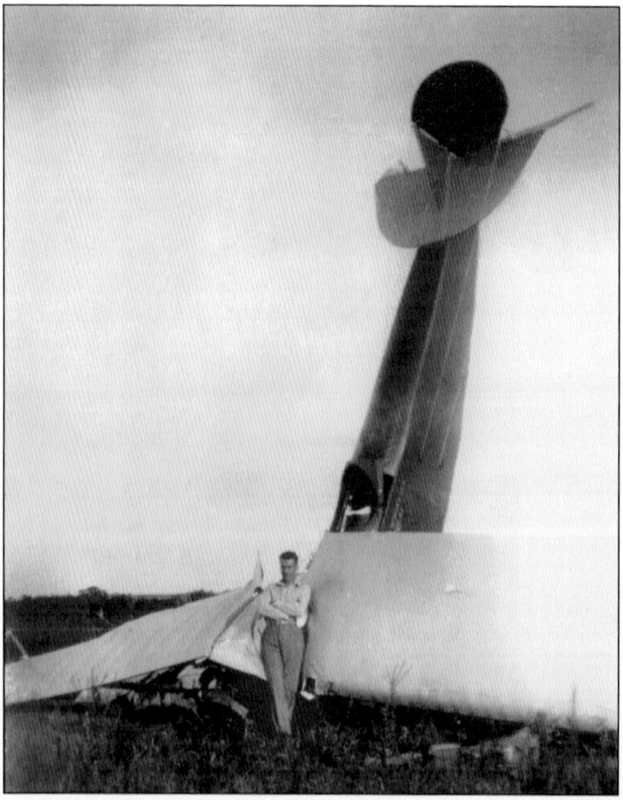

Henry Wisener is shown here with his wrecked JN4-C "Canuck" airplane when engine failure on takeoff caused a "hard" landing.

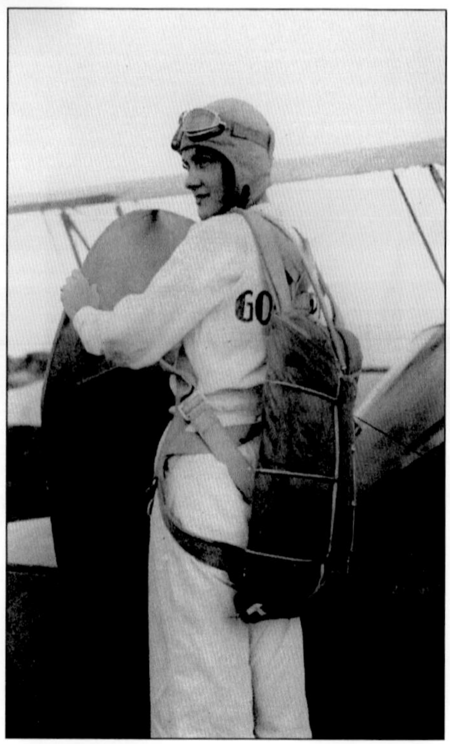

Miss Faye Lucille Cox, a professional parachute jumper shown here in full gear, set a world's record for consecutive jumps (over 100) during an air show in Mineola. Henry Wisener flew the plane for her jumps.

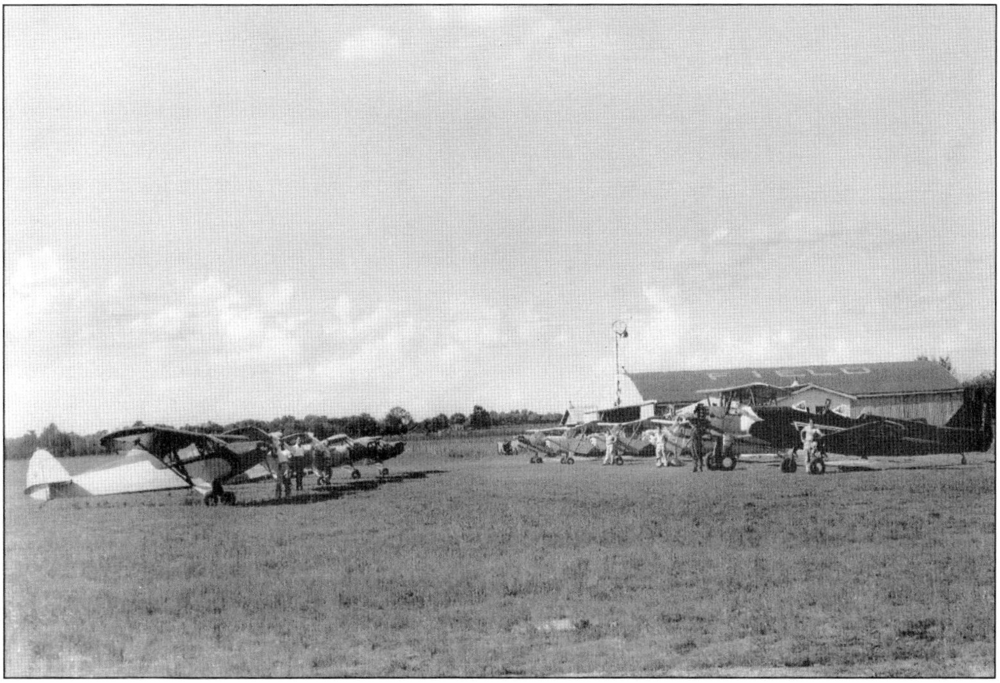

Pictured here in the late 1940s is the Wisener School of Aeronautics. Displayed are a Fairchild PT-19, a Boeing PT-17m Aeronca Champion, a Chief, and a Piper PA-12 Super Cruiser.

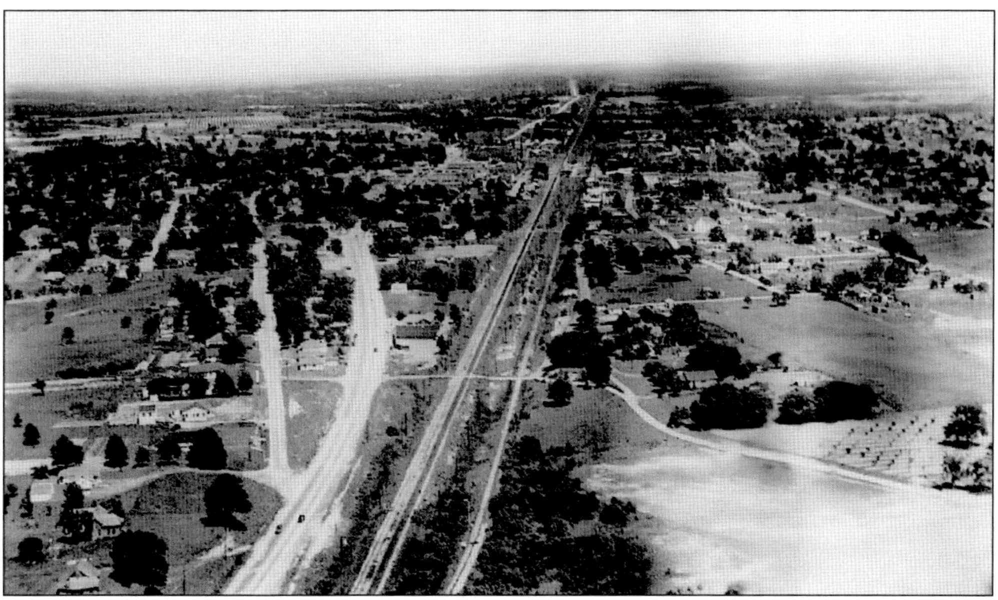

This aerial photograph of Mineola, *c.* 1945, shows Highway 80 and the railroad to the east.

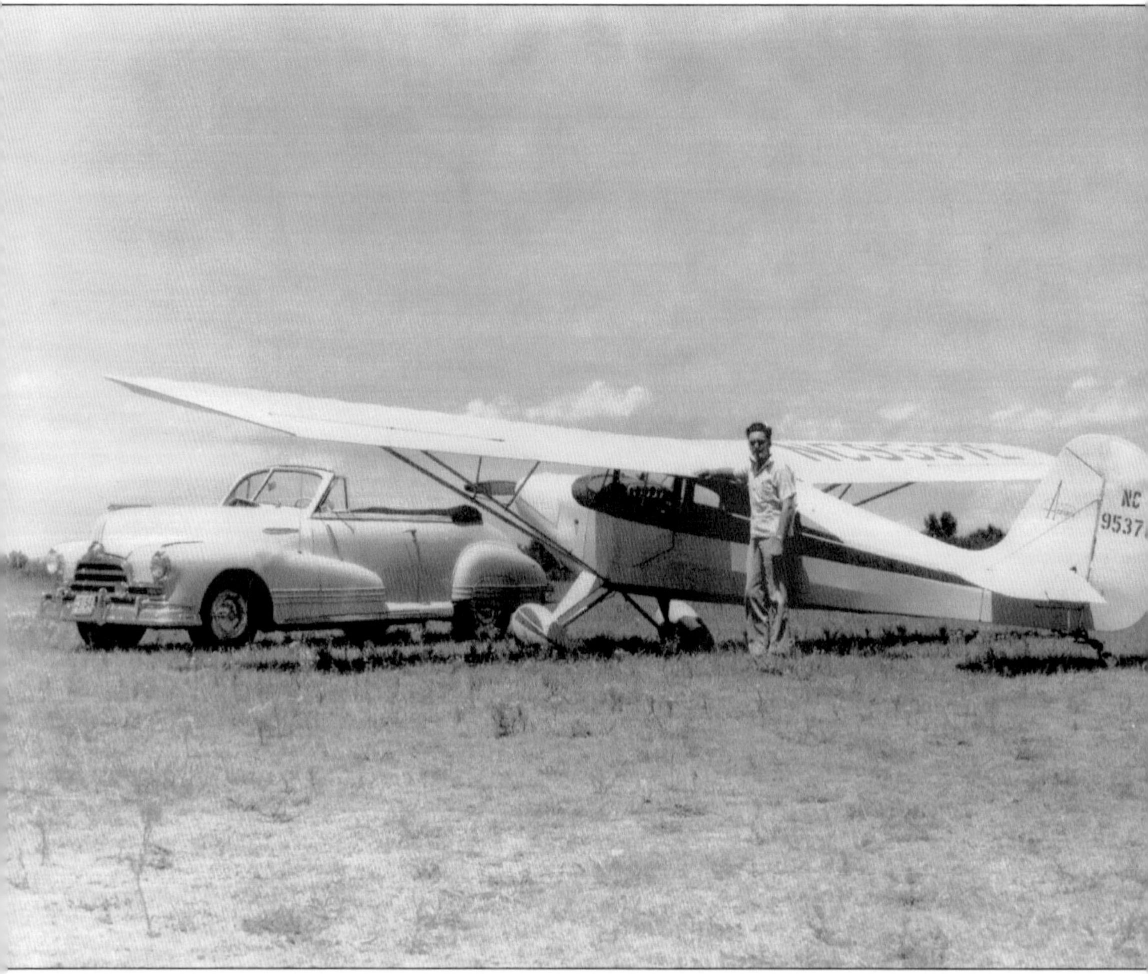

Everett Nix, chief instructor at the Wisener School of Aeronautics, is pictured here with a new Aronca Chief in the 1940s. The son of Maude Nix and the nephew of Henry and Bryce Wisener, Nix later became the chief pilot for Delta Airlines in Atlanta, Georgia.

Three

Country and Religious Music

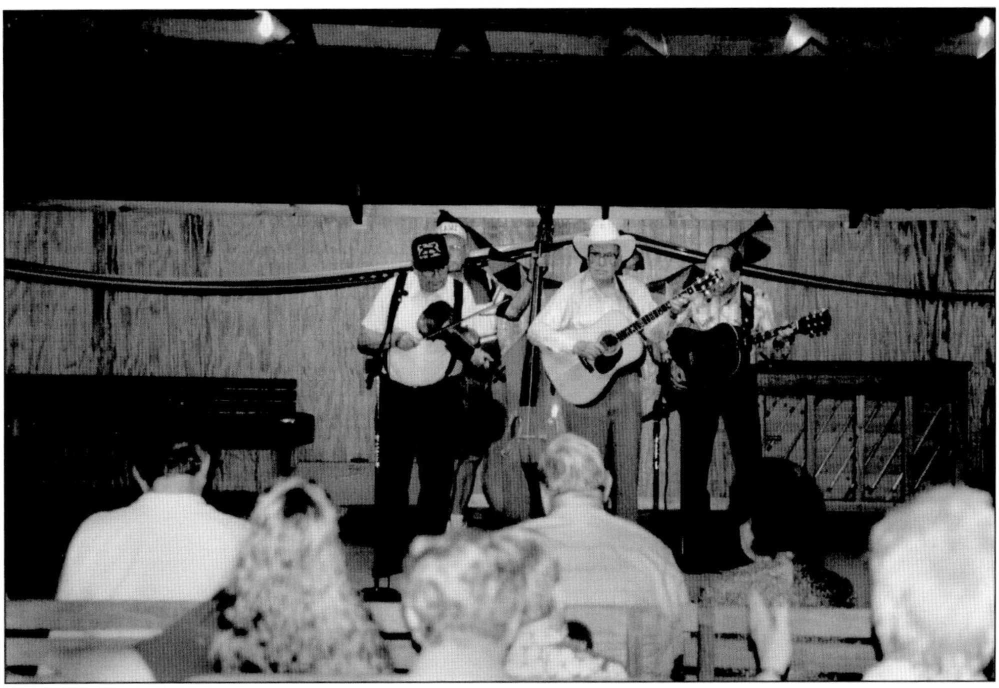

From the beginning, East Texas has been home to musicians who enjoy playing guitars or stringed instruments to entertain themselves and those around them. Most if not all of these musicians had no formal training but simply the desire and the ability to play by ear. They composed much of their own music, mainly country, bluegrass, or religious music. Through the years Wood County has produced singers, songwriters, movie stars, and performers, who by using their talents have made a name for themselves.

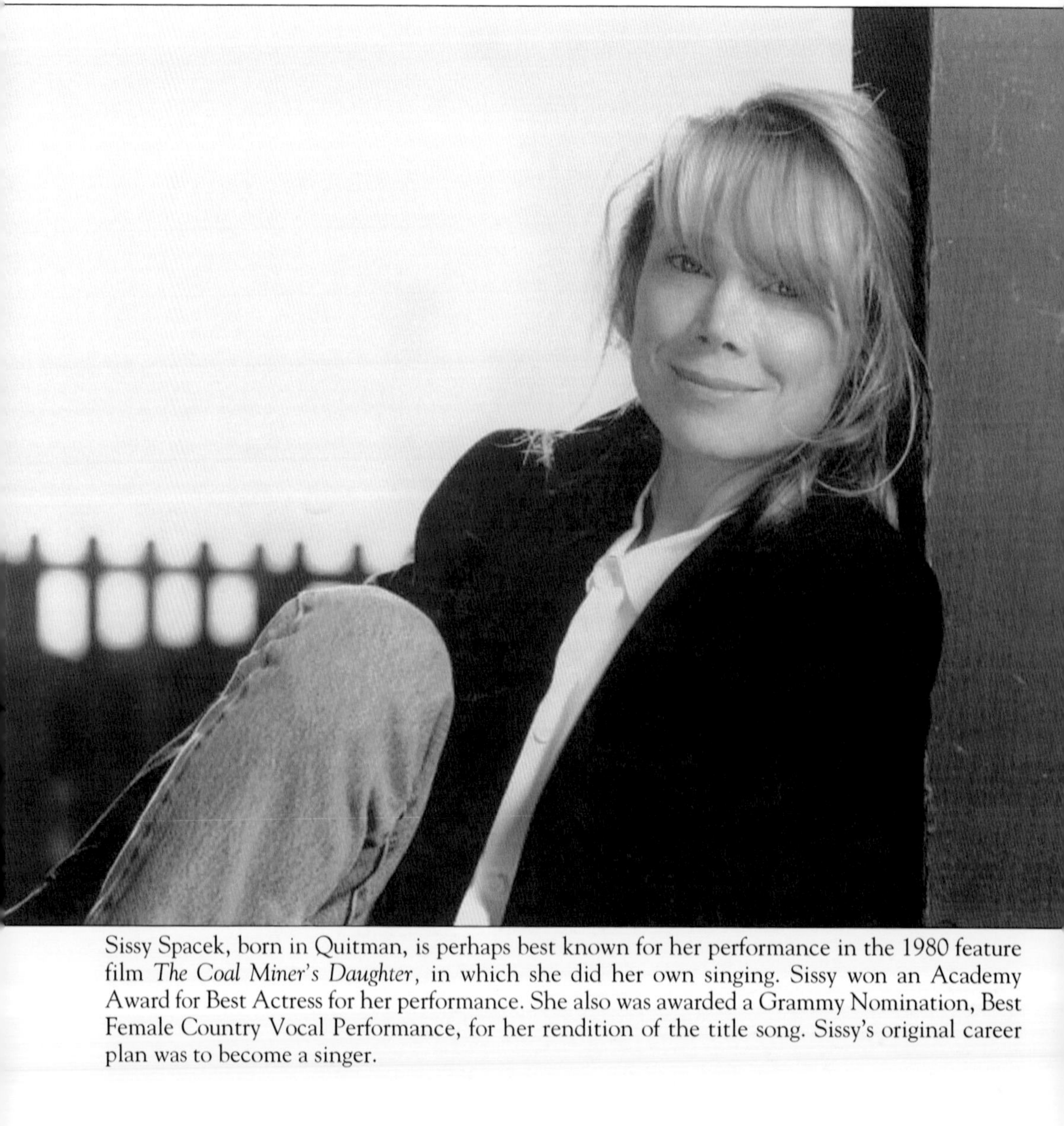

Sissy Spacek, born in Quitman, is perhaps best known for her performance in the 1980 feature film *The Coal Miner's Daughter*, in which she did her own singing. Sissy won an Academy Award for Best Actress for her performance. She also was awarded a Grammy Nomination, Best Female Country Vocal Performance, for her rendition of the title song. Sissy's original career plan was to become a singer.

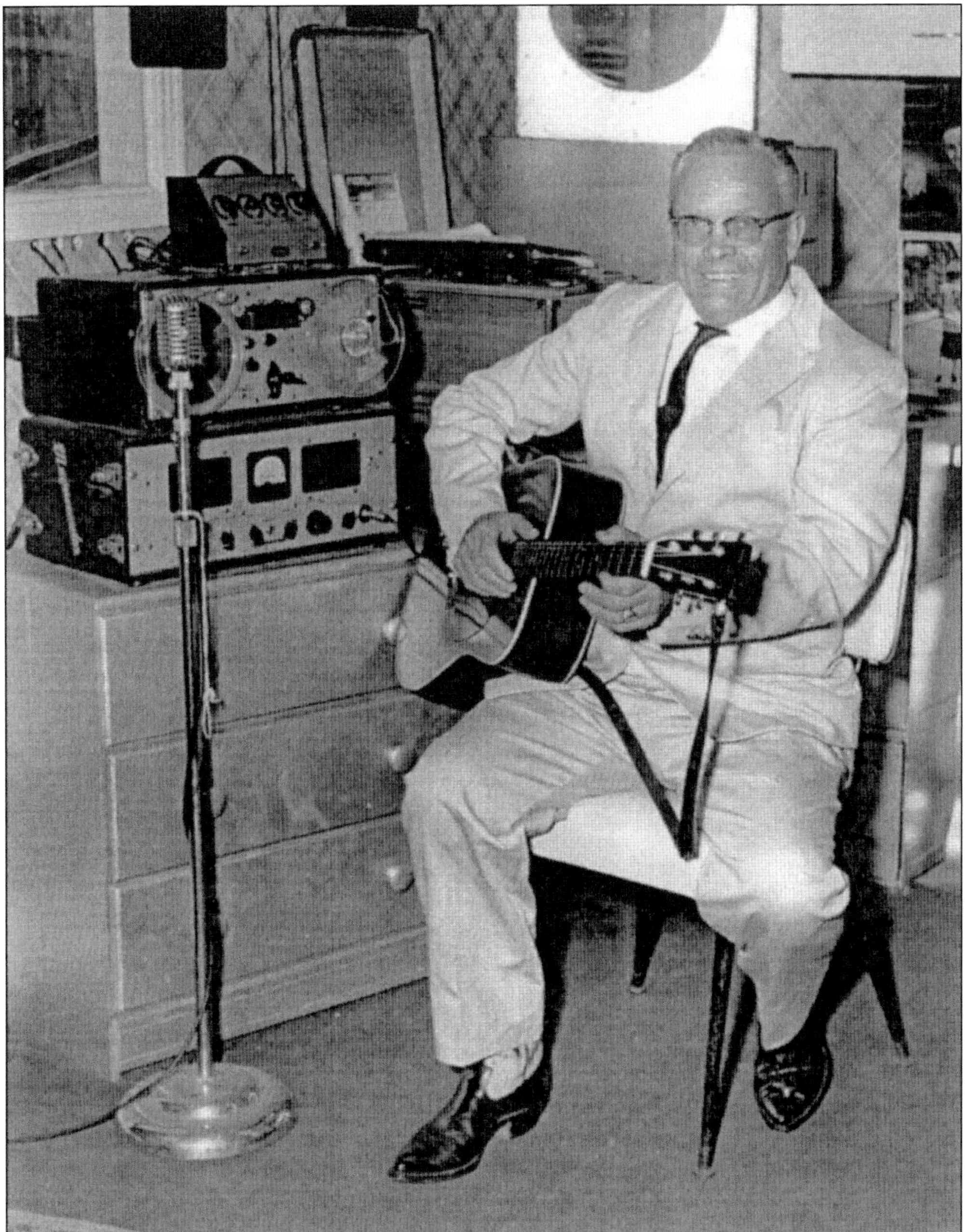

Country music performer/writer Andrew Jackson (Jack) Rhodes was born in Mineola. Jack played and sang with various groups over the years but he is best known for the many compositions he wrote. After his death in Mineola at the Trail 80 Motel and Café, several scribbled-on pieces of paper containing the words of songs he had written were found stuffed in his clothing, in desk drawers, and any other place he could find.

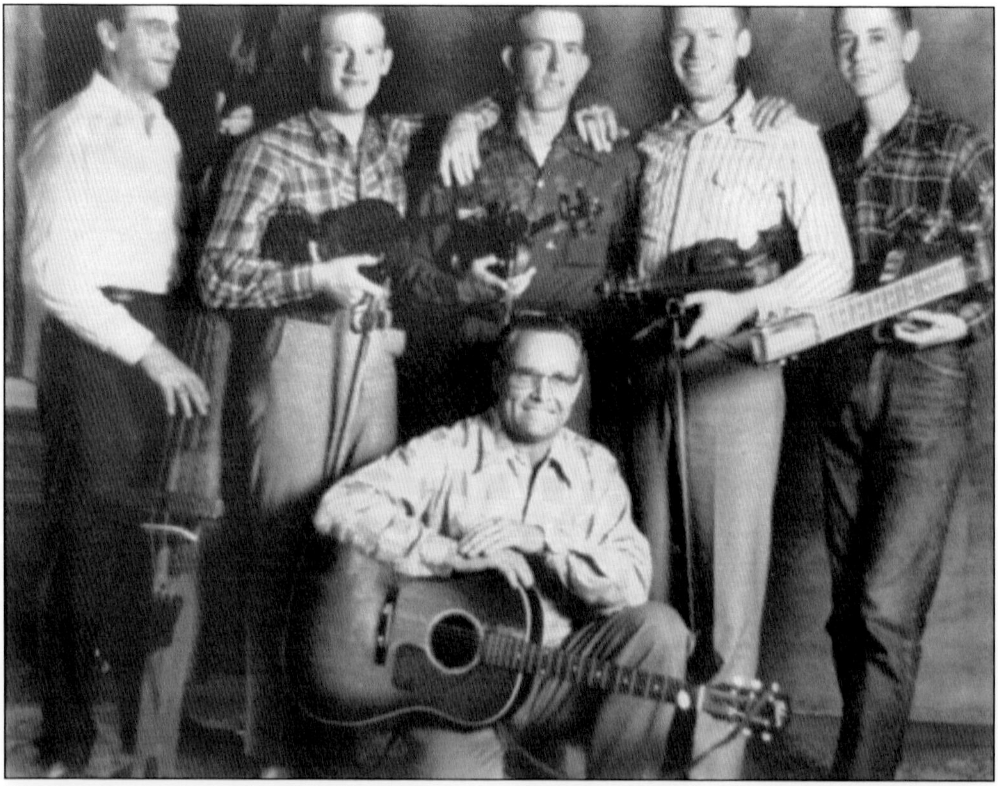

Rhodes, shown above playing with a group, never became a household name as a musician, but was recognized for his songwriting. He was inducted into the Country Music Hall of Fame in 1972. Some of his best-known songs include "Beautiful Lies," "Satisfied Mind," "Conscience," "I'm Guilty," and "Too Young To Settle Down." The lyrics below are from his most famous song, "Silver Threads and Golden Needles."

Silver Threads And Golden Needles

Jack Rhodes, Dick Reynolds

Silver threads and golden needles cannot mend this heart of mine
And I'll never drown my sorrow in the warm glow of your wine.
You can't buy my love with money, for I never was that kind,
Silver threads and golden needles cannot mend this heart of mine.
Go ahead!

I don't want your golden mansions with a tear in every room,
All I want's the love you promised, beneath the halo moon.
But you think I should be happy with your money and your name
And hide myself in sorrow while you play your cheatin' game.

Silver threads and golden needles cannot mend this heart of mine
And I'll never drown my sorrow in the warm glow of your wine.
You can't buy my love with money, for I never was that kind,
Silver threads and golden needles cannot mend this heart of mine.

Leon Payne was born on June 15, 1917 in Grit, a small community near Alba. He was blind in one eye at birth and lost the sight of the other eye in a childhood accident. Payne attended school at the Texas School for the Blind and began his music career at a radio station in Palestine, Texas. He played the guitar and several other stringed instruments and sang, according to his critics, "in the smooth style of Eddie Arnold."

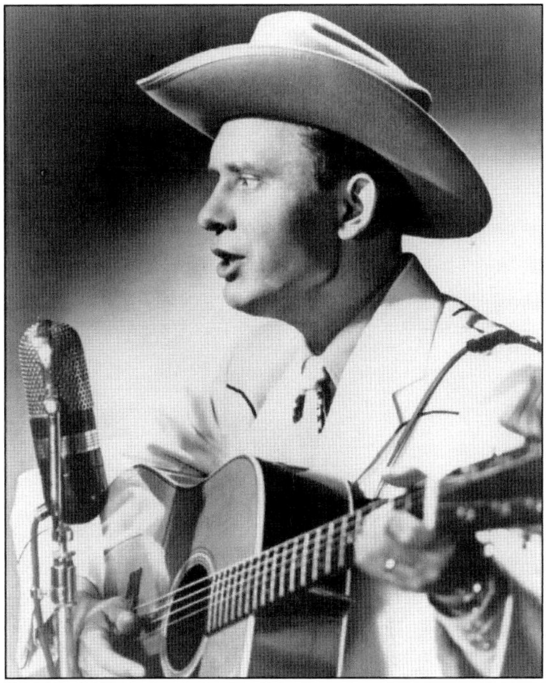

Leon Payne, country and western song writer and singer. Leon was born and raised at Grit, his parents were Jess and Gert Payne. Leon was blind. Mrs. Laura Speer took an interest in Leon and helped with his education. He attended a school in Austin where he learned Braille. *Courtesy- Audrey Flowers and Writing- Saundra Burge.*

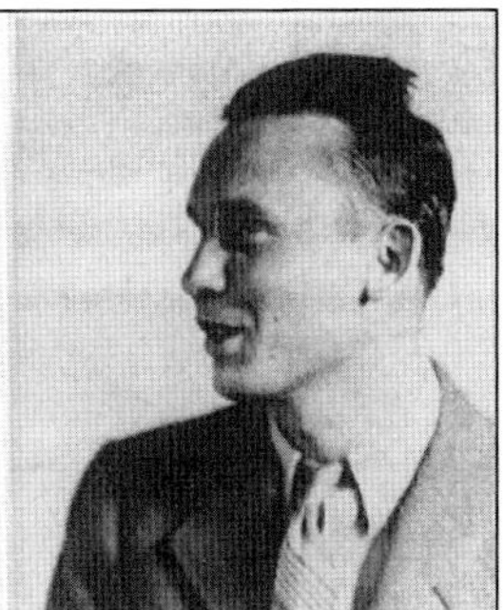

"I Love You Because" was one of Leon Payne's biggest hit songs. He wrote dozens of others which were recorded by Bing Crosby, Perry Como, Jim Reeves, Gene Autry and others. Leon was a member of the Louisiana Hay Ride and the Grand Ole Opry. *Courtesy- Elvis and Francine Allen*

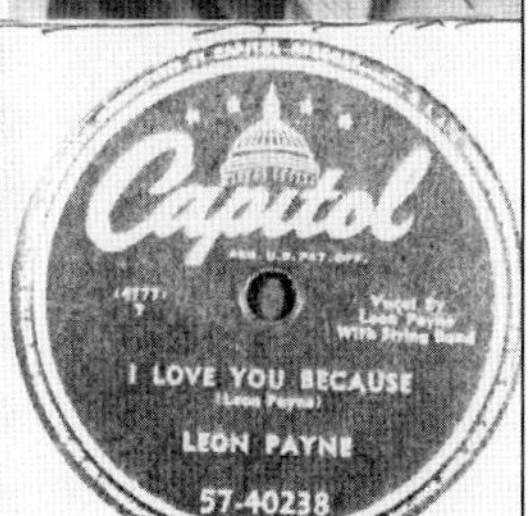

"Lifetime To Regret" by Leon Payne and Jack Rhodes. Leon and Jack wrote many great country and western songs. Jack lived in Alba when he was young. He built Trail 80 Motel and Cafe at Mineola. *Courtesy- Elvis and Francine Allen*

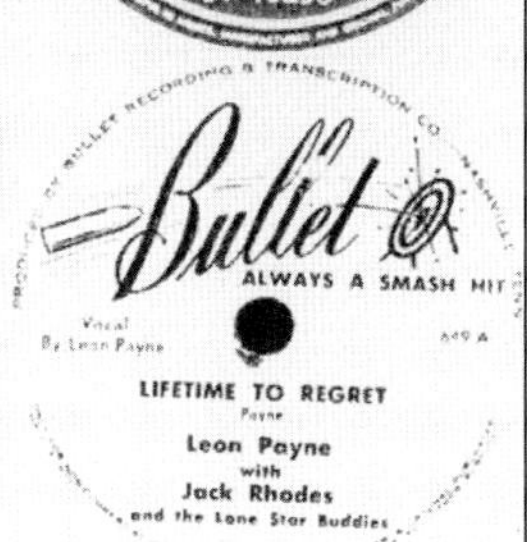

"I Love You Because" was one of Leon Payne's biggest hits; it was recorded by big-time stars such as Bing Crosby, Perry Como, Gene Autry, and others. Hank Williams Sr. made Leon's song "Lost Highway" a national hit. The song "Lifetime to Regret" was written by Payne and Jack Rhodes who had also lived in Alba when he was young.

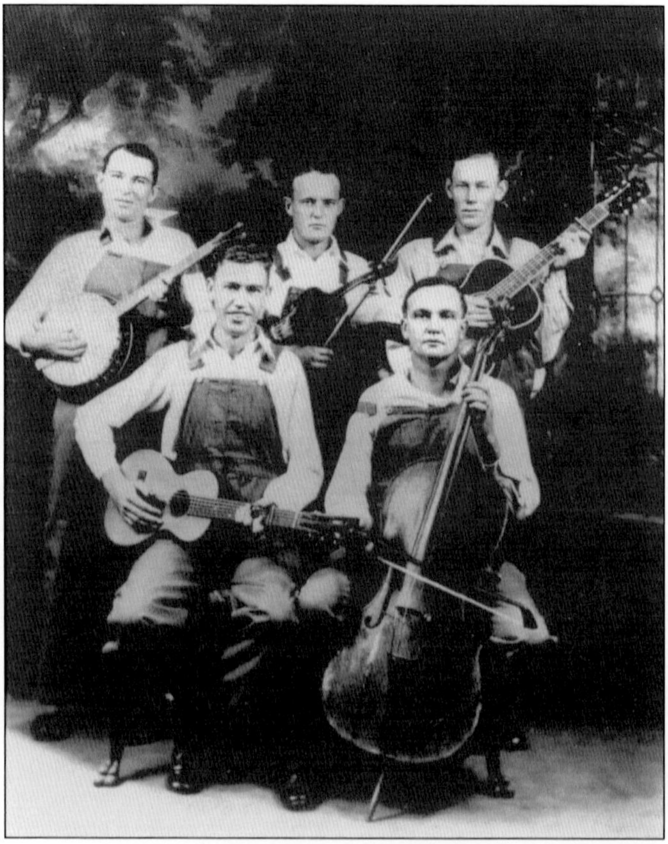

These men, all from the local area around Mineola, composed a string band, the East Texas Serenaders, which provided music and entertainment. The group played mostly rags, waltzes, and two-steps—dance music for moving in a circle around the floor. They recorded for Brunswick, Decca, and Columbia Record Companies from 1927 to 1937.

Bill Boyd and the Cowboy Ramblers was a popular Texas band in the 1930s and was composed of residents of the county. The exact time and place of the photograph below is unknown.

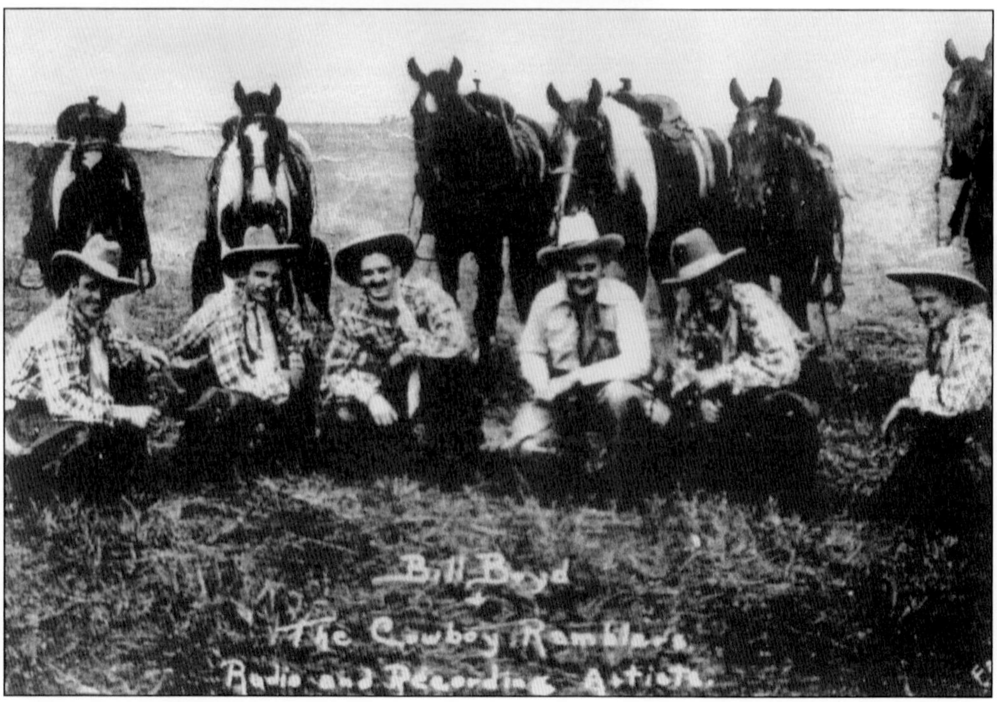

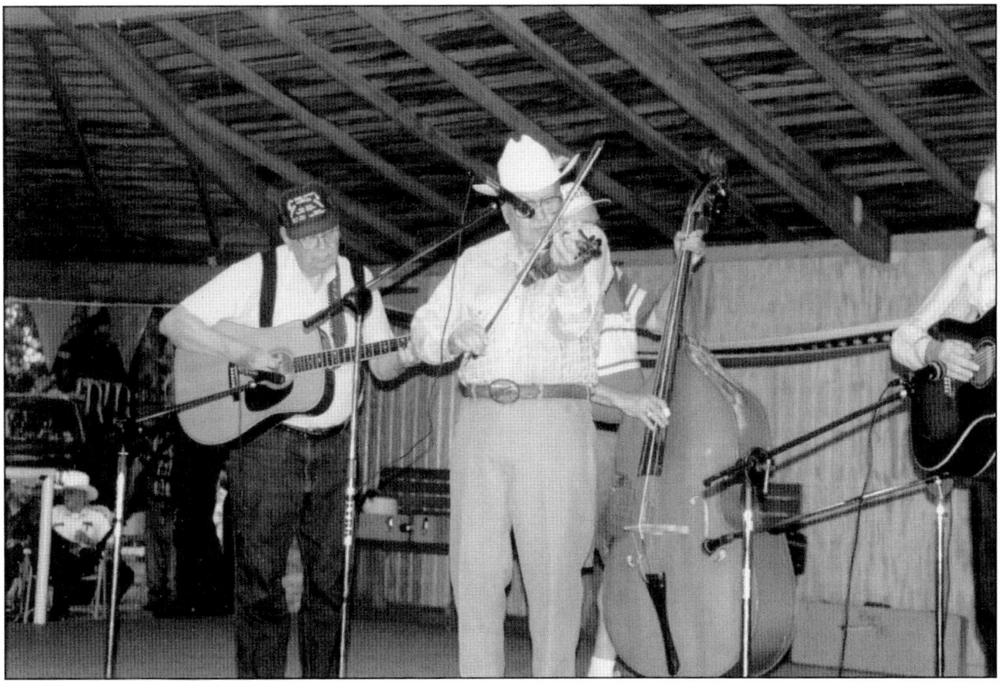

The group performs at a recent reunion. A fiddling contest has always been a part of the festivities and draws the largest crowd during the week-long Old Settlers Reunion held in Quitman each year.

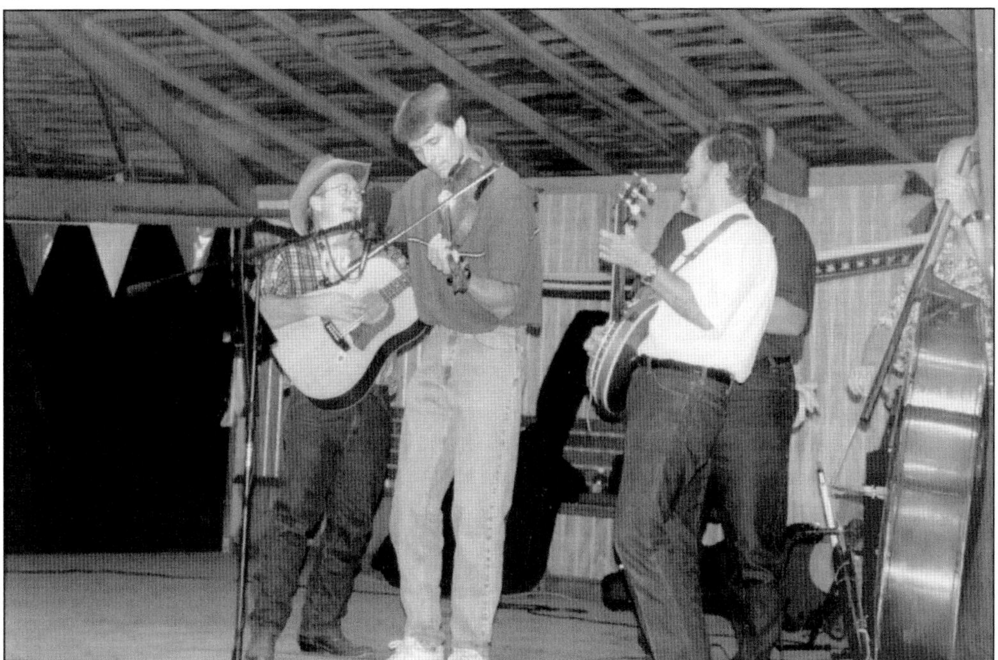

Many of the same people compete in the fiddling contest from year to year. The contestants come from all over Texas and surrounding states to compete and their ages range from children to senior citizens.

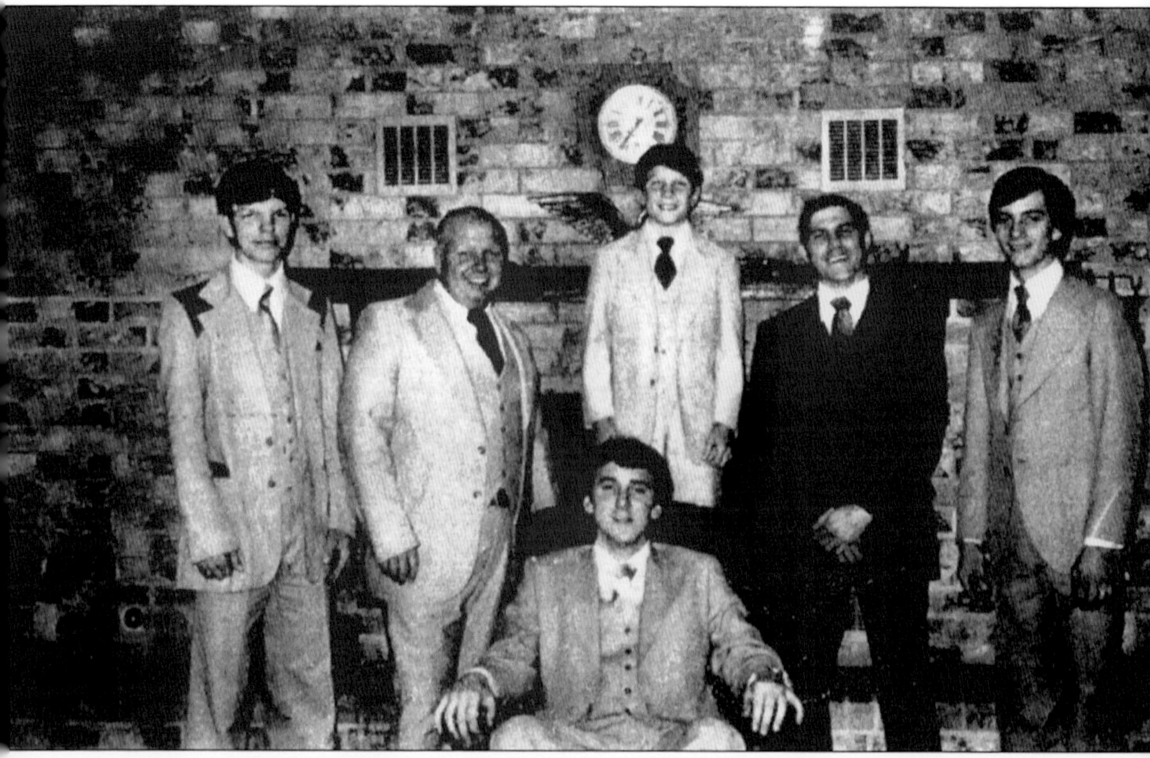

Religious and gospel music arrived with the early settlers to the area and continues to be loved by East Texans. Singing conventions were held all over the surrounding area early in the 20th century, and today many rural churches still sing the old gospel songs. The group in this photograph is from the Golden area.

Four

Fishing and other Recreational Activities

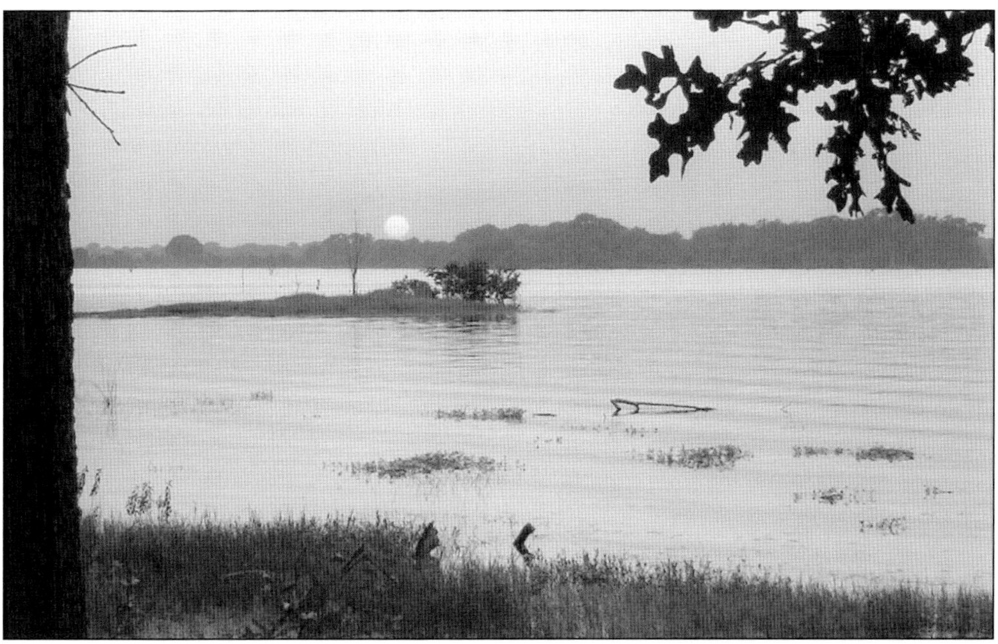

Wood County abounds with many different kinds of recreational activities, such as hunting and fishing, water sports, high school athletics, soccer, summer and fall leagues in baseball and softball, and golf. There is something for everyone. Lake Fork, pictured here, is a paradise to fishermen and is known as the bass capital of Texas. The state record bass was caught out of Lake Fork in 1992. Wood County has four county lakes used for recreational purposes. The Sabine River marks the southern border of the county and provides a great place for hunting, fishing, and bird watching.

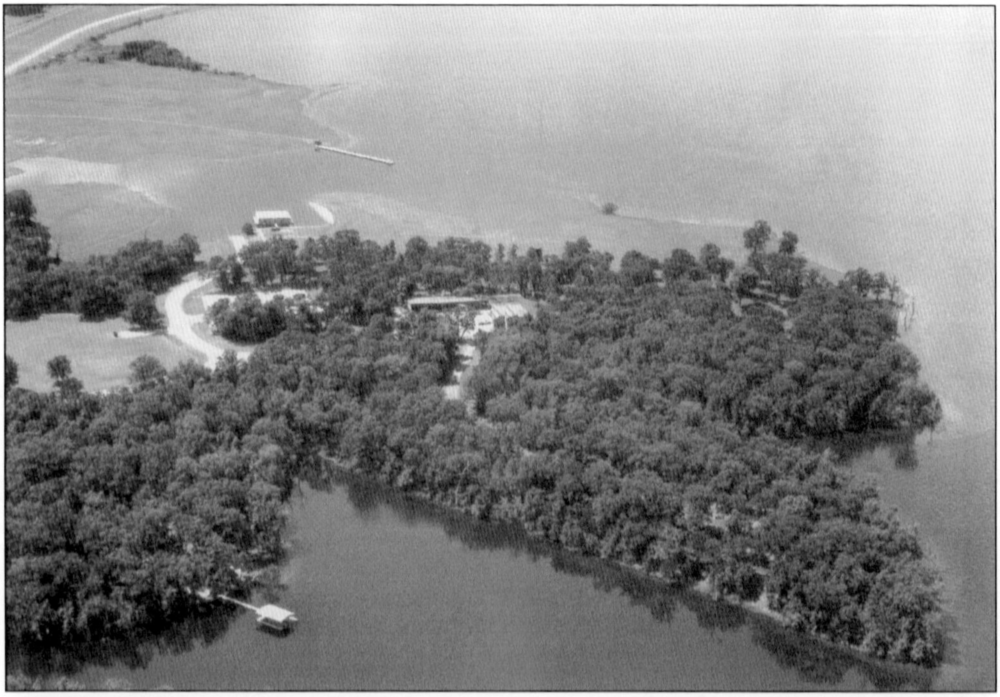

Lake Fork construction began in 1975 and the dam was closed in 1980. Lake Fork was constructed and funded through a water supply agreement with Texas Utilities Generating Company to provide water for municipal and industrial users. Texas Utilities, Dallas, Longview, Kilgore, Henderson, and Quitman have contracted to purchase water from the reservoir; other water corporations are making plans for future use of the water. (Courtesy of Texas Department of Wildlife.)

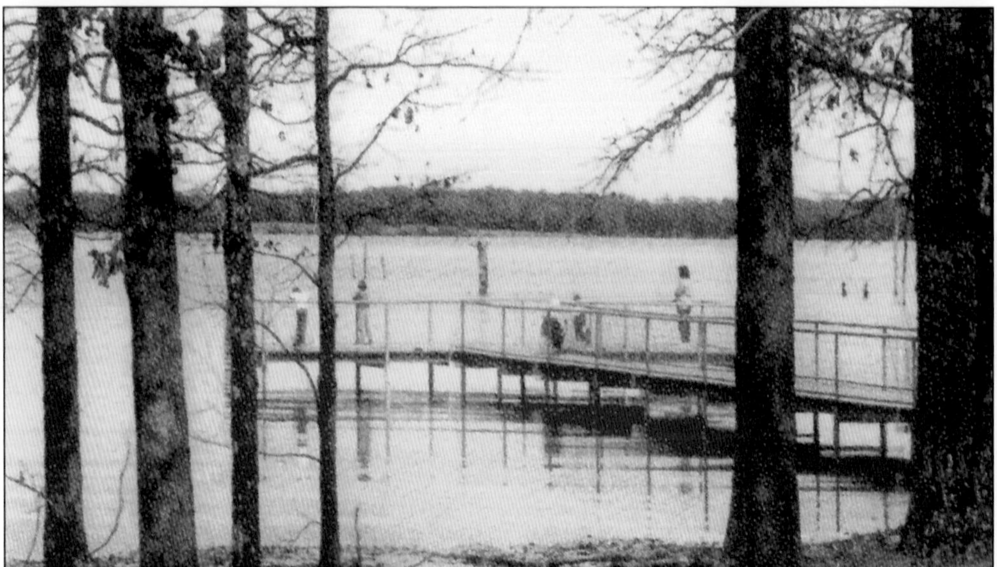

Lake Fork is known worldwide as the finest trophy bass fishing lake in the United States. The lake has attracted fishermen from all over the United States and abroad. (Courtesy of Texas Department of Wildlife.)

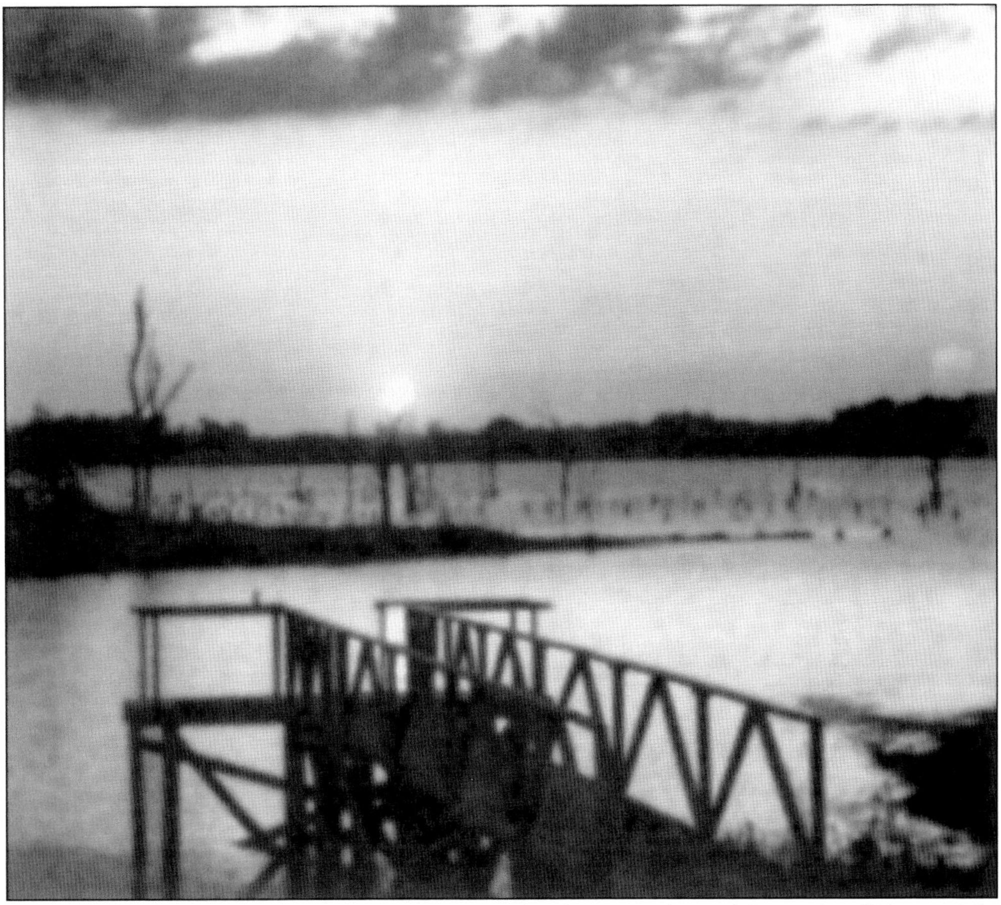

Lake Fork is known mainly for big bass, but it also has large numbers of channel and blue catfish. Other fish, such as naturally occurring populations of yellow bass, crappie, bluegill, and red-ear sunfish, create an interest for some anglers. (Courtesy of Texas Department of Wildlife.)

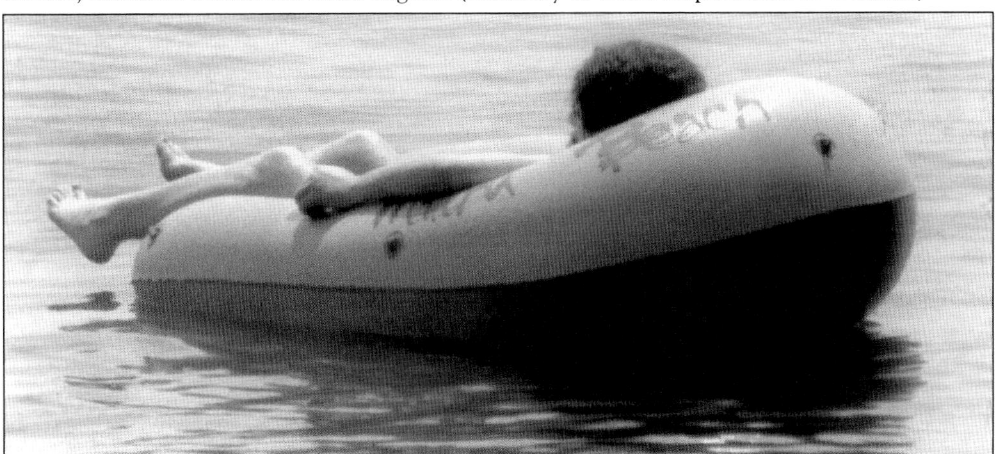

Lake Fork is enjoyed by thousands of water sport enthusiasts each year. The long summers and mild winters are an attraction to many visitors, along with the picturesque views and abundant wildlife, especially the eagles. (Courtesy of Texas Department of Wildlife.)

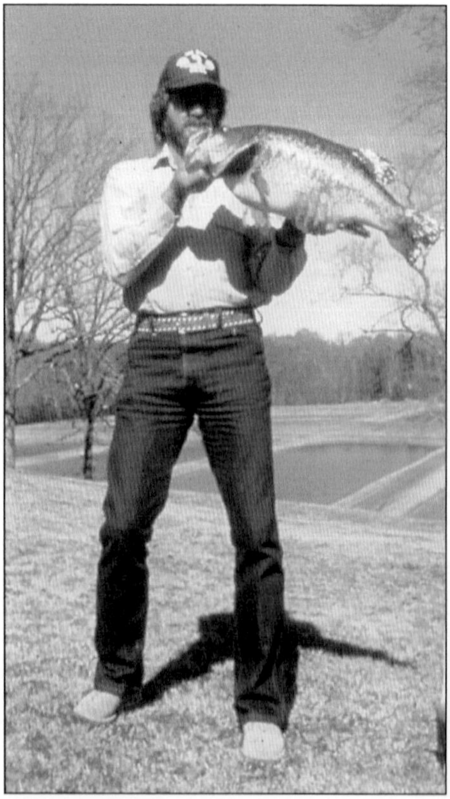

Barry St. Clair poses with his state record large mouth bass. The fish weighed 18.18 pounds and was caught in January 1992. (Courtesy of Texas Department of Wildlife.)

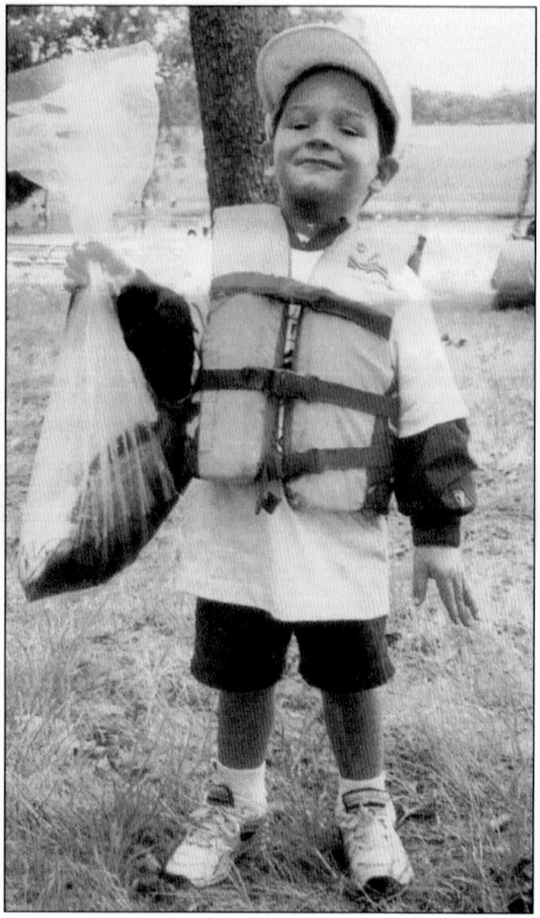

Even the little ones enjoy fishing at Lake Fork. Several organizations in Wood County operate special programs that take children out on the lake for a day of fishing. (Courtesy of Texas Department of Wildlife.)

Mark Stephenson is pictured with his 17.67-pound large mouth bass caught out of Lake Fork. (Courtesy of Texas Department of Wildlife.)

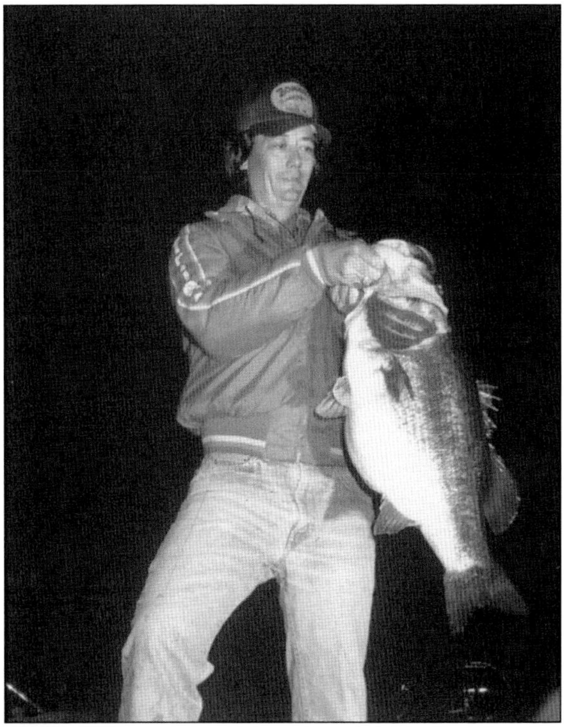

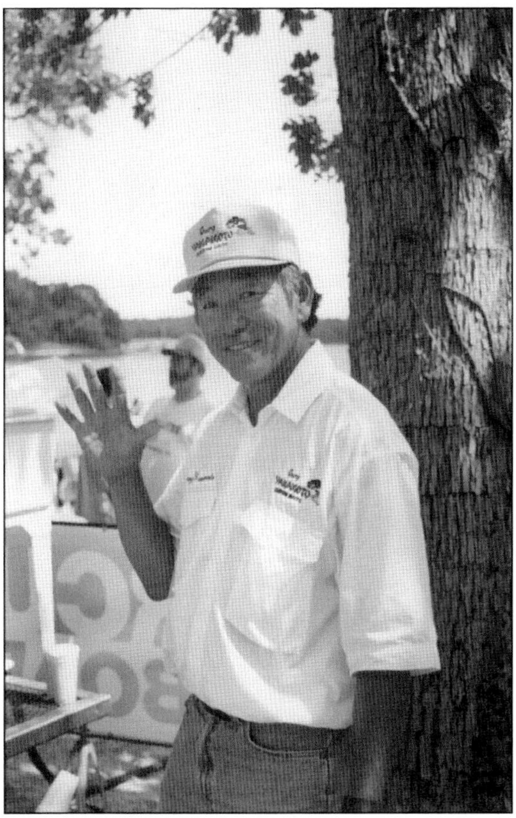

It was quality fishing that lured Arizona bait manufacturer Gary Yamamoto to Texas. A noted western tournament pro, Yamamoto wanted to test and develop baits for bass-fertile Texas water, so in 1997 when the Lone Star State cast its lure toward Gary and Beverly Yamamoto, they bit. World-class fishing and the couple's plans to build a private fishing resort led them to Mineola. The resort that stands there today is Sugoi Lakes. Sugoi is a Japanese word meaning "perfect."

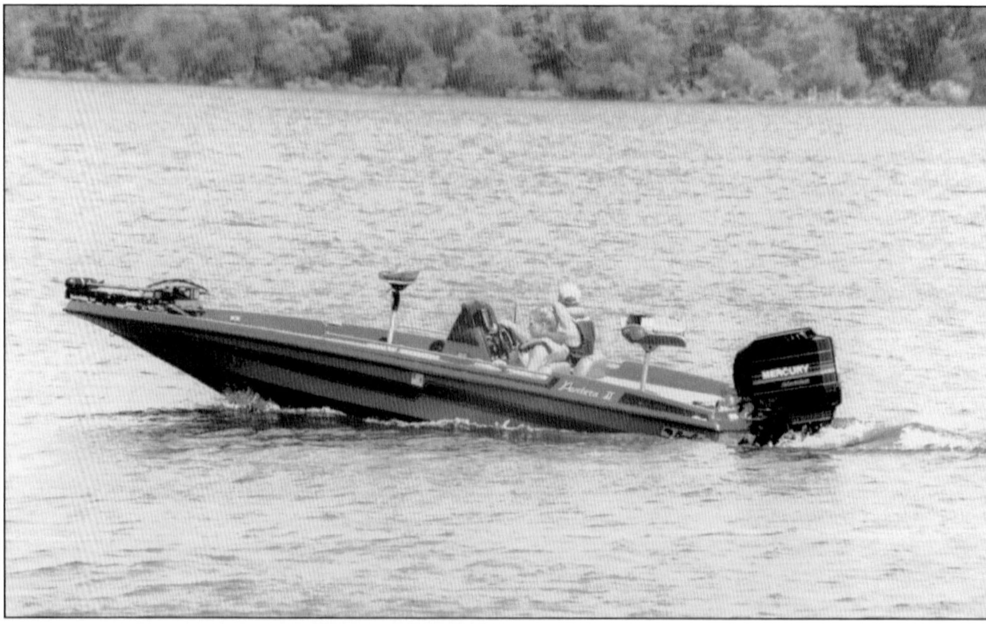

Boaters enjoy one of the many lakes in Wood County.

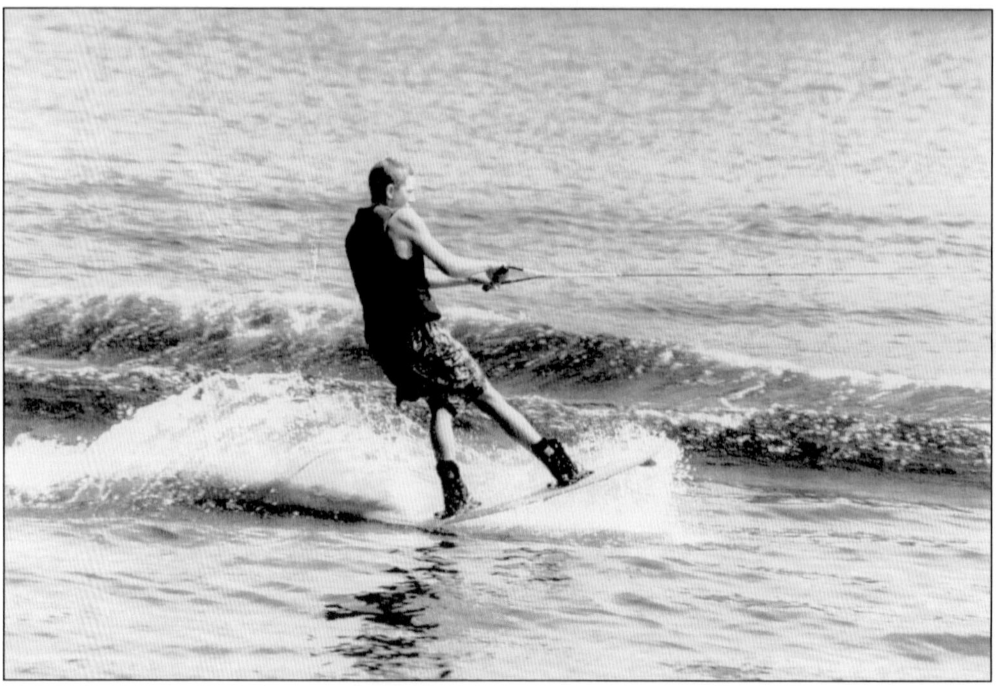

Water skiing on Lake Fork is another one of the water sports enjoyed by many. Jet skiing is also a very popular sport on the lake.

Shirley Madsen was fishing with Randy Bennett on Lake Fork when she reeled in this nice bass. (Courtesy of Texas Department of Wildlife.)

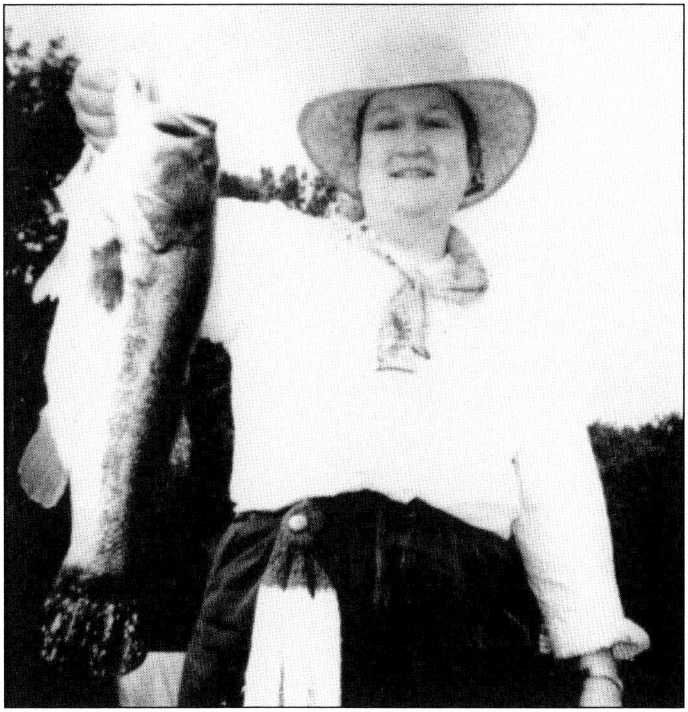

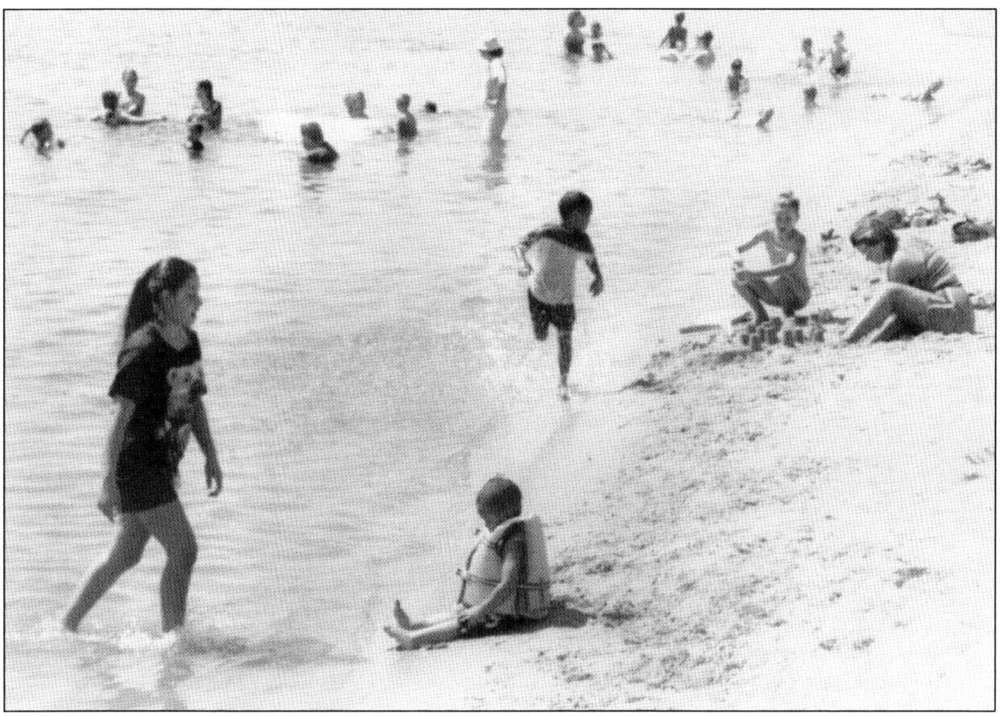

Swimming is enjoyed at one of the county's many lakes. In the early 1960s, Wood County built four lakes for recreational use. The lakes all have beaches with swimming areas along with picnic and camping areas.

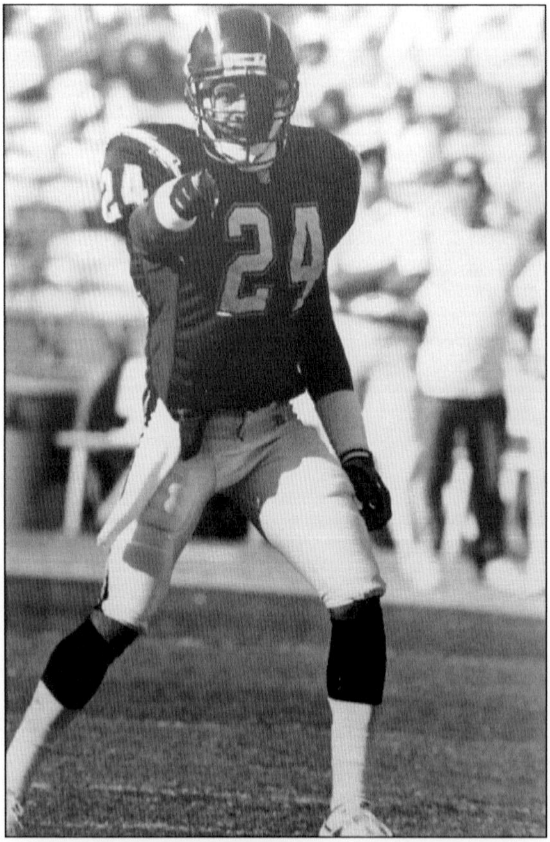

Stanley Palmer Richard was born in Mineola in 1967, was raised in the Fouke community, graduated from Hawkins High School, and was named East Texas athlete of the year. Stanley was awarded a full athletic scholarship to the University of Texas at Austin and was named to the Associated Press's All-American Football Team. In 1990 he was named MVP and player of the year. He was later drafted by the San Diego Chargers, where he played from 1991 to 1994. In 1995, Stanley became the only Wood County resident to play in the Super Bowl.

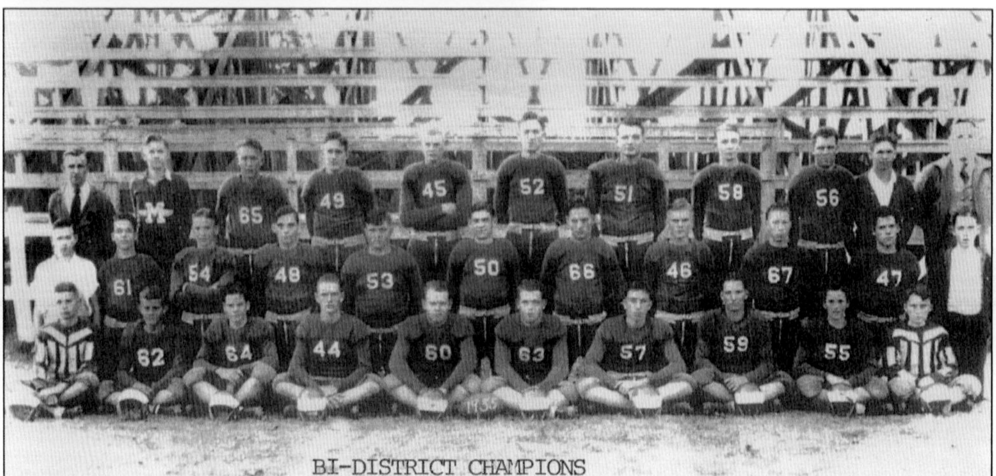

The members of the 1935 Mineola team and Bi-District champs are pictured here, from left to right: (front row) John Cowan, Larry Colvin, Hugh Pennal, Bruce Welch, Bedford Parker, Ledford Parker, Dallas Lankford, H.L. Hargraves, John Shirey, and Robert Rogers; (middle row) Bill Dugan, C.J. Tiner, Gerald Shirey, Hershall Dean, L.D. Lester, Jack McReynolds, and Joe Ford Mayberry; (back row) Coach Paul Snow, Milford York, Forrest Colvin, Henry Blankenship, Roscoe Lindley, Worth Bruner, Guy Moseley, Paul Shirey, Henry Speights, Al Snyder, and Coach Red Moore.

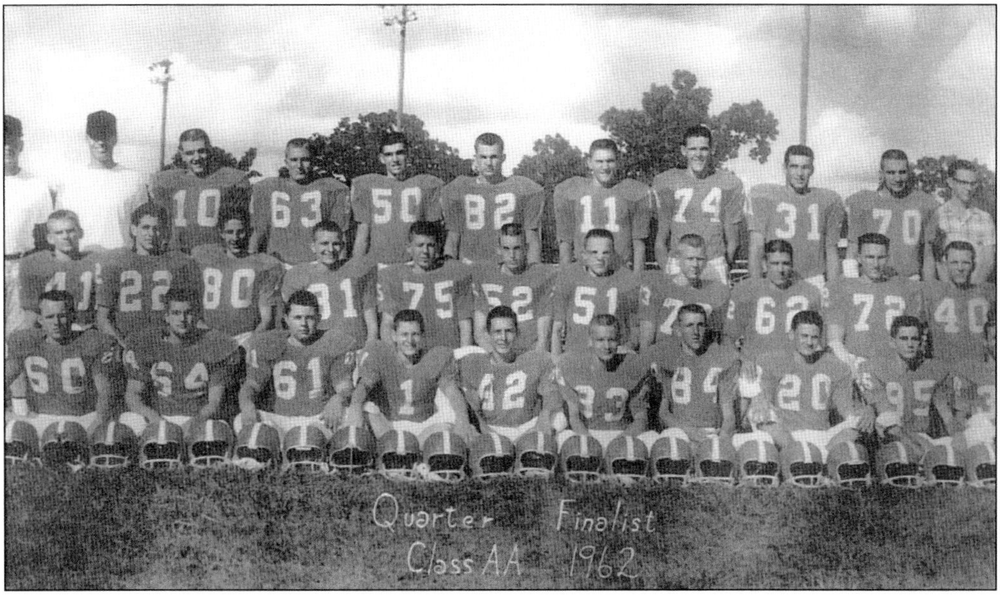

Pictured, from left to right, are members of the 1962 Mineola quarterfinalist football team: (front row) Jeff Smith, Jack Williams, Mike Scroggins, Lovic Williams, Woody Weimer, Johnny Cobb, Jimmy Allen, Jimmy Moody, Richard Ellison, and Skipper Hortman; (middle row) Ronnie Oglesby, Tom Harrison, Chris Molnari, Doug Robertson, John Evans, Ray George, Mike Fisher, Larry Pool, Larry Williams, Glen Dossett, and Scotty Smith; (back row) Coach Charles Lyles, Coach Phil Jones, Mike Phillips, Perry McDonald, Jay Barlow, Dean Childres, Jimmy Williams, Anthony Bruner, Doug Cannon, Elvis Dobson, and Manager C.R. Evans.

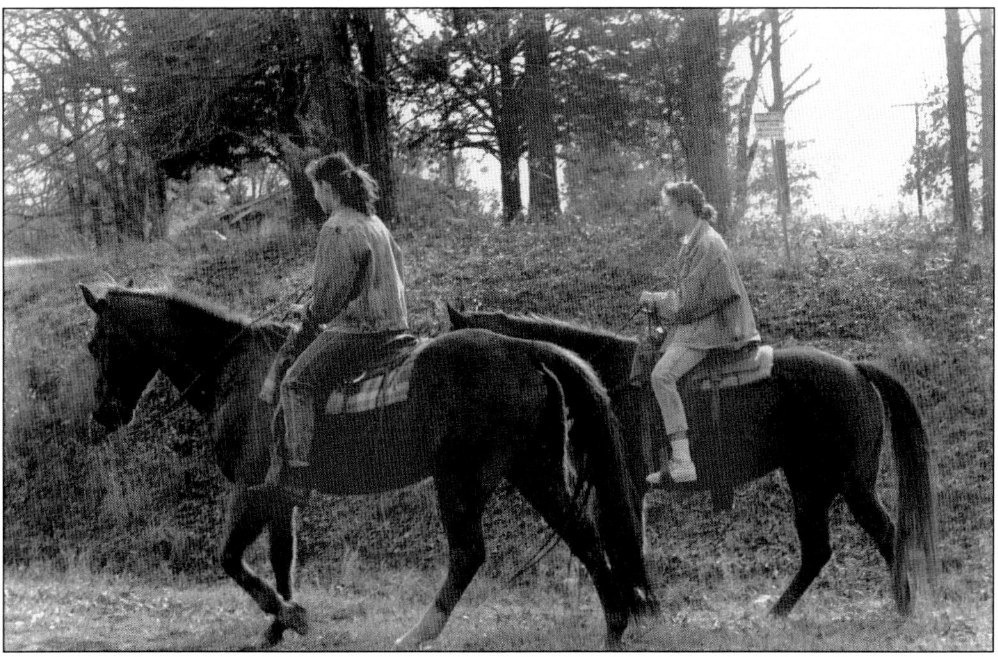

Horseback riding is another very popular sport in Wood County, and several trail rides are held throughout the year. Horses and riders are a big attraction at the many parades held in the different towns.

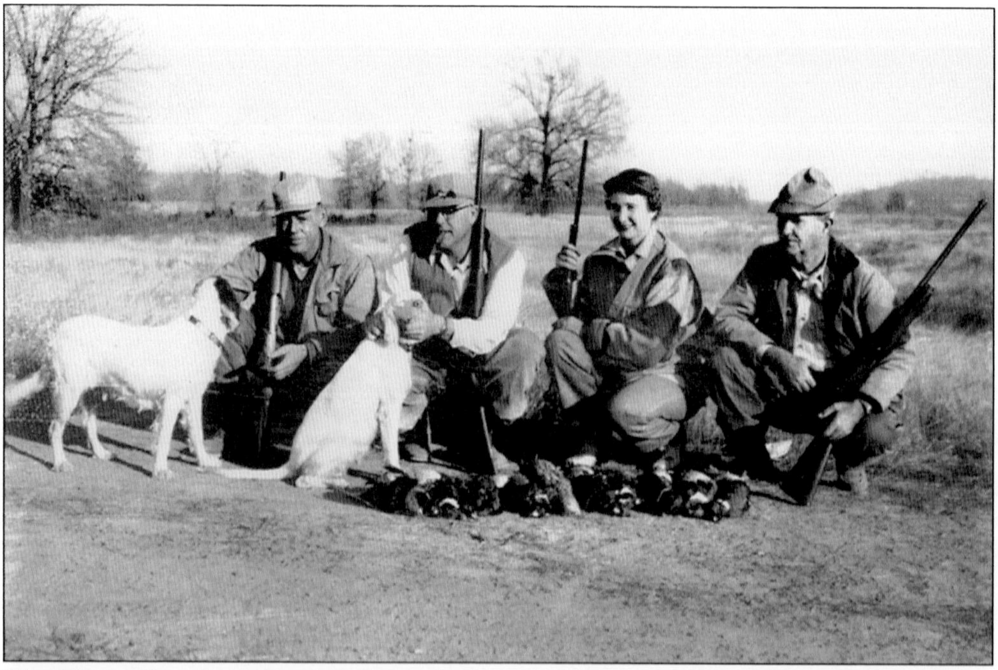

Wood County loved to go hunting. Pictured here is a local group, c. 1950, including M.E. Peppeard, Ruth Lott, David Lott, and Howard Lott.

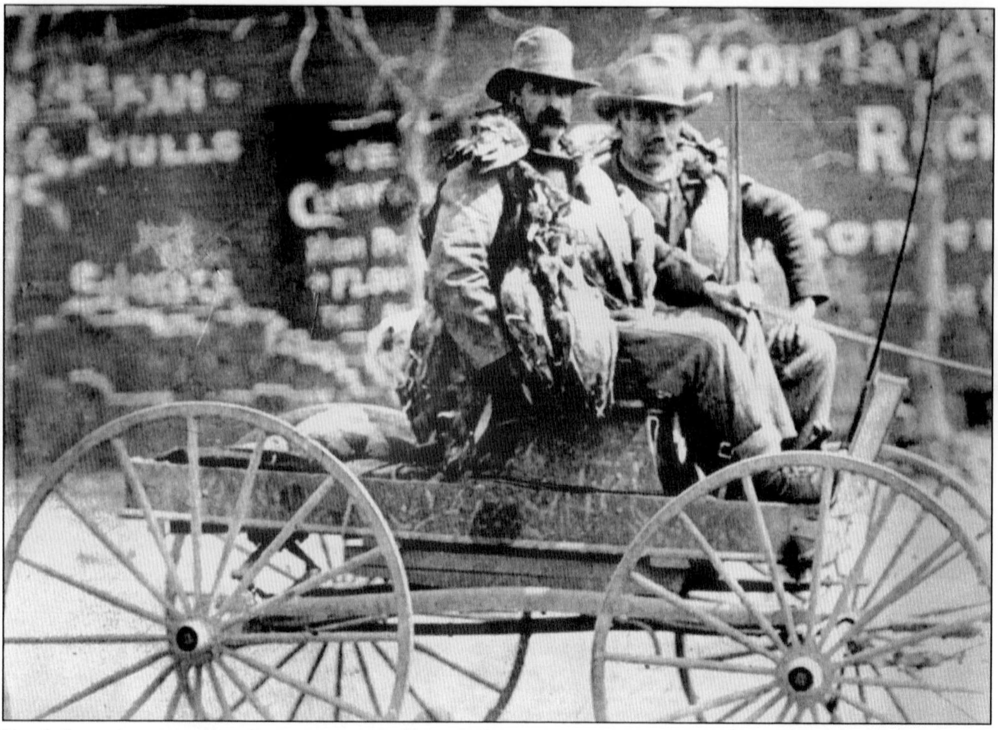

Duck hunting is still as big a sport in Wood County now as it was when this photograph was taken at the turn of the century. Lake Fork is a hot spot for hunters.

Land's End is Wood County's newest golf course, located near Yantis along the shore of Lake Fork, and 13 of its 18 holes are directly along the waterfront. Land's End was inspired by the original Land's End on the southwestern tip of England. An elegant clubhouse and English-style pro shop welcome visitors.

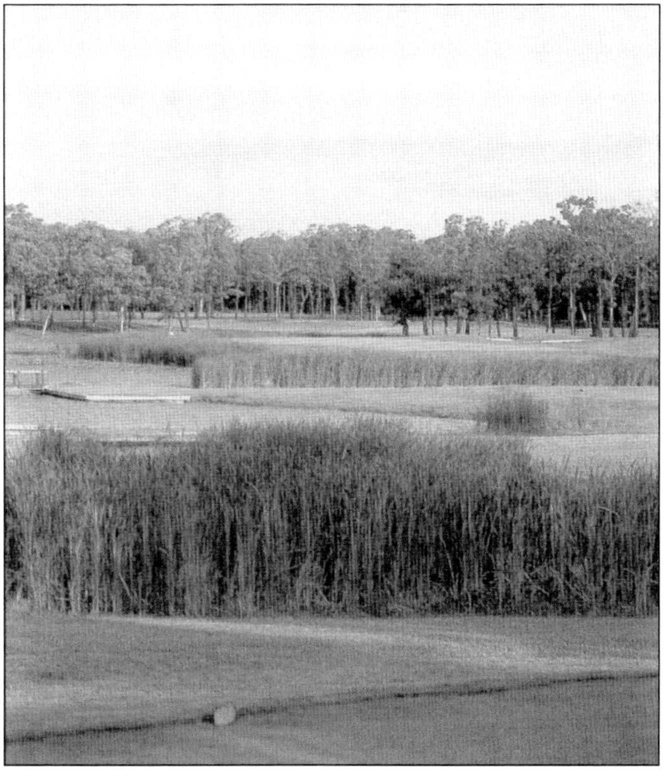

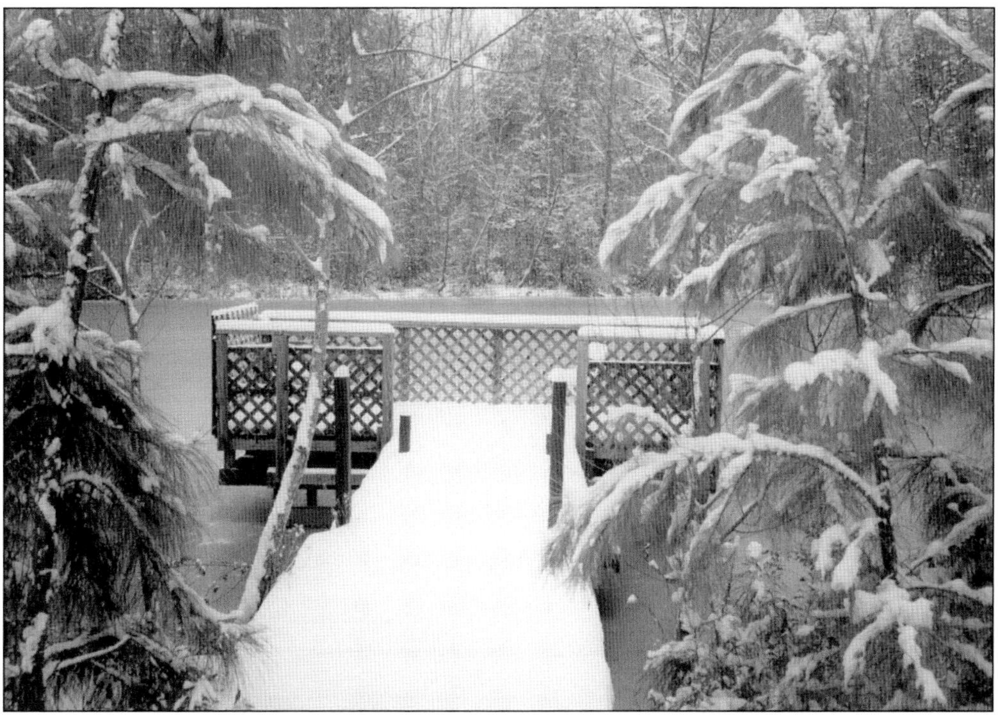

This beautiful wintry lake scene at Pine Mills is not repeated often in Wood County, and snow is an exciting event for local residents.

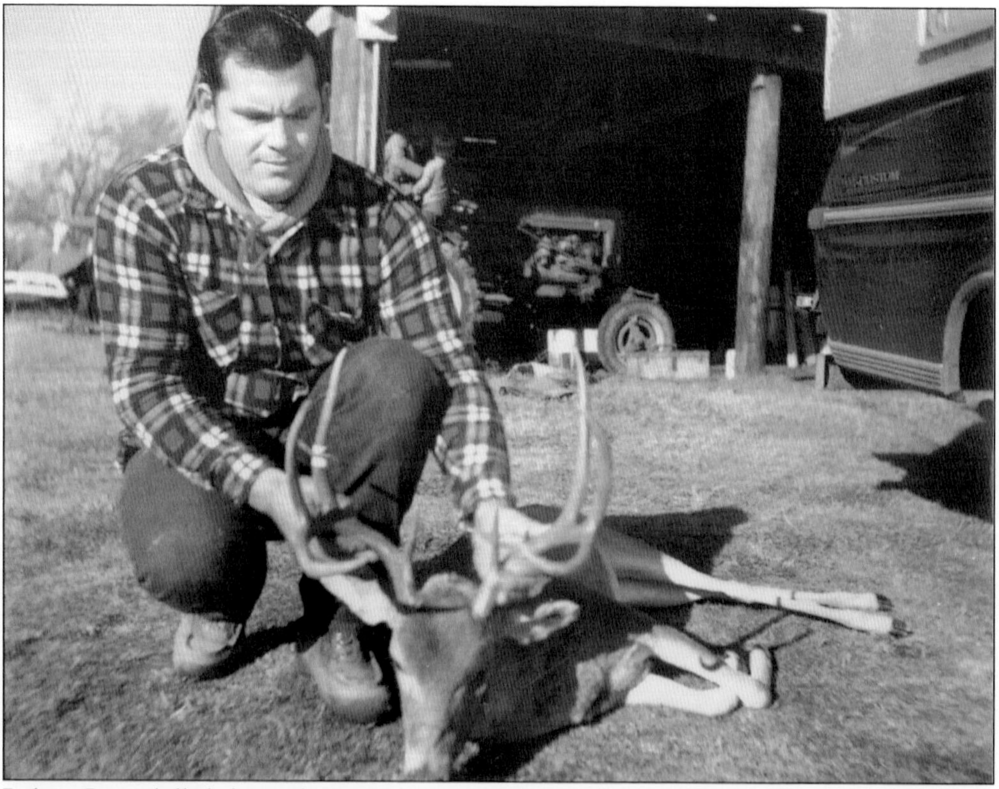

Robert Burge killed this eight-point buck near Hainesville in Wood County in 1972. Deer hunting is the favorite sport of many in Wood County. Whitetail deer can be found in every area of the county.

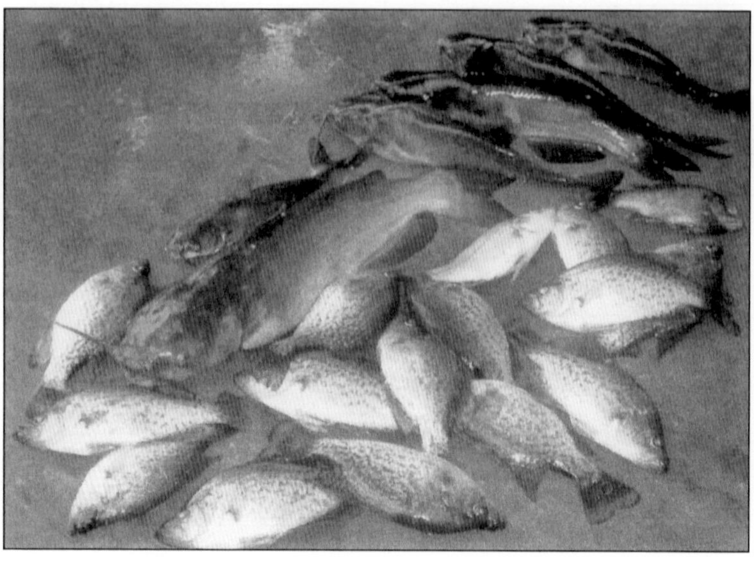

Pictured here are crappie and catfish caught by Joe Spaits out of Lake Fork on July 12, 2002. The fish were caught on a $^1/_{16}$-inch flashtail gig using a 6-pound test line and ultra rod. (Courtesy of Texas Department of Wildlife.)

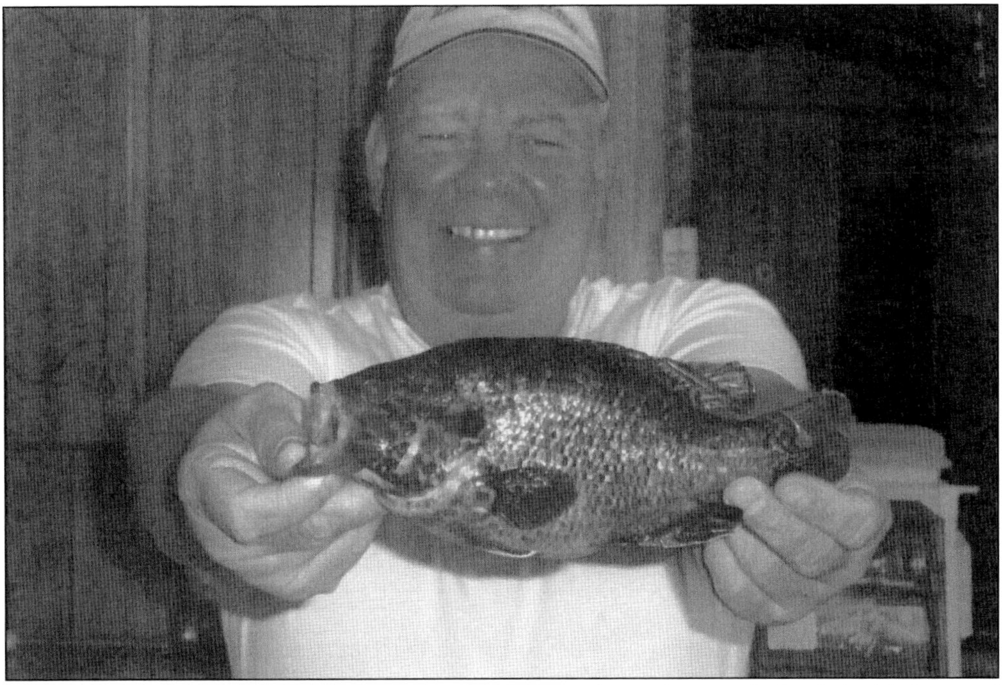

Joe Spaits, owner of Weedless Lures on Lake Fork, is shown here with his Lake Fork record warmouth caught on May 16, 2004. He used a flashtail crappie girt. Weighing in at 1.84 pounds and measuring 9½ inches long and 9 inches in girth made the fish the new lake record. (Courtesy of Texas Department of Wildlife.)

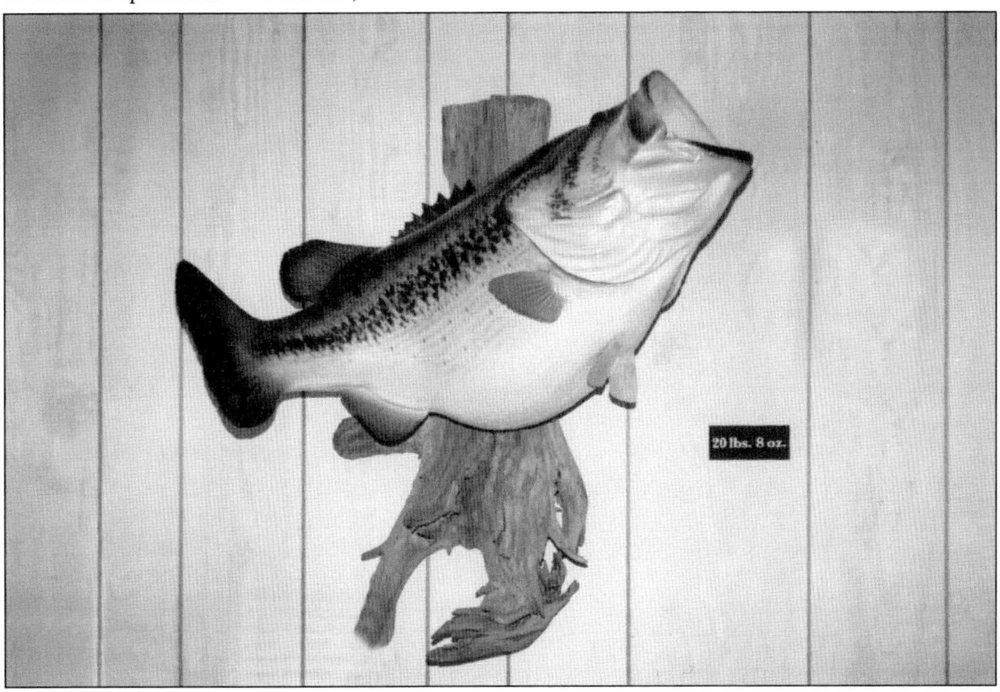

This 20-pound, 8-ounce bass was found dead floating near Mustang Resort on Lake Fork in the early 1990s. (Courtesy of Texas Department of Wildlife.)

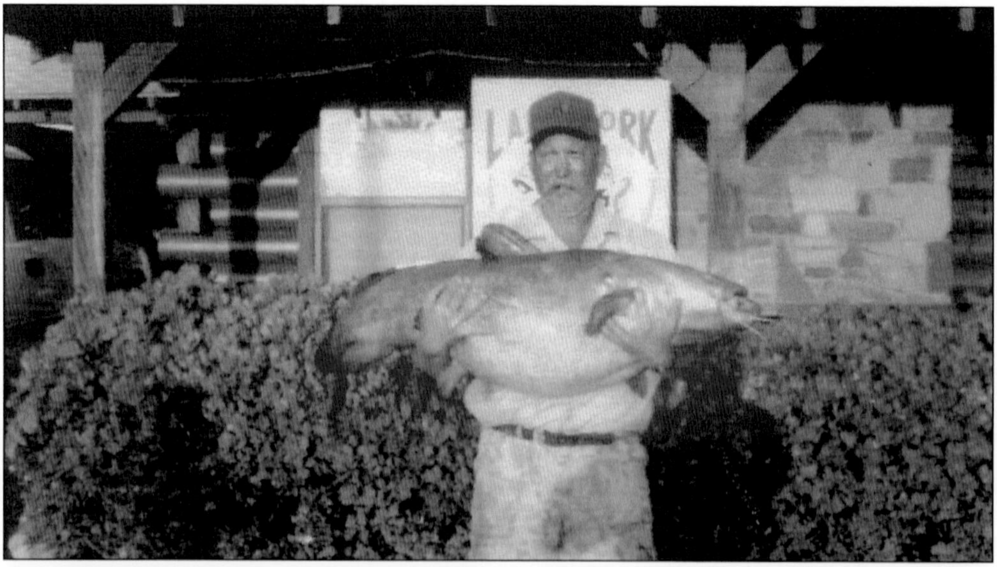

Dwain Hamilton of Tyler caught this 88-pound, Lake Fork record flathead in late April 2004 on a trotline baited with a pound-and-half carp. Dwain said he has caught at least a dozen weighing over 50 pounds and a half-dozen over 65 pounds on Lake Fork. (Courtesy of Texas Department of Wildlife.)

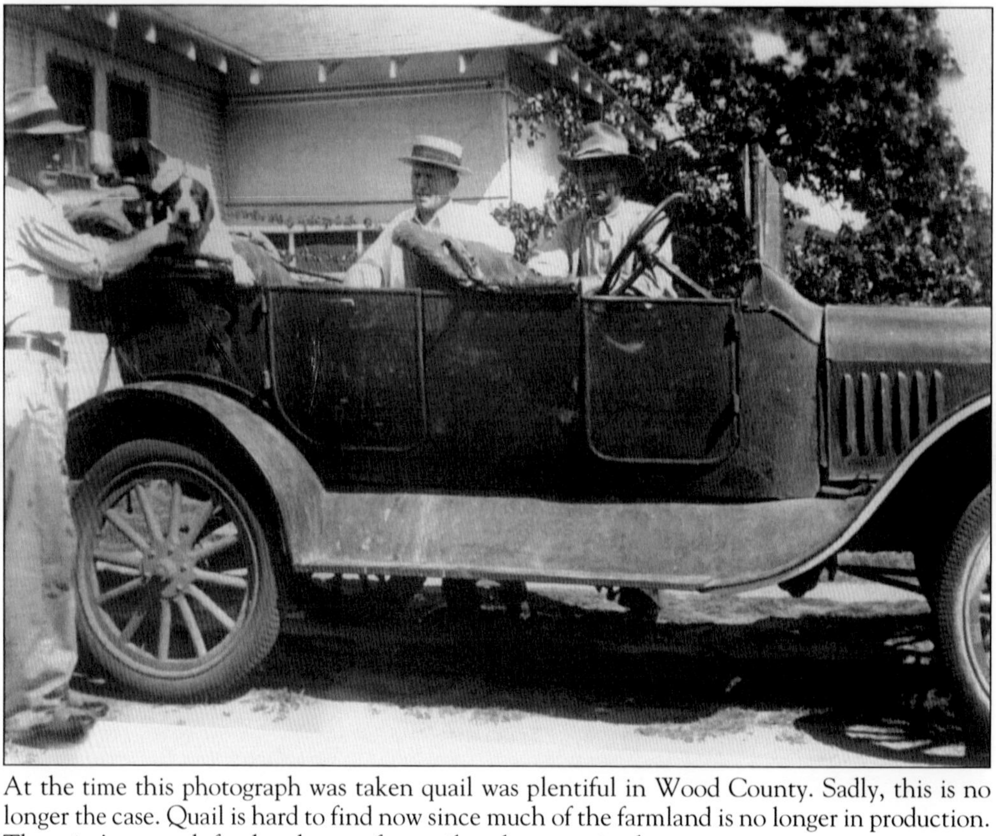

At the time this photograph was taken quail was plentiful in Wood County. Sadly, this is no longer the case. Quail is hard to find now since much of the farmland is no longer in production. There isn't as much food and cover for quail as there was in the past.

Larry Clanton killed this 21-point trophy deer in 1970 at Redland in Wood County.

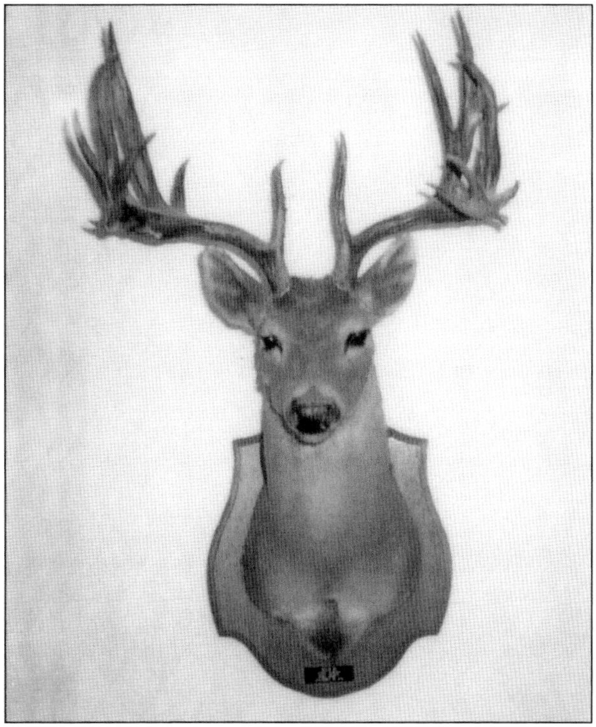

Pictured in the photograph below is the Mineola High School boys basketball team of 1929.

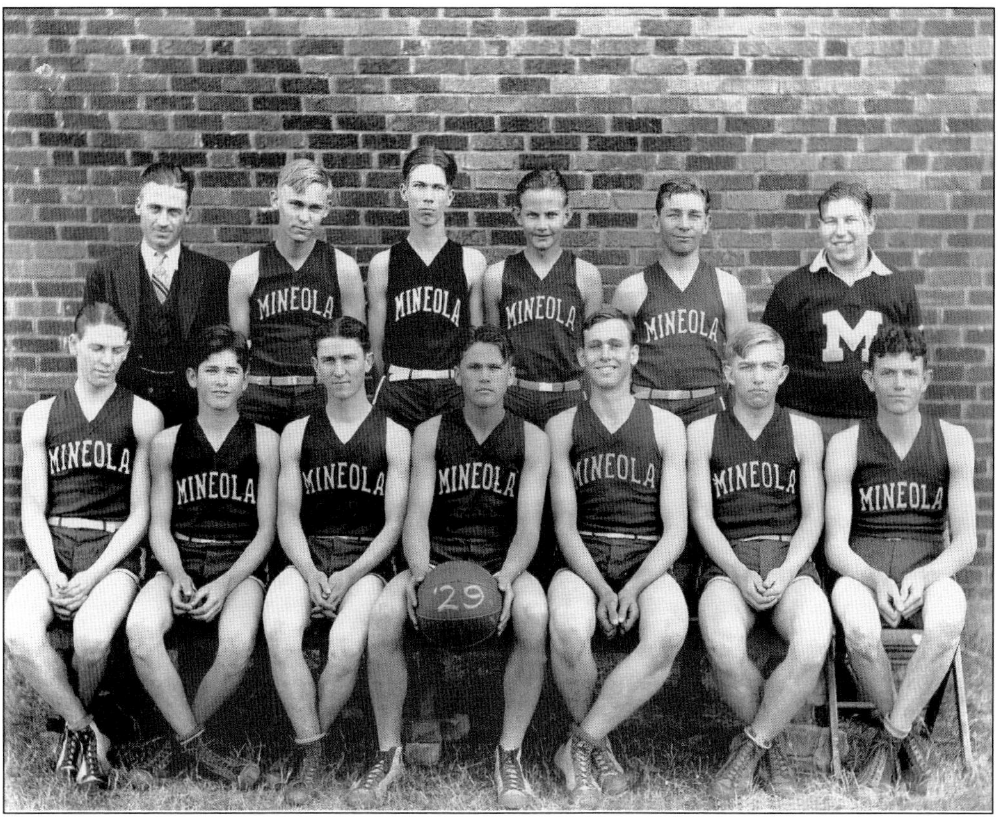

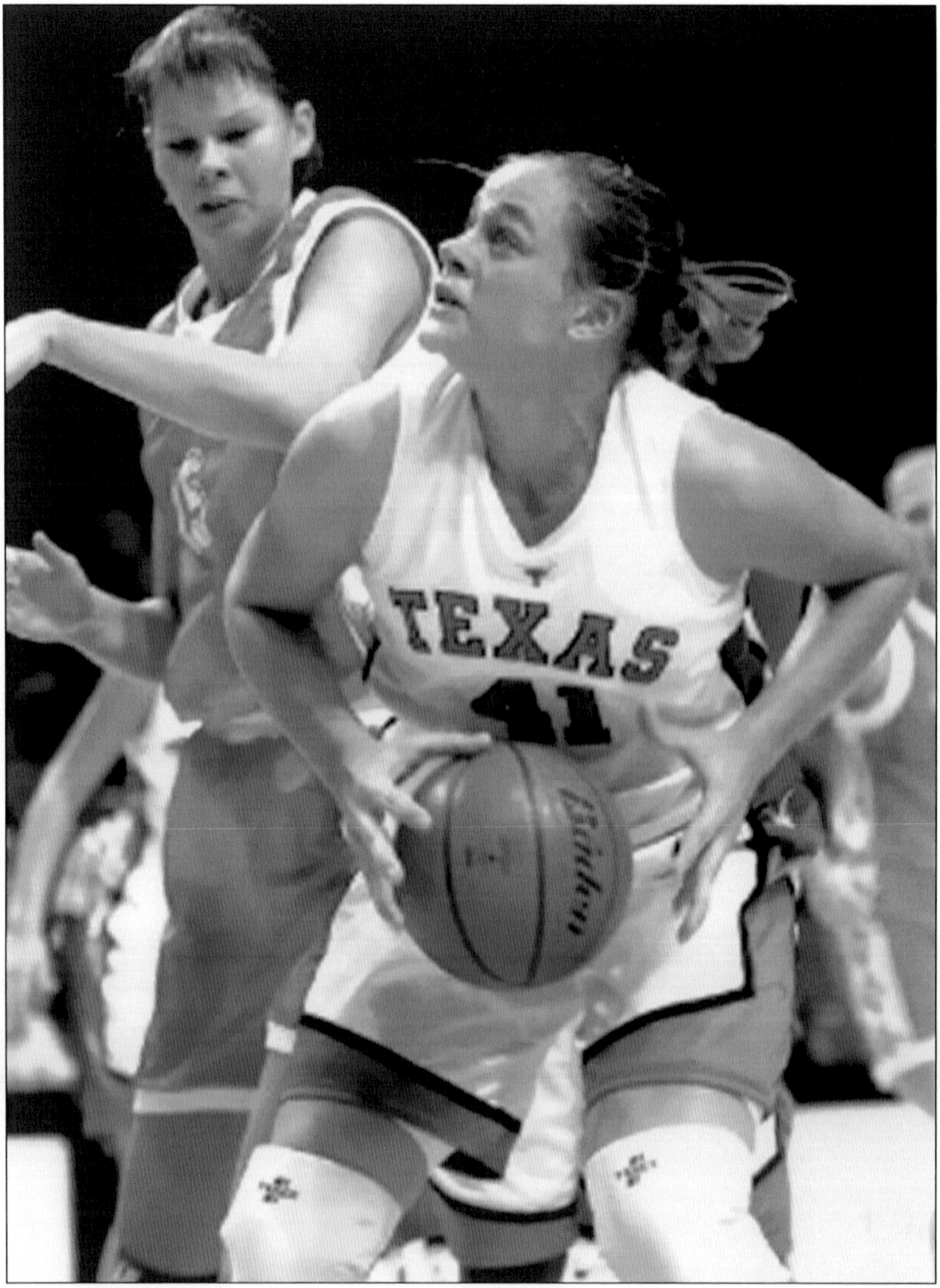

Pictured here is Stacy Stephens, a graduate of Winnsboro High School and a member of the 1999 and 2000 Winnsboro's 3A state champion girls basketball team. Stacy was named the most valuable player of the state basketball championship both years. Also in 1999–2000, Stacy was named an All-American by *USA Today*, Nike, Adidas, and *Parade Magazine*. Stacy accepted a scholarship to play basketball at the University of Texas at Austin, where she has won even more awards.

Five

Entertainment

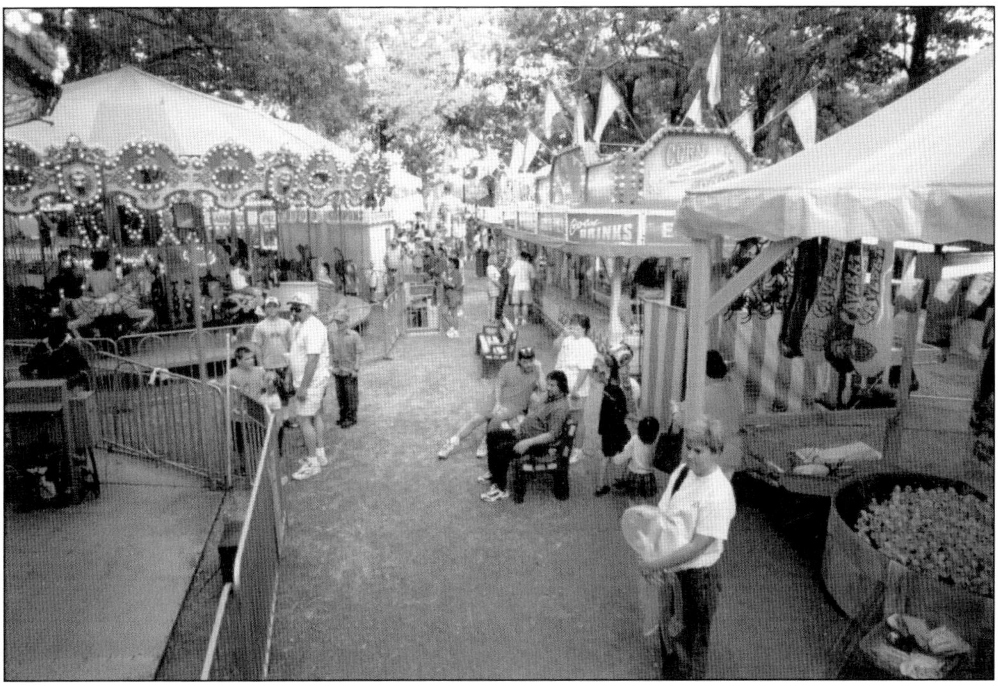

The early settlers were ambitious and hard-working people. Nevertheless, they enjoyed fine arts, good music, and lively entertainment. After the rail lines came through the county, opera houses flourished and nationally acclaimed performers traveling from the East Coast to the West Coast by rail stopped and performed for local residents. The county also has had an abundance of local talent to provide entertainment. County residents could also see a movie at one of the local theaters. In 1900 the Old Settlers Reunion began, and each August, at the park in Quitman, both old and young gather to enjoy fiddling, gospel music, and a carnival for the young and the young at heart.

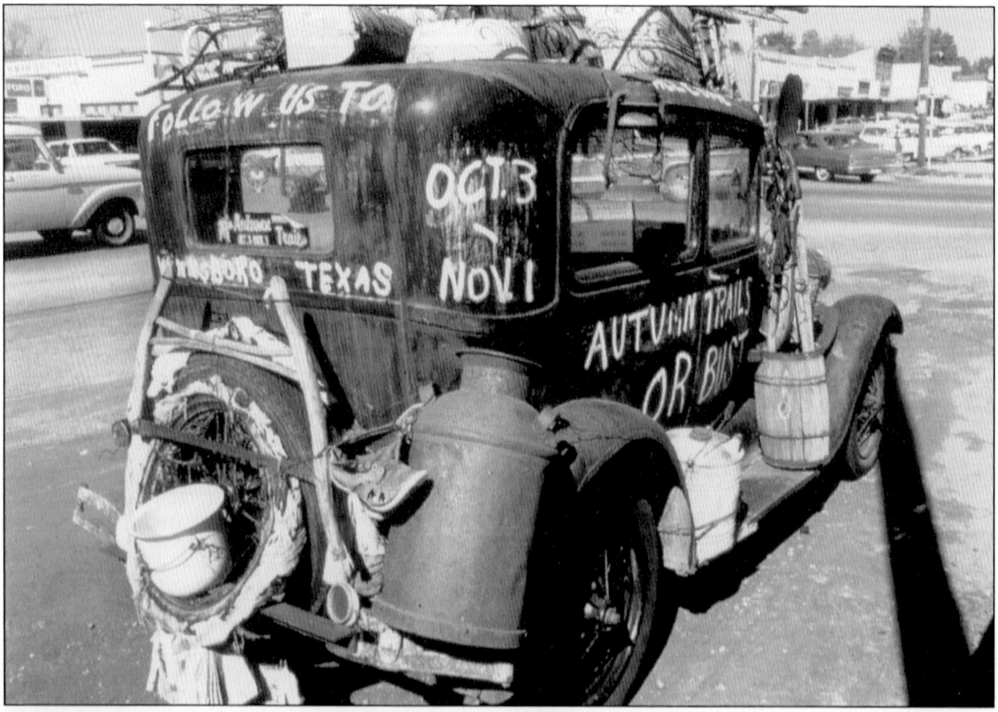

This antique car advertises Winnsboro's Autumn Trails held each fall during the month of October.

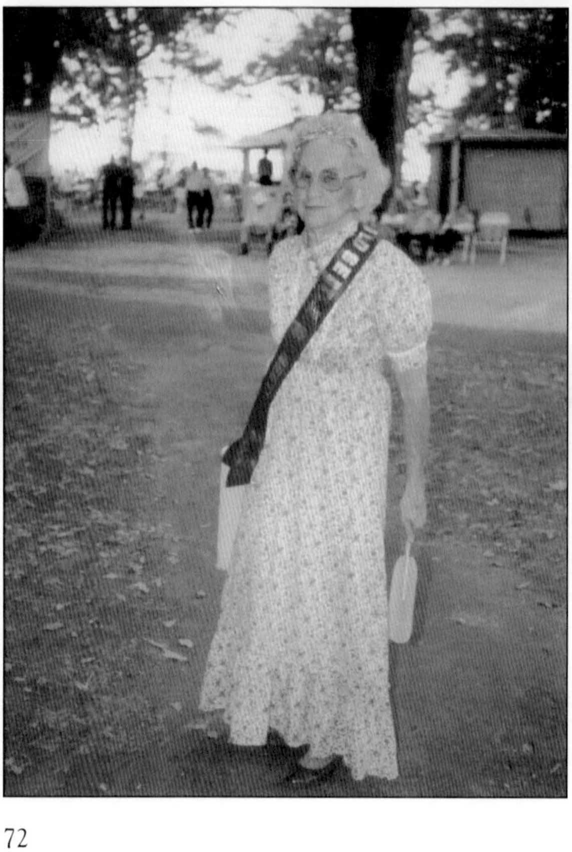

Mrs. Lillian Cathey, a longtime Wood County resident, is pictured after being crowned queen at the Old Settlers Reunion in 1993. The celebration, organized in 1900, is held each August at Governor Hogg Park in Quitman.

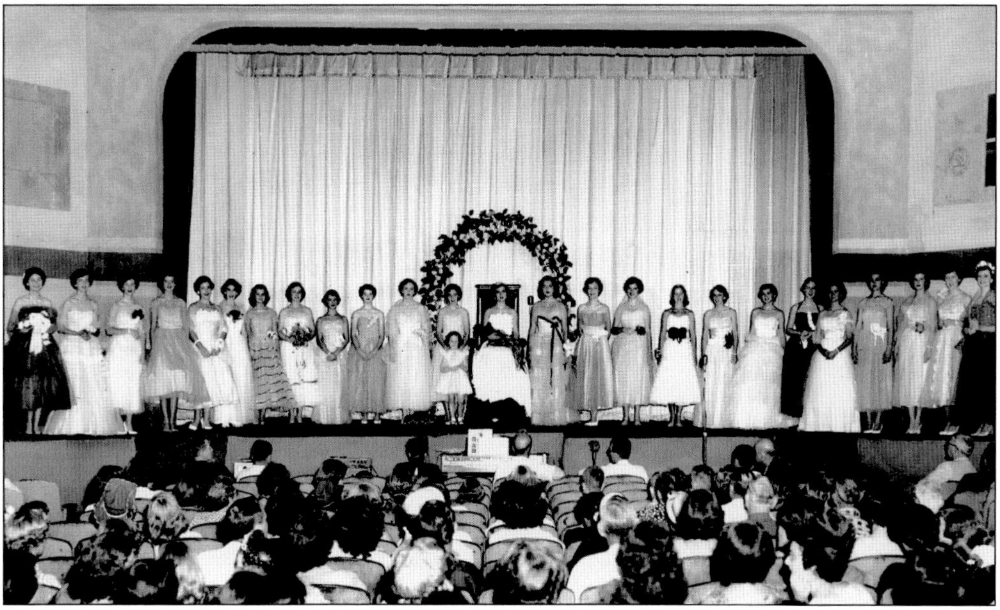

Beginning in 1949 Mineola hosted a Watermelon Festival each summer. A queen was selected at the coronation, and a parade was always held with beautifully decorated floats. Perhaps the most interesting event took place on Festival Day, when participants stopped out-of-town cars as they approached the Farmers' Market on U.S. Highway 80 and invited them to stop and eat watermelon. It has been estimated that as many as 15,000 were served on this day.

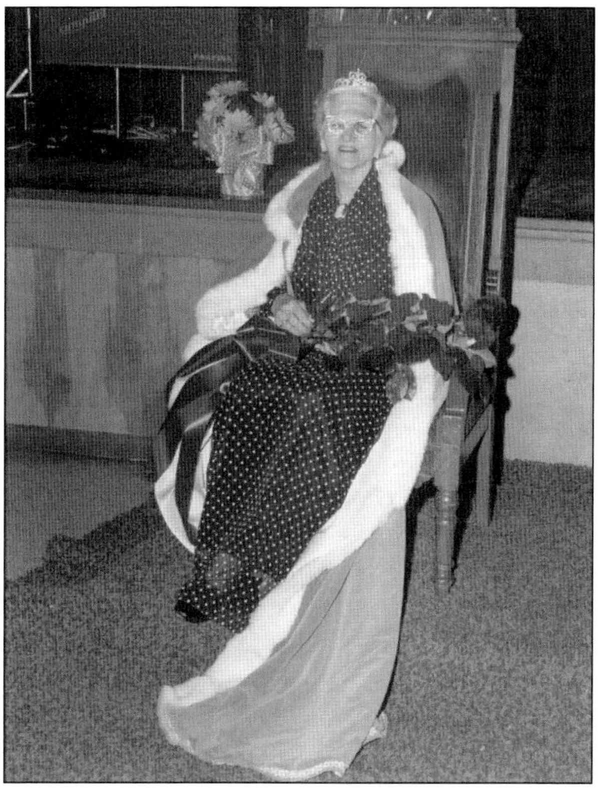

Mrs. Howard (Vivian) Lott, a native of Mineola, was chosen queen of the centennial festivities in 1973; she is shown here wearing the tiara and banner declaring her queen. Mineola had a host of activities that lasted the entire month of May.

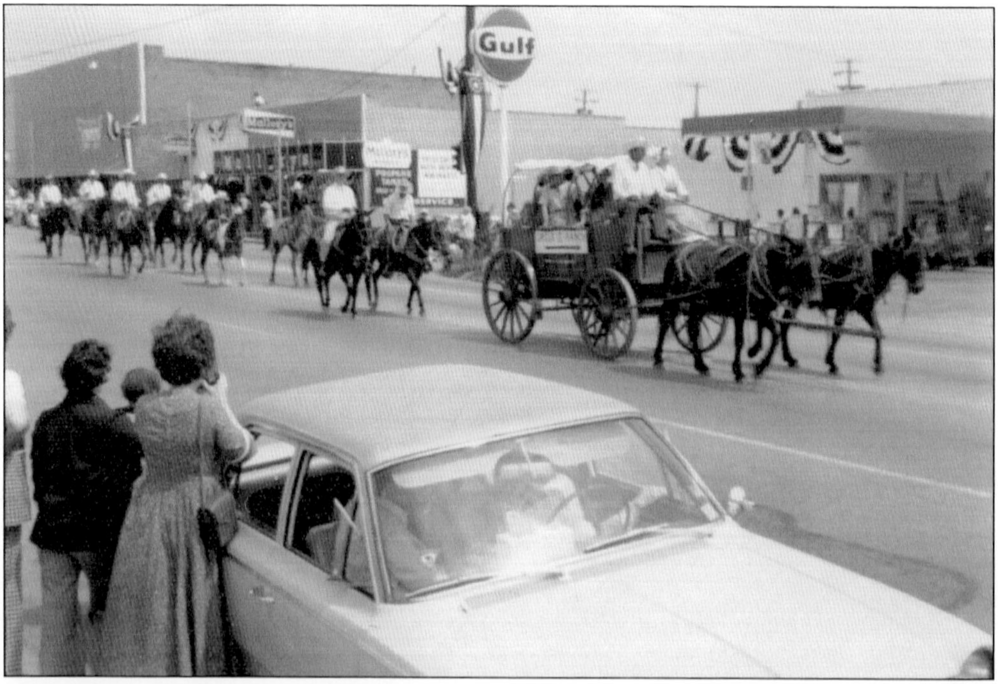

The parade for the centennial in Mineola featured floats, antique cars, bands, and mounted horse groups.

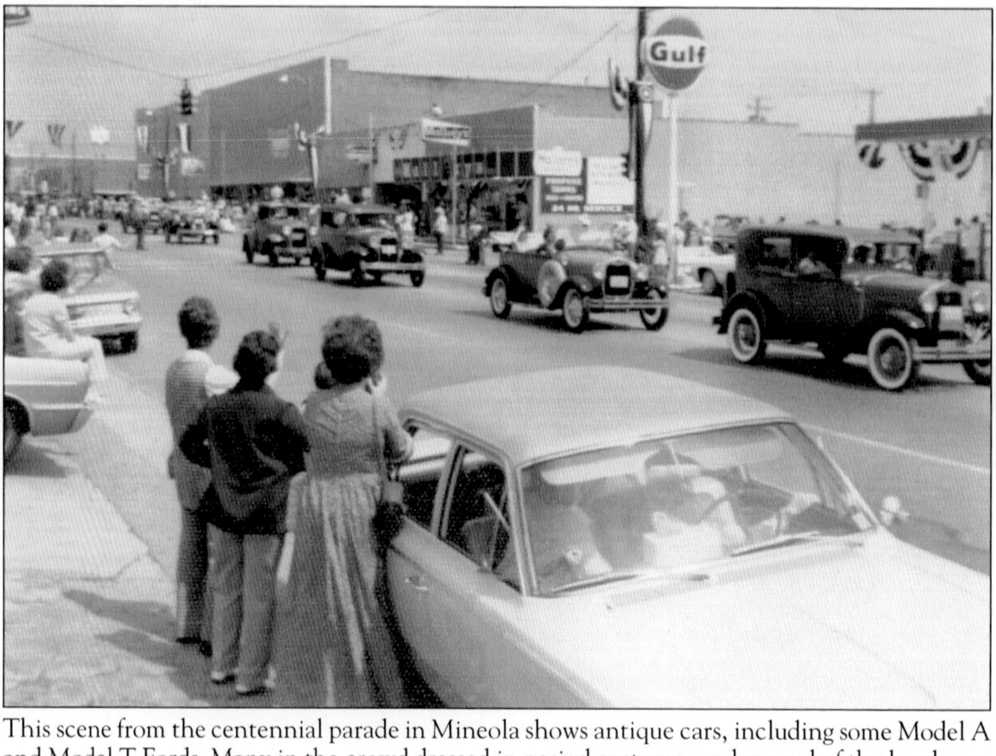

This scene from the centennial parade in Mineola shows antique cars, including some Model A and Model T Fords. Many in the crowd dressed in period costume, and several of the local men grew beards for the occasion.

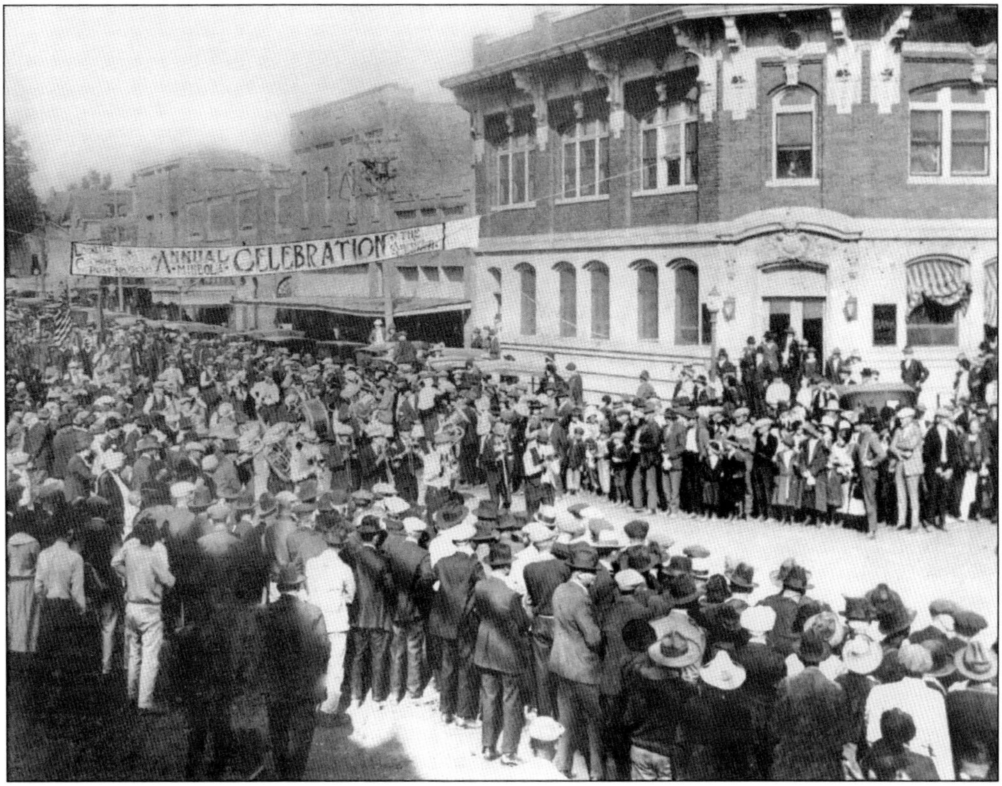

Armistice Day on November 11, now known as Veterans' Day, was observed in Mineola starting in 1919 with a day of activities. At least one block of downtown would be roped off for games, speeches, contests, and band music. A parade was held in the afternoon and was usually followed by a football game.

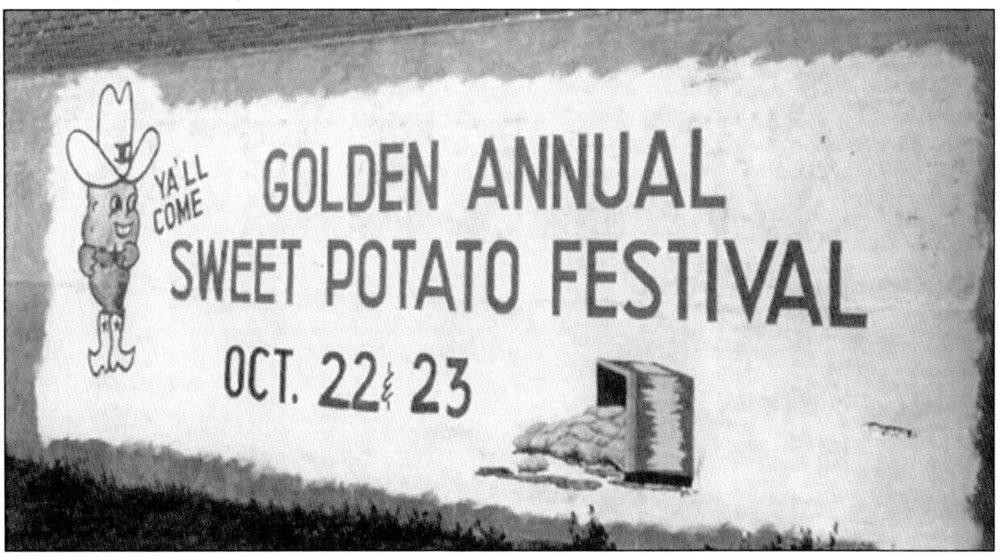

The Sweet Potato Festival is held each October on the fourth weekend. Sweet potatoes have been grown in the county for many years, and the festival celebrates the financial benefits they have provided this community.

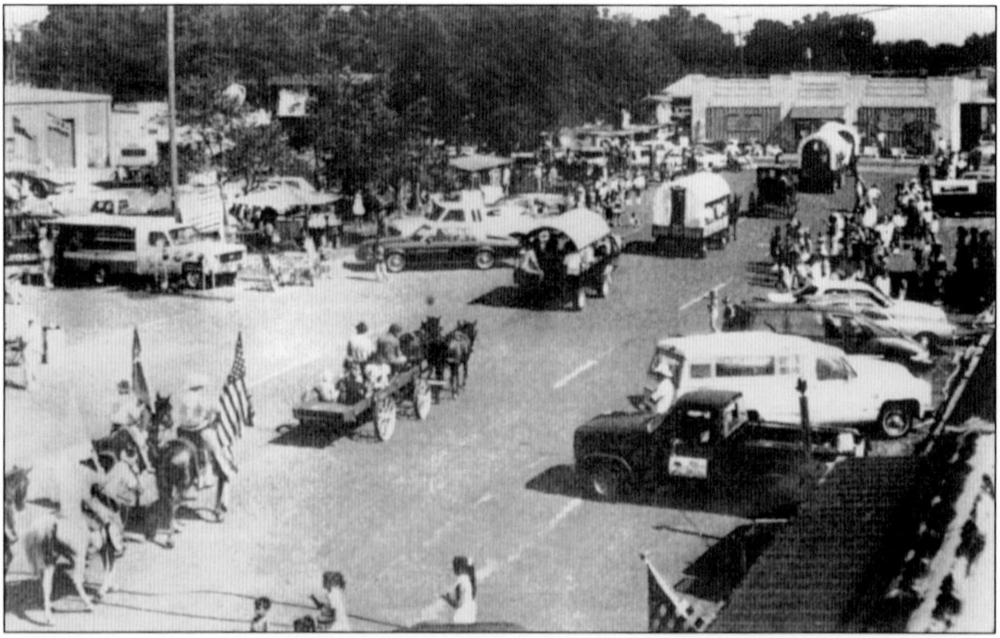

In September, the Alba Ladies Club sponsors "Country Fair" held downtown around the square. A parade, as well as lots of food, crafts, and entertainment, are a part of this annual event.

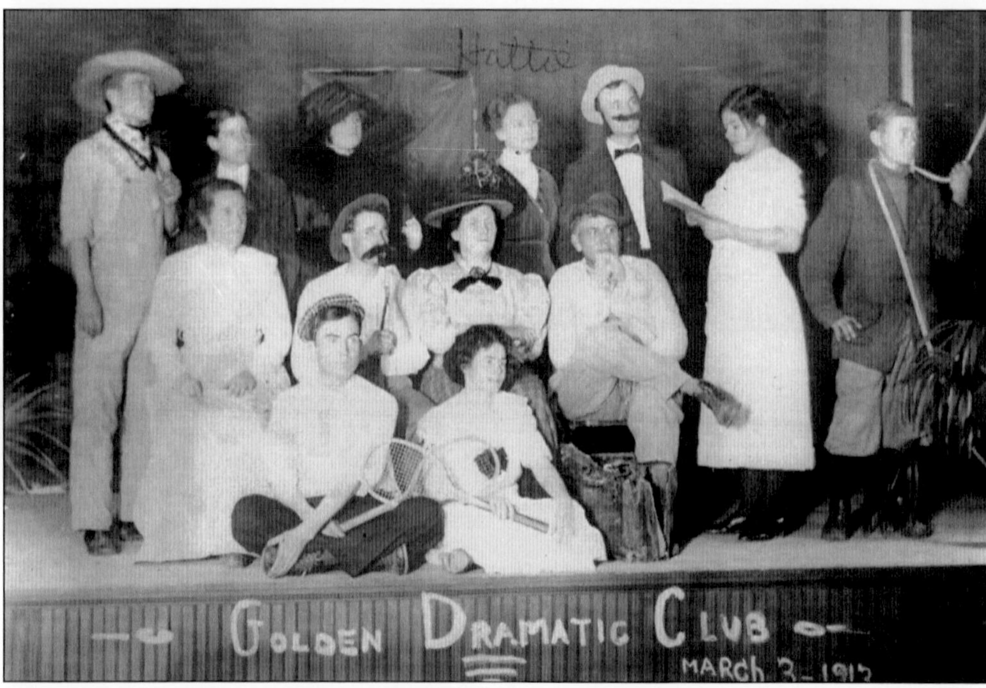

The Golden community northwest of Mineola has always been a farming area and early on had a bank, a newspaper, and good schools. Residents appreciated the arts, and here, members of the community are shown in costume apparently for one of their productions. Names of the performers and location are unknown.

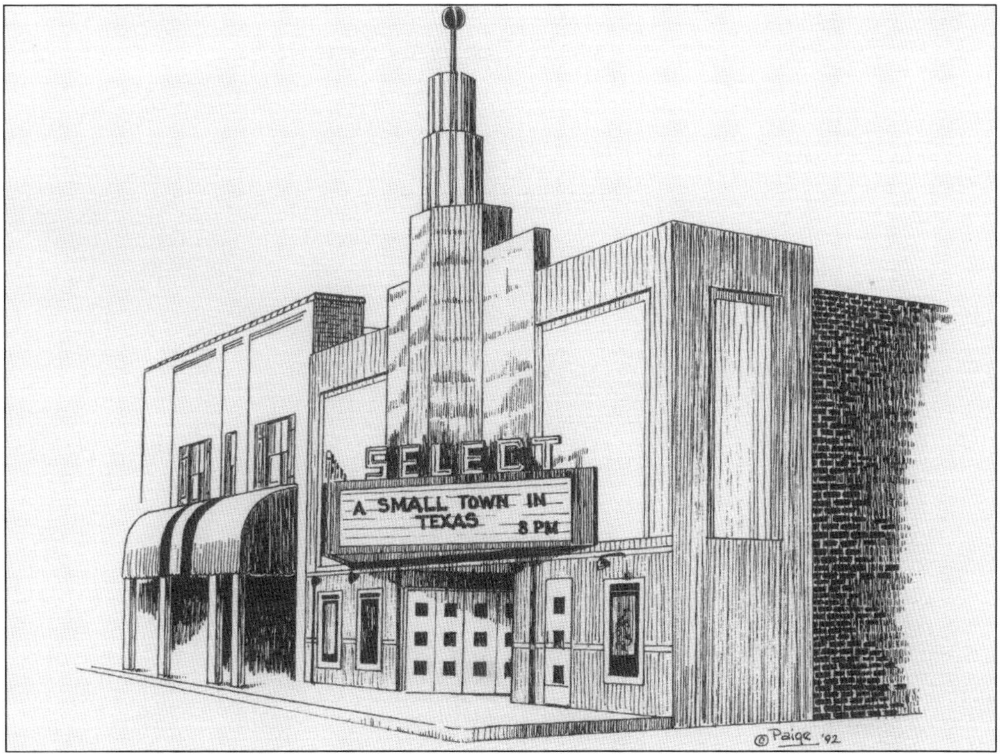

The Select Theater in Mineola is thought to be the oldest continuously operating movie theater in Texas. The theater was remodeled in 1948 and again in 2001. Today, the Select is the home of the Lake Country Playhouse, a live drama group that performs during the year but shows movies on the weekends that plays are not scheduled.

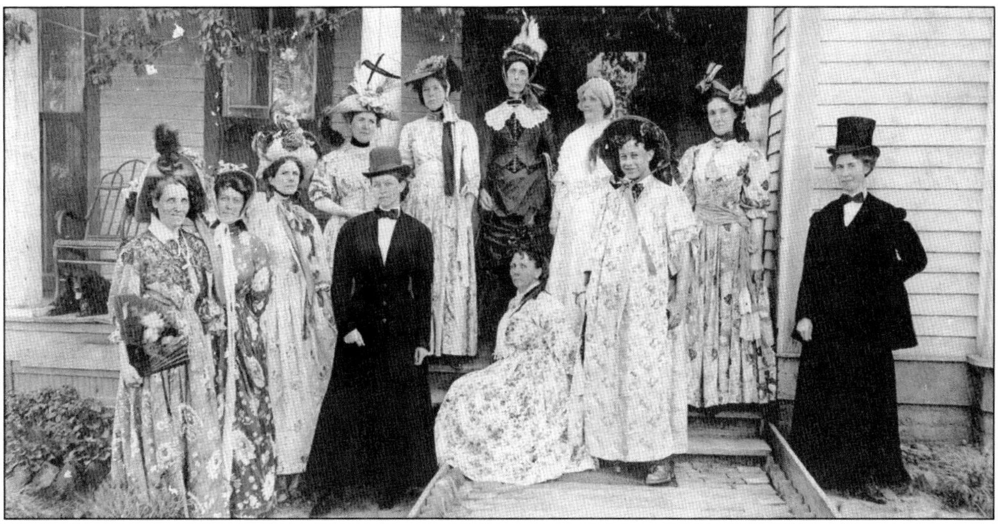

The oldest literary club in Mineola, the 20th Century Club, was organized on February 18, 1913, with 14 founding members, and is still an active organization with a membership of 26. Eleven of the founding members are shown wearing costumes at one of their early meetings. The philosophy of the club has always been one of continued learning and cultivation of the mind—as necessary as food for the body.

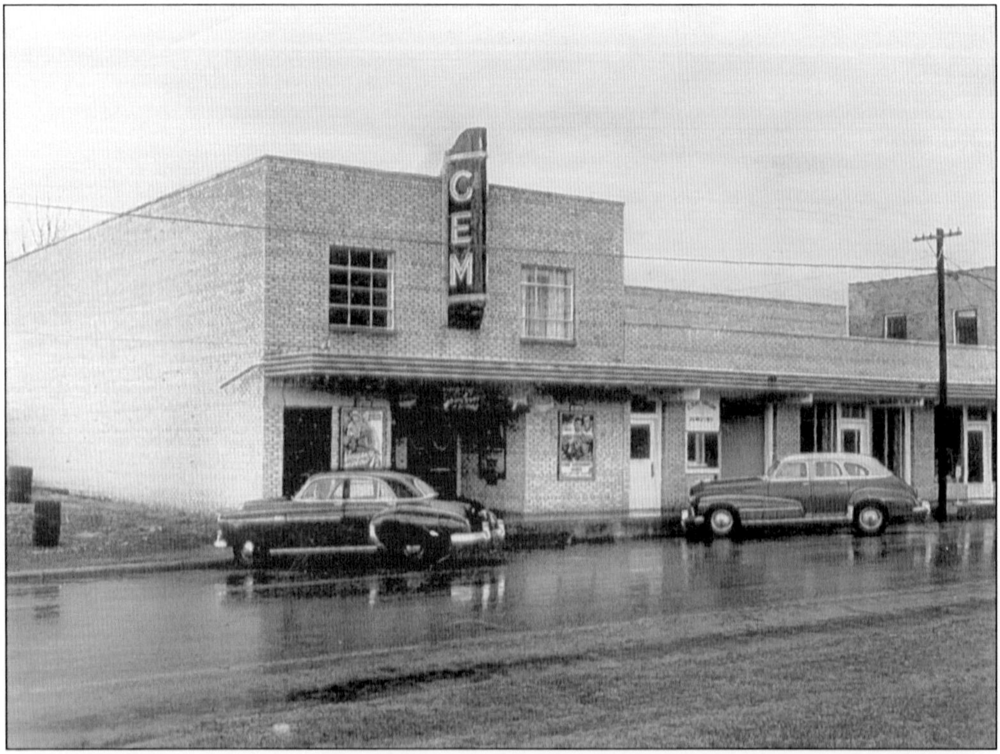

The Gem Theater, located on Main Street in Quitman, was a popular source of entertainment during the mid-20th century. The business was owned and operated by Theo and Mildred Miller.

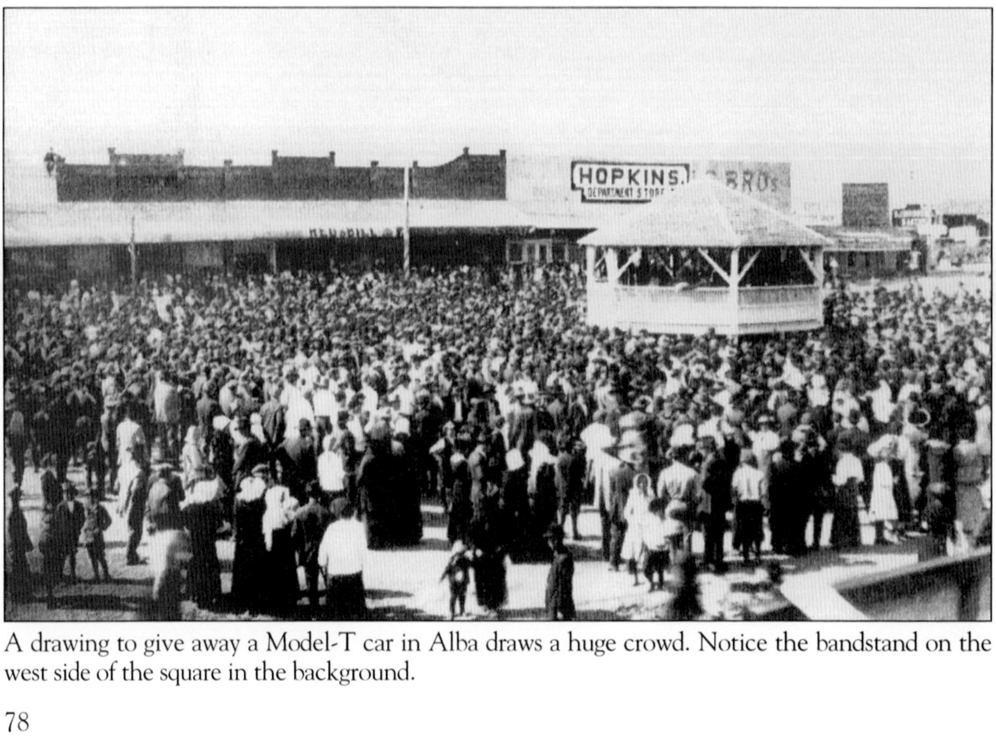

A drawing to give away a Model-T car in Alba draws a huge crowd. Notice the bandstand on the west side of the square in the background.

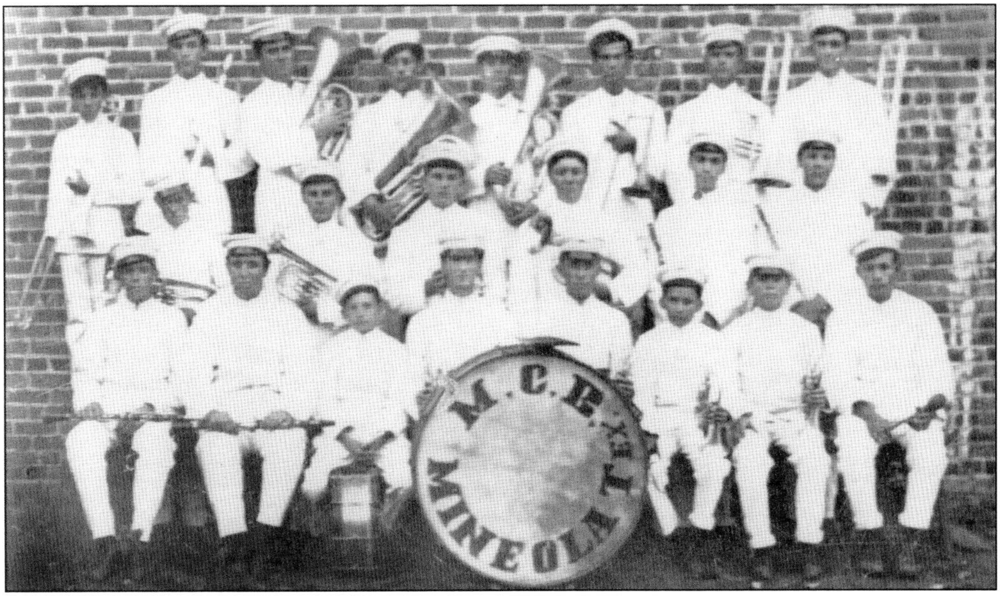

Members of the Mineola Concert Band are shown with their instruments. The exact date is unknown but it is believed to be from the early 20th century. Notice the member in the middle of the front row who appears to be wearing a helmet while all the others sport hats. Concerts provided entertainment for local citizens, and some of the concerts were held at the bandstand surrounding Mineola's downtown water well. The well and the bandstand have been torn down and removed.

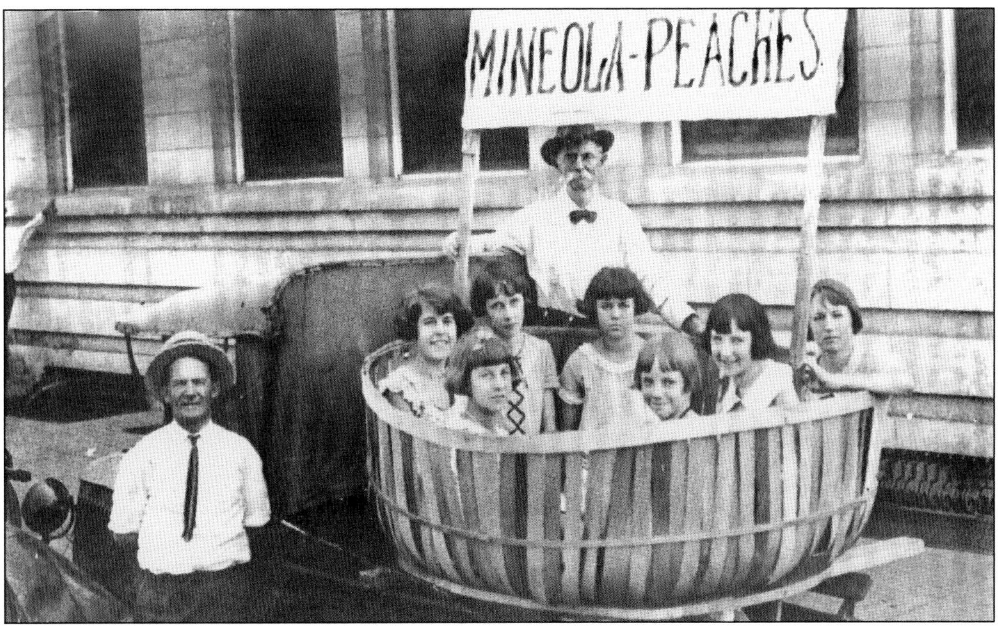

W.C. Dubose was elected mayor in 1924, and this picture was taken later that same year. Mineola and Wood County have long been known for their agricultural products. The area had numerous peach orchards, and in this photo the mayor and George C. Reeves, who long promoted Wood County agriculture, are shown with some of Mineola's best "peaches"—from left to right, Donie Humphreys, Abilene Huff, Ruth Land, Lola Mae Hendrix, Frances Copeland, Margaret Bogan, and Lera Mae Scott.

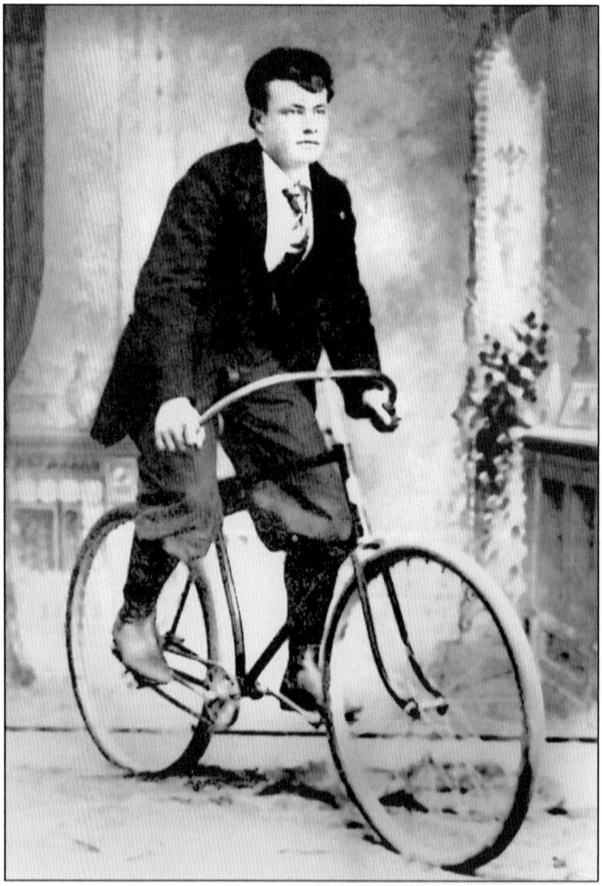

R.J. Smith is shown riding Mineola's first bicycle in 1908. In 1906, the City of Mineola ammended the ordinance on bicycle riding on the sidewalks: "Bicycles may be ridden on sidewalks outside the fire limits provided due respect is shown footmen, blowing their whistles when approaching and in all cases to dismount when meeting ladies."

The Lions Club was organized in Mineola in 1952, and this banquet was held in September of that year to install the new officers. The location for the banquet is unknown.

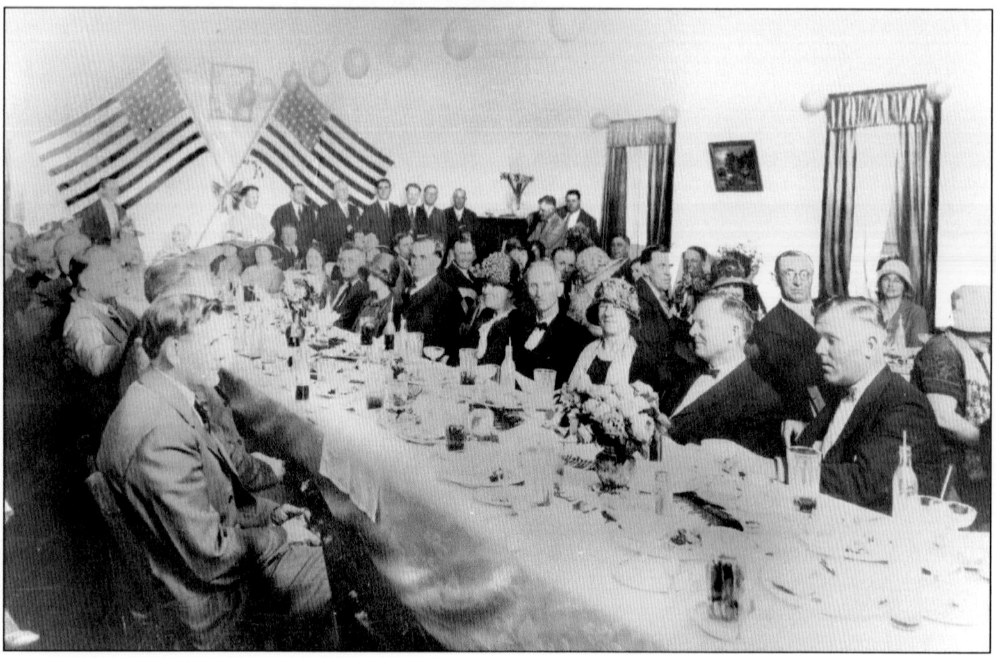

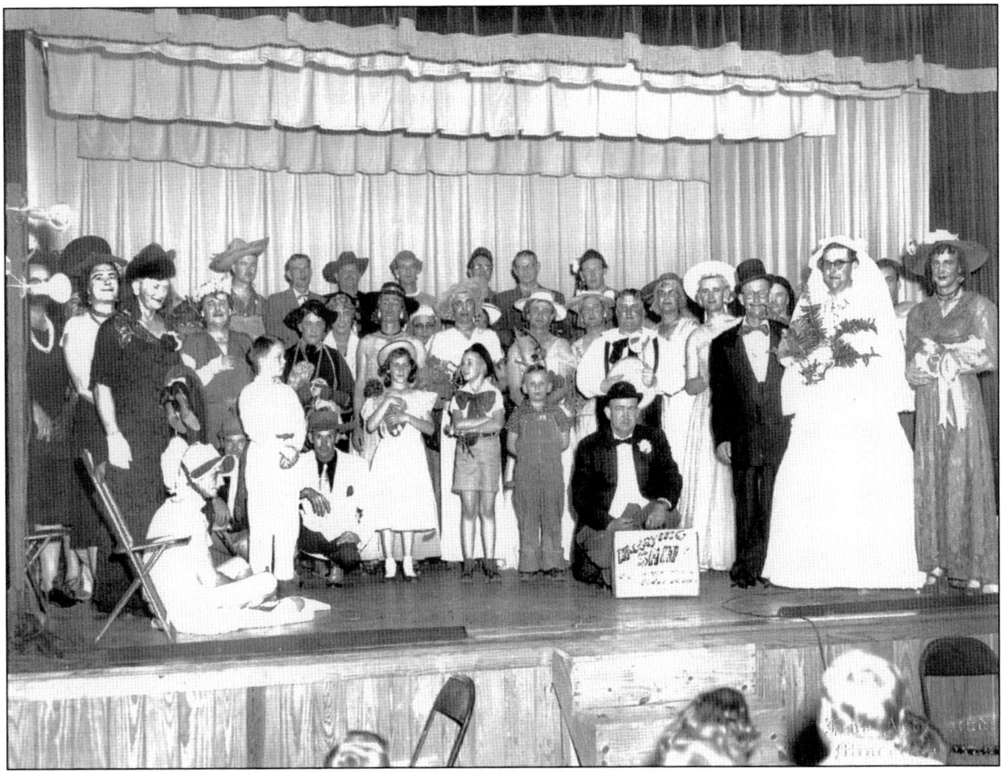

Local clubs and organizations in each of Wood County's communities sponsored events during the year. This "womanless wedding" was staged at the junior high school auditorium in Mineola. The cast consisted of several local businessmen dressed in costume, as well as some local children. The bride was David H. Lott and the groom was played by Brady Mills.

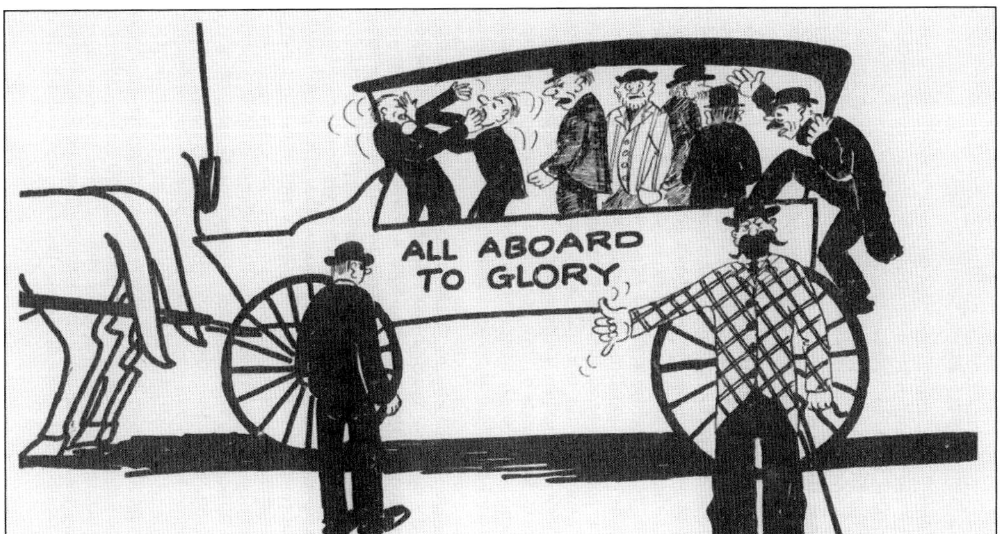

Saloons were a thriving industry in the area as early as 1898. Pictured here is the hack that offered Wood County citizens rides, free of charge, to the saloon in Franklin County just north of Winnsboro.

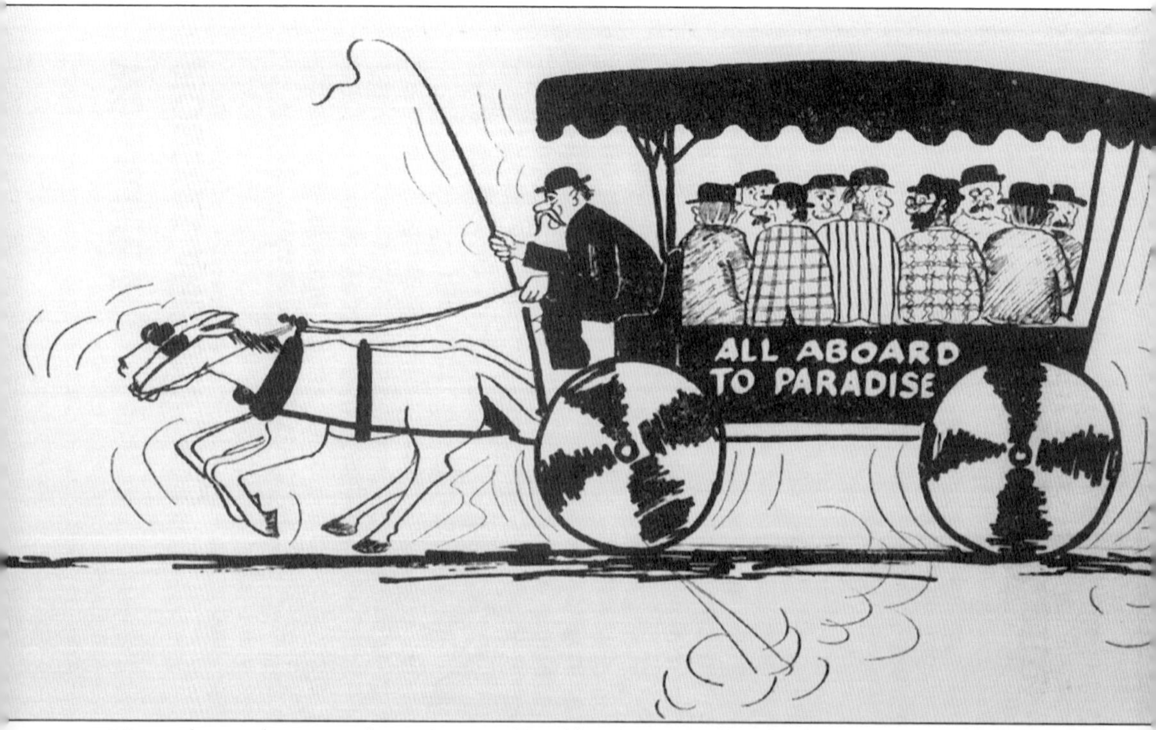

Not to be outdone, another saloon in Franklin County offered rides to their establishment to residents of Wood County.

Six

Education

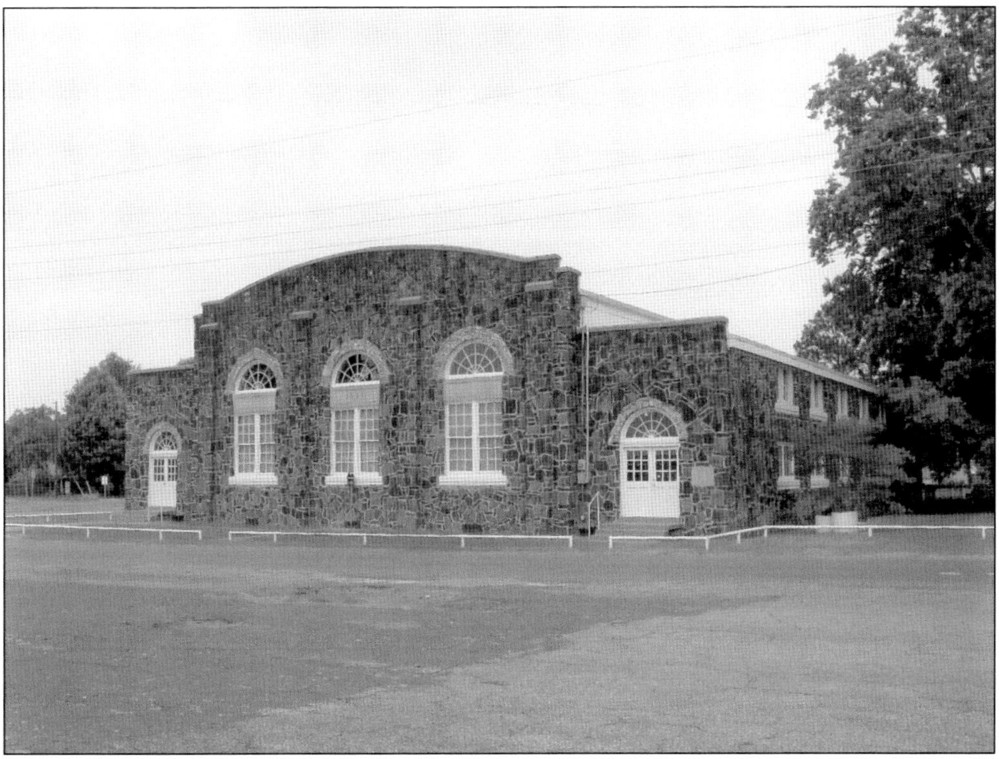

Public education was one of the primary goals of the first settlers to Wood County, but that goal proved hard to attain. From around 1850 to 1884, there were no public schools. It was not until a special session of the Texas legislature convened in Austin on January 8, 1884 that Wood County was divided into school districts. The county, as a result, had 34 white school districts and 9 African-American school districts. The Rock Gym in Winnsboro, pictured here, was a WPA project built in 1939. The Rock Gym is the scene of many activities for the school district and the community.

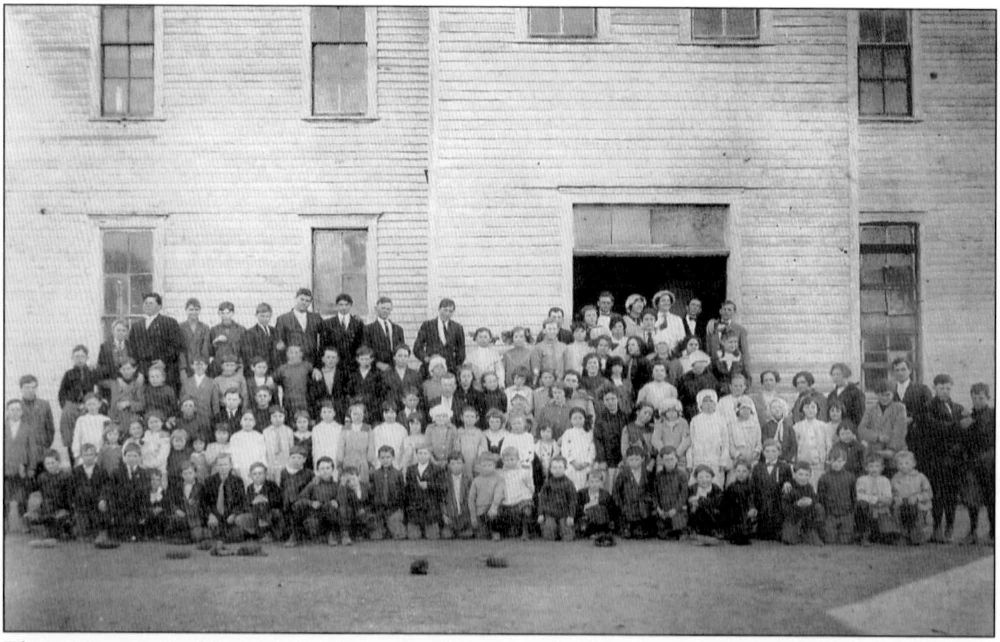

This two-story, white frame school building in Quitman was constructed in 1907, and T.O. Craddock was the first superintendent in this building. At the time this picture was taken in 1914, W.E. Cox was superintendent. The structure was condemned and torn down, and in 1919 a two-story brick building was erected at a new location on Morris Street.

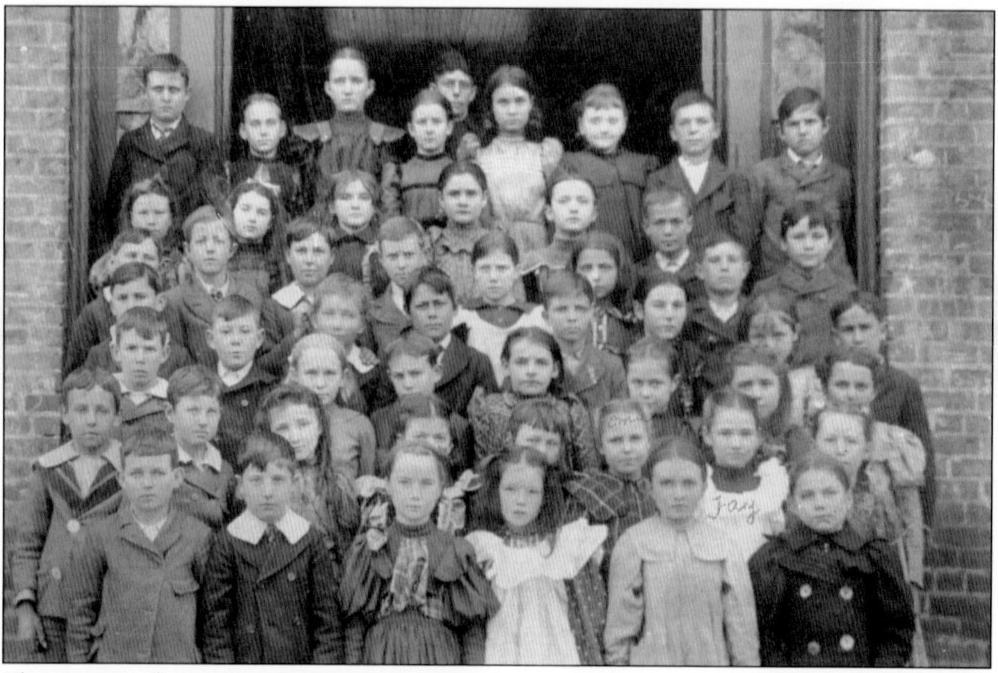

This picture shows the charges of teacher Mrs. Mary B. Good between 1897 and 1899. C.L. Turner was superintendent at this time.

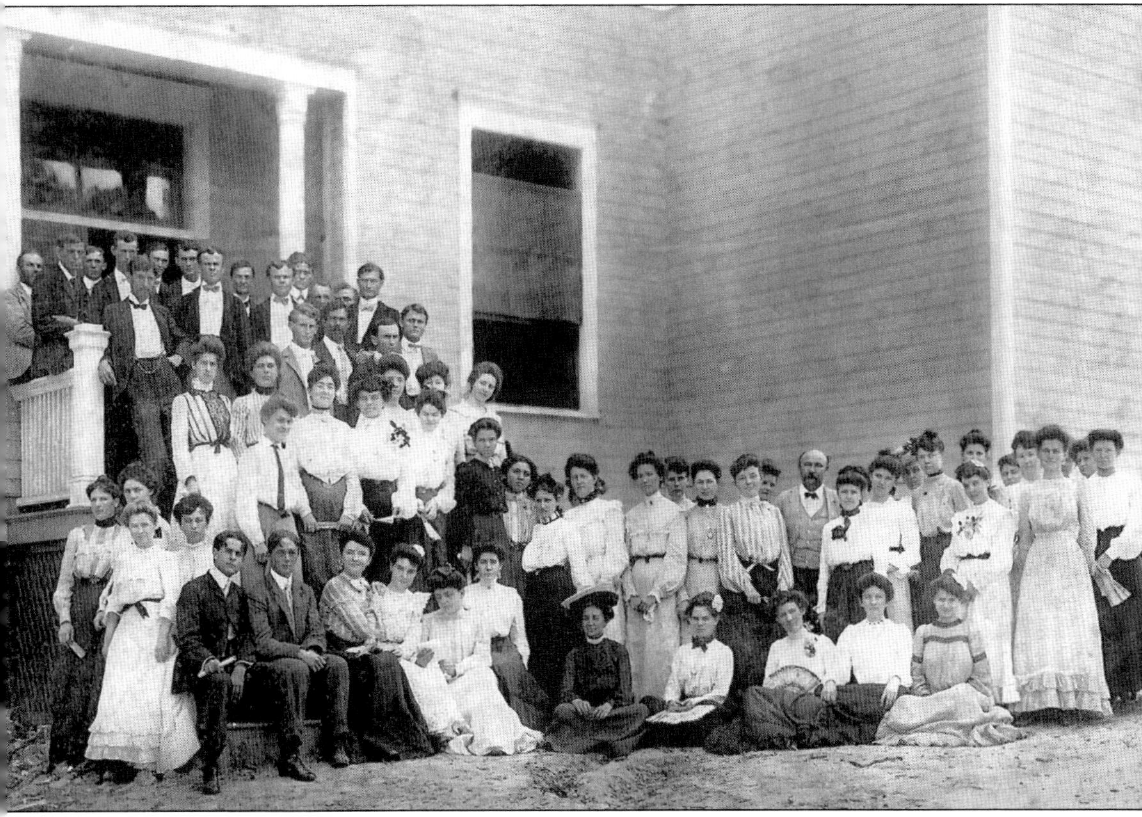

Dressed in fashionable attire of the turn-of-the century, these women and men attended the Mineola Normal School in 1903.

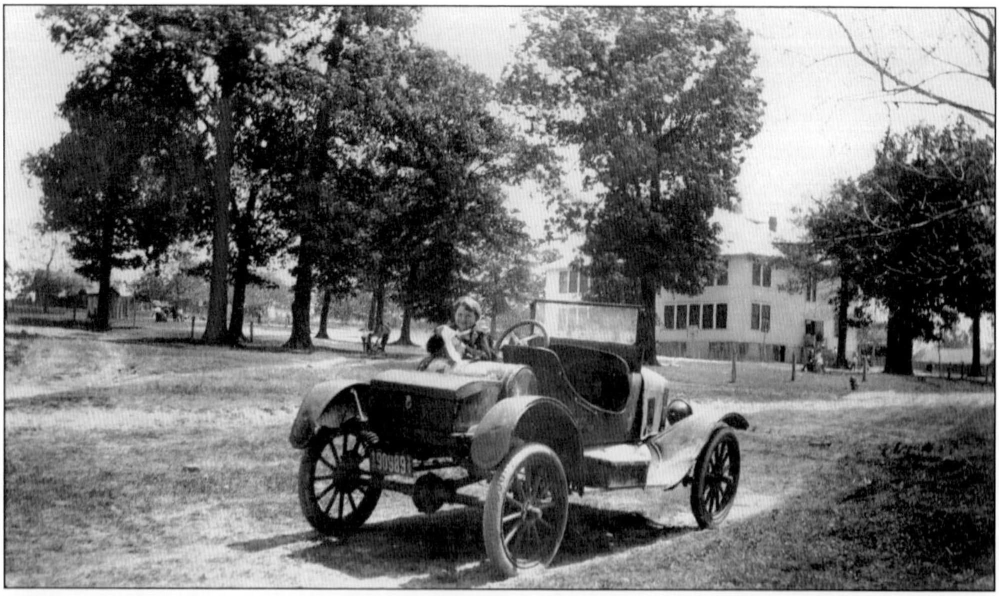

In the background is a two-story frame school building that was constructed in 1901 for all grades to attend until a high school was built in 1914. The elementary grades continued to use the building until 1933, when a two-story brick elementary school building was erected on North Newsom Street in Mineola.

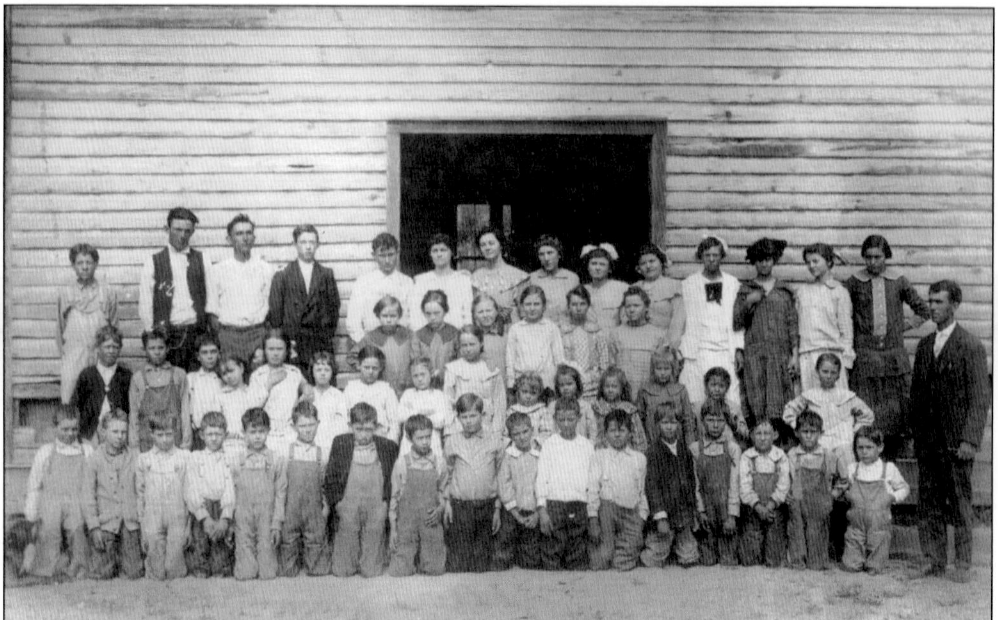

Reinhardt students and principal George McAlister pose for a picture c. 1916. Reinhardt was located to the north of Quitman. In the early 1940s that district consolidated with the Quitman Independent School District (ISD).

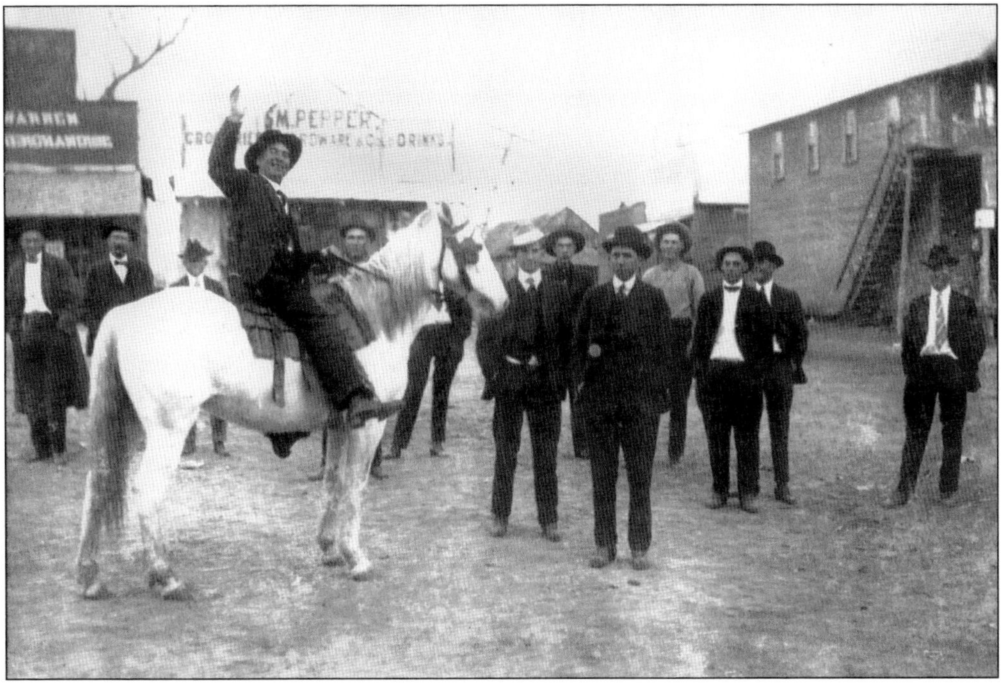

Students and teachers congregate for a picture in the late 1920s in front of the Bellafonte School located between Quitman and Golden. Mr. J.U. Searcy was principal at the time.

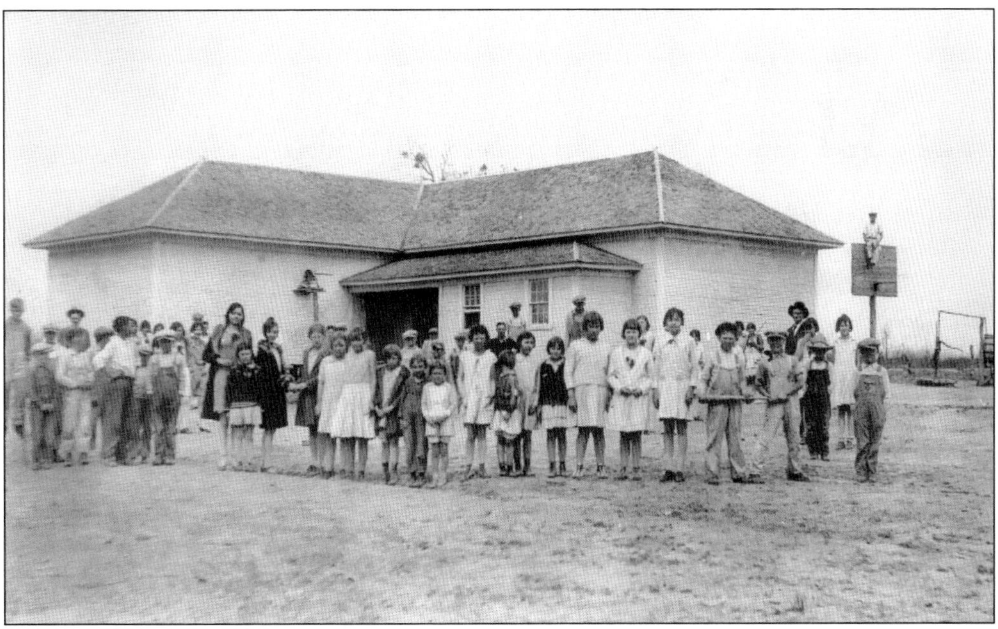

This street scene of Yantis in 1925 shows the first school, a two-story structure, to the right in the background. The building was used as both a school and a post office.

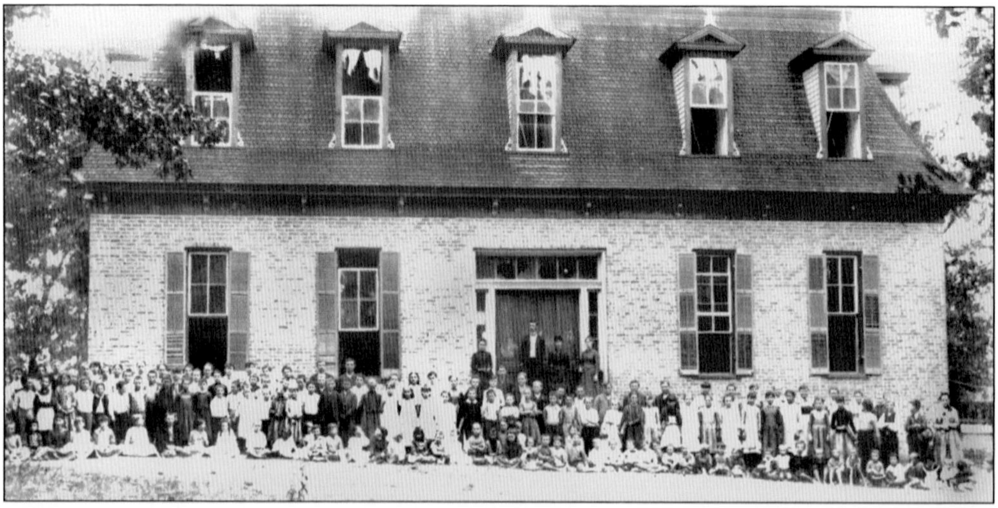

Citizens, dissatisfied with the way the schools had been run, voted in 1885 for the second time to have the city run the schools. This Mineola Public School Building was located on the southwest corner of the intersection of Line and McDonald Streets, *c.* 1895. During this period, graduation exercises were a very special event. The graduation invitation for the class of 1899 contained eight pages.

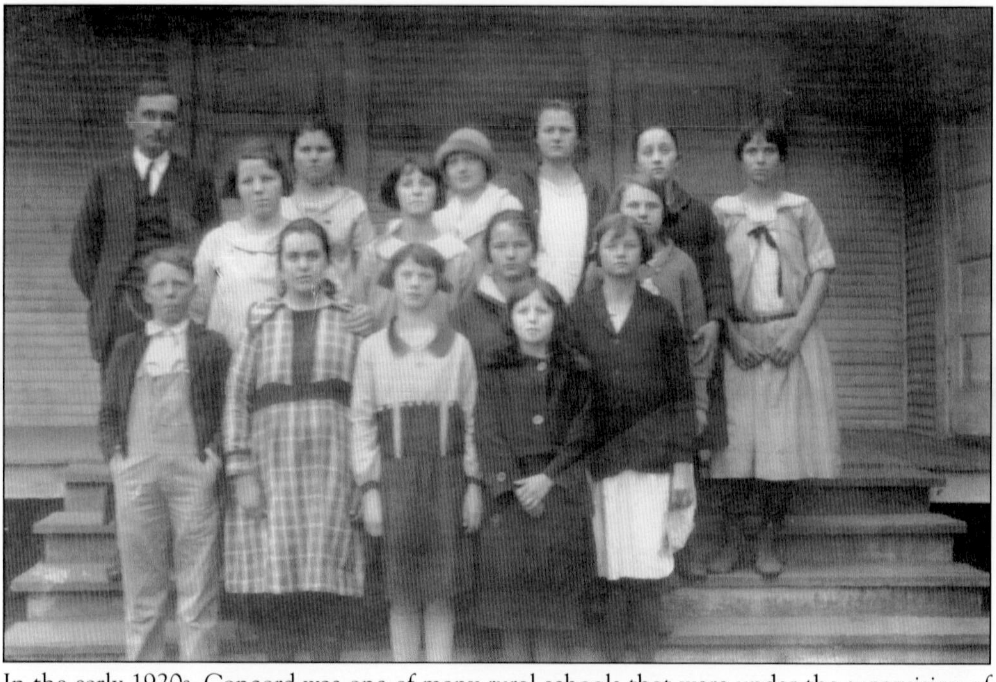

In the early 1920s, Concord was one of many rural schools that were under the supervision of the county school superintendent. Concord was located between Hainesville and Quitman. In Wood County in the early 1920s, Horace Cathey served as the principal as well as teacher of the upper grades at Concord.

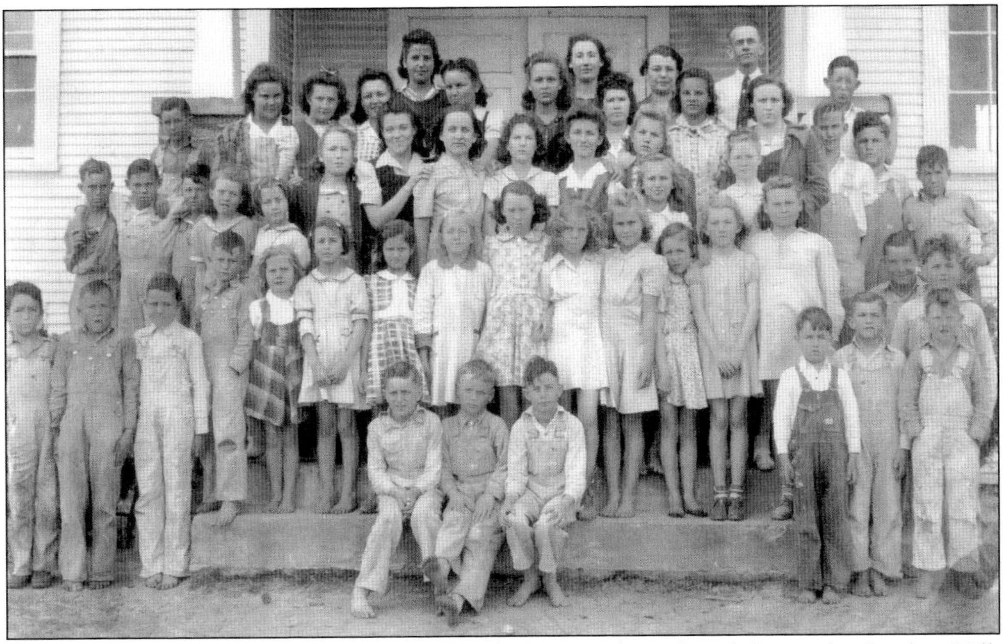

Students at Rock Hill School are pictured with their teachers, from left to right, Lindsey Hill, Thelma Hill, and Lois Cade, who taught in the 1940s. Rock Hill School was located seven miles north of Quitman. During the 1930s there were 11 grades in the school with six to eight teachers employed. In the late 1940s the school closed and students then went to Yantis and Quitman.

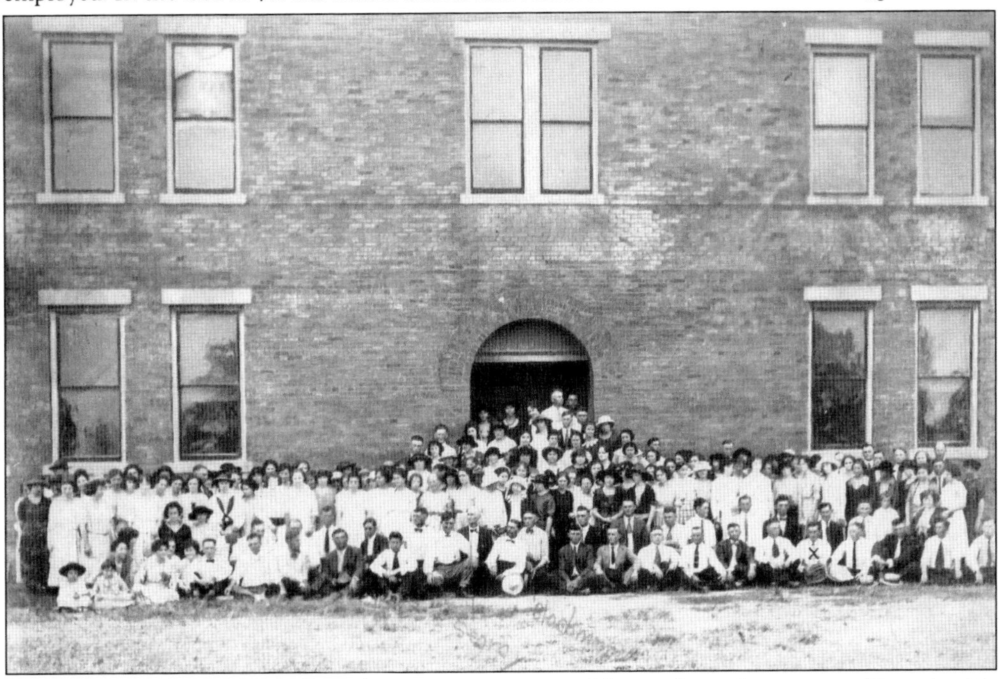

In the early 20th century a college degree was not required for teachers. A person could teach with a second- or third-grade certificate earned by written examination. Teachers were also required to attend a countywide institute where methods of teaching were discussed. They were paid for attending. Pictured are teachers attending an institute at Alba School in the early 1920s.

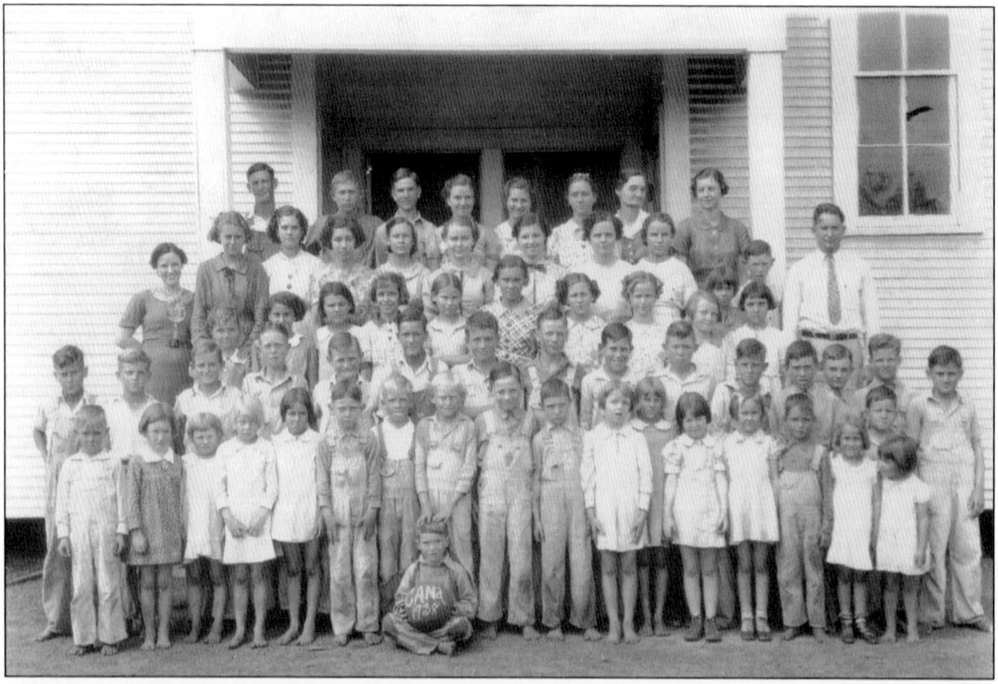

Cana School scholars line up for a picture in 1938. Cana was located to the north of Quitman on Farm to Market Road 2225. The white frame building in the picture burned and was replaced by a rock structure built by the WPA. Mr. and Mrs. Cowan were the teachers that year.

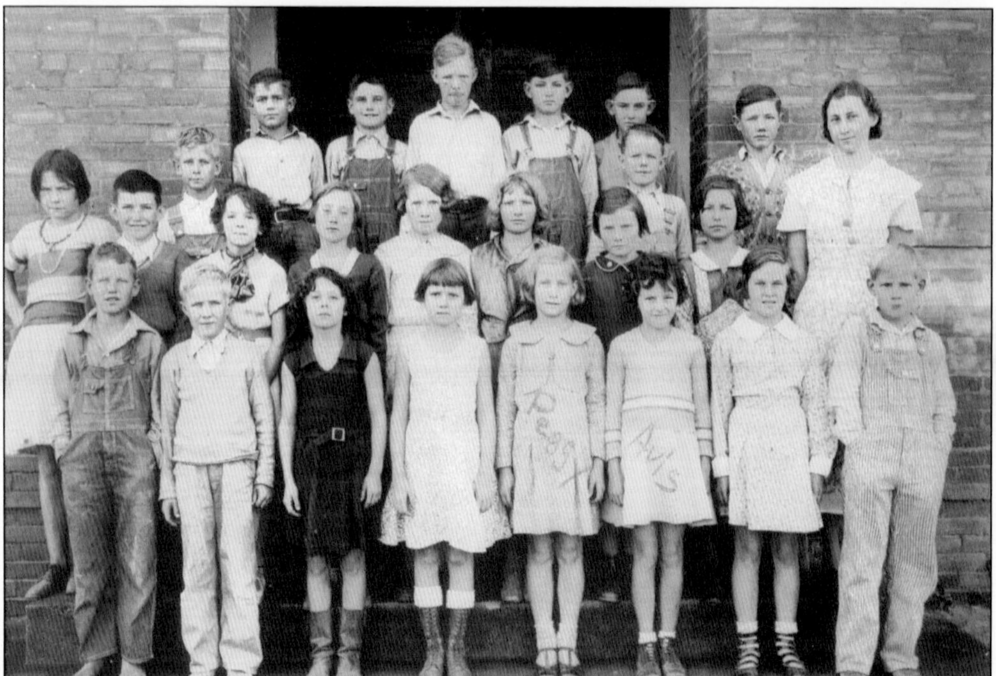

Students in the third and fourth grades at Alba Elementary School are pictured with their teacher, Mrs. Lillian Cathey, in 1933.

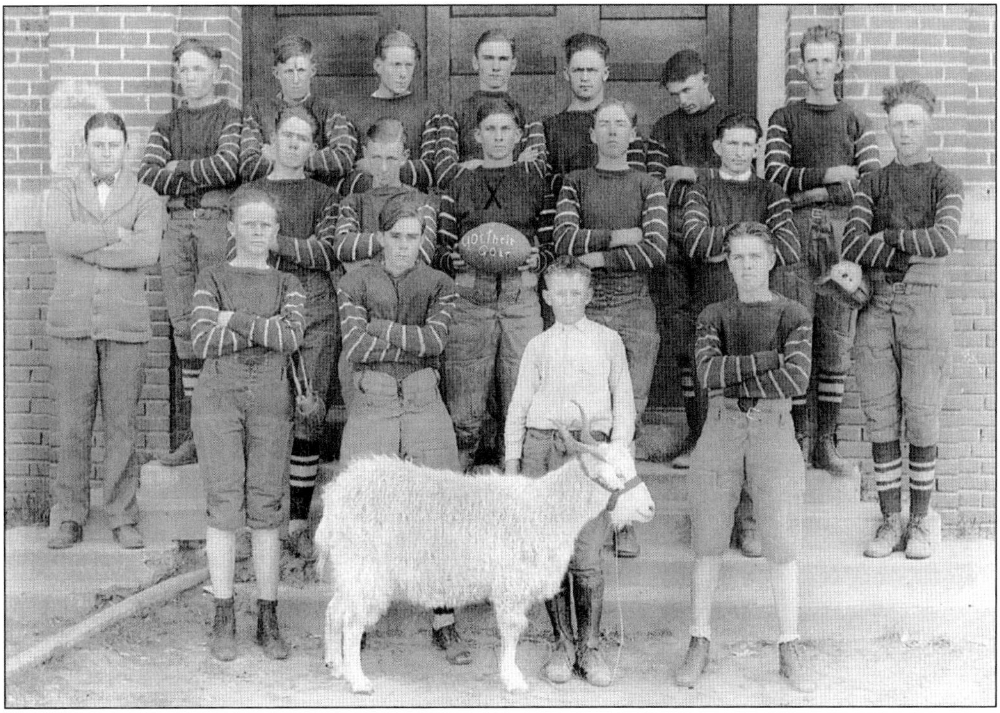

Quitman's first football team, c. 1926, included, from left to right (front row) Ernest Frank Smart, Loman Bozeman, Paul Conger with the mascot, and Thomas Corley Hart; (middle row) Clyde Lawrence, J.U. Searcy, Campbell Cathy holding the ball, James Wright, Marvin Taylor, and A.L. Dyer; (back row) Edison Blalock, Howard "Slim" Walker, Orsburn Sanders, Pet Green, John Ingram, William Rainwater (captain) and Theo Wilder. Don Hamm served as their coach.

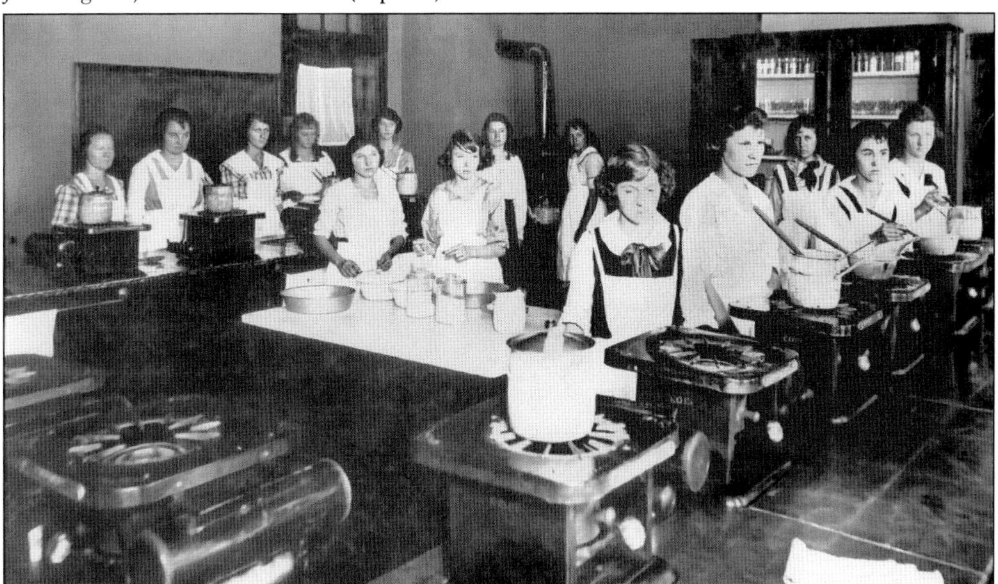

The photograph shows the Mineola High School home economics class of 1922. Home economics was a course in the public school curriculum that most girls took during their high school years. They learned skills in sewing, cooking, and childcare.

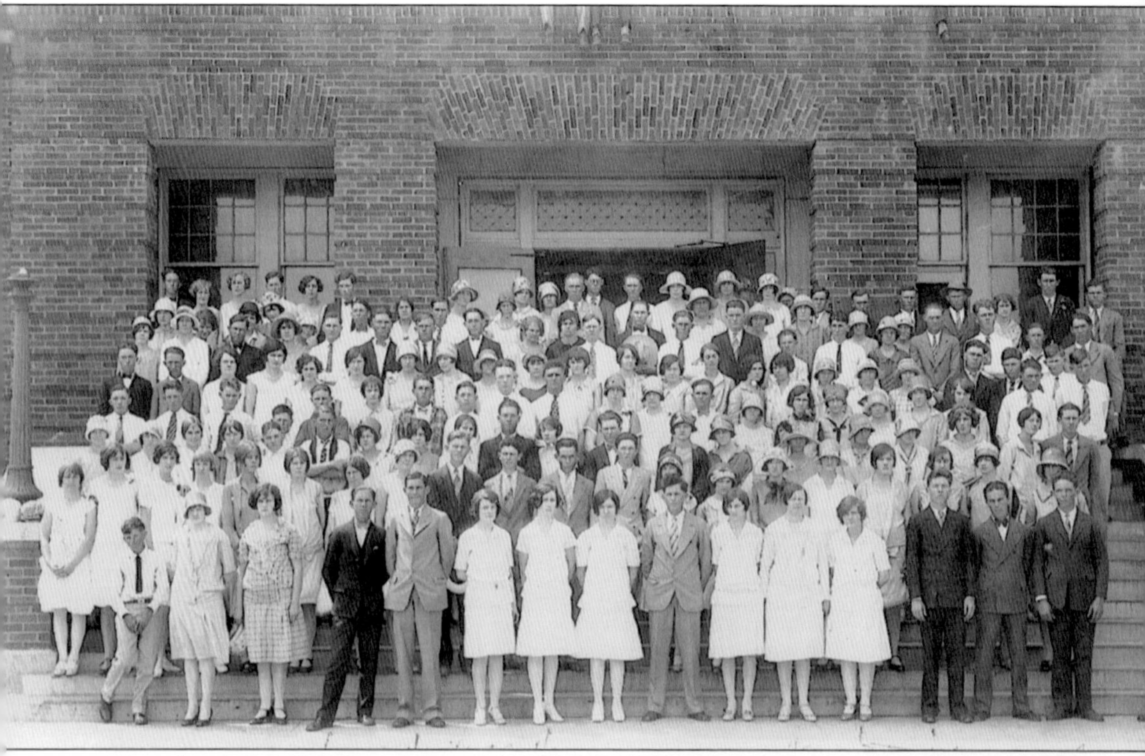

This photograph, taken in front of the Wood County Courthouse in 1927, shows of all the tenth grade students in the county, representing several rural school districts, who participated in the county graduation.

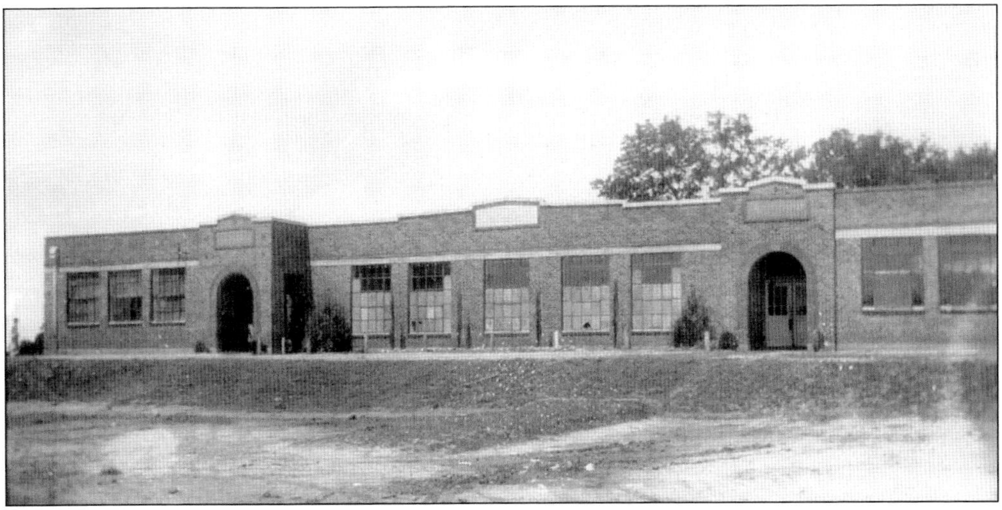

This structure built in 1928 was the second red brick school building to serve the children of Quitman. It replaced the first red brick building that had been built in 1919 and was destroyed by fire. Both structures were located on the same site on Morris Street.

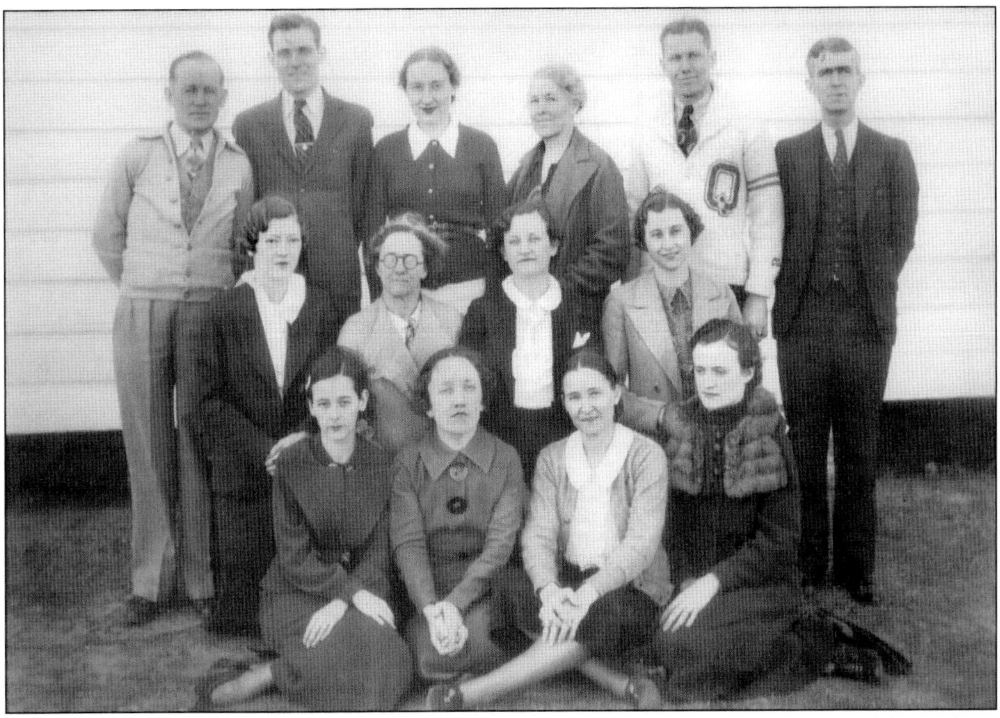

Members of the Quitman ISD faculty for the 1933–1934 school year are pictured here, from left to right: (front row) Mrs. Hall, Reba Richards, Mrs. W.C. Proctor, and Mrs. Slayton; (middle row) Gladys Powers, Olga Wright, Mozelle Wright, and Lillian Cathey; (back row) Superintendent W.C. Proctor, Mac McMillium, Imogene Black, Eva Garvin, R.E. Slayton, and George McAlister.

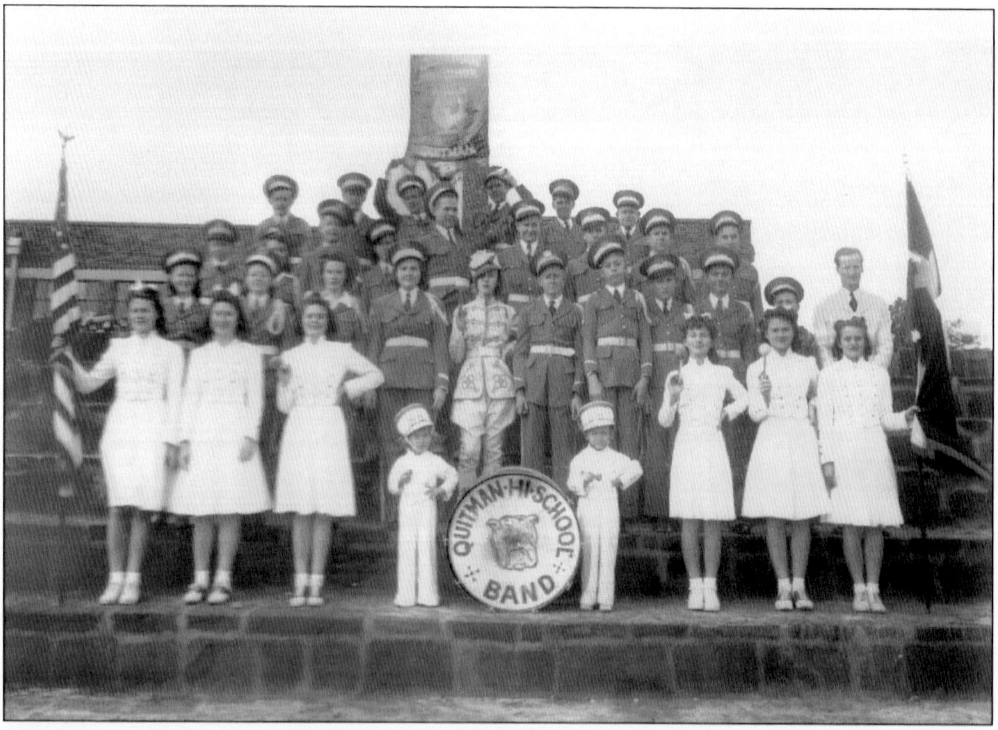

The Quitman High School Band is pictured here in the early 1940s on rock bleachers that were built by the WPA. Soon afterward the band director left to serve in World War II. Because so many people served the war effort in some capacity, there was a severe shortage of teachers. The band program was discontinued and was not reorganized until 1947.

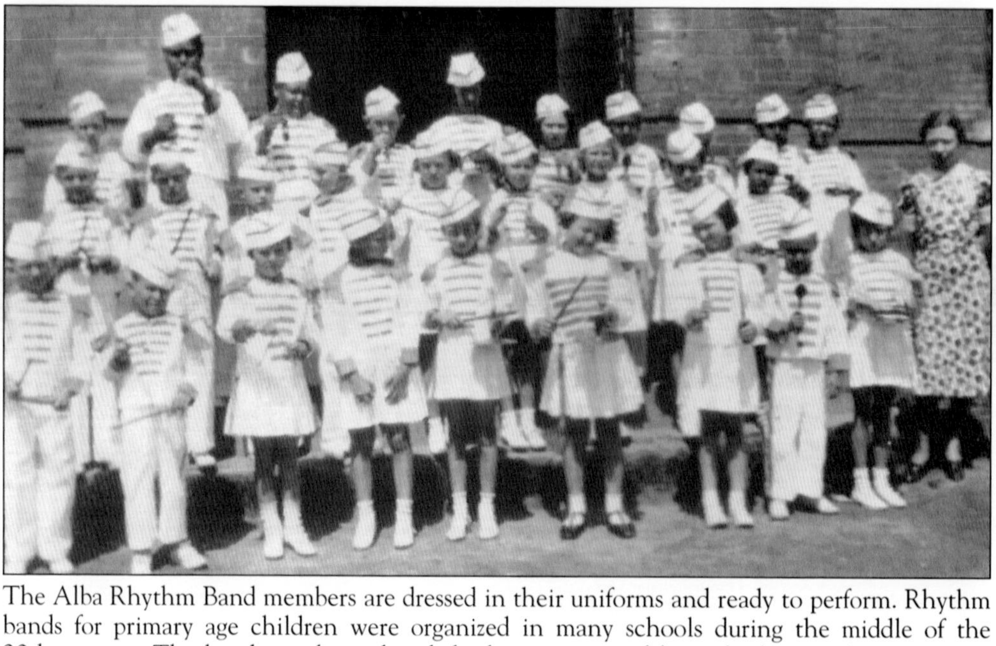

The Alba Rhythm Band members are dressed in their uniforms and ready to perform. Rhythm bands for primary age children were organized in many schools during the middle of the 20th century. The band members played rhythm patters and kept the beat with a variety of rhythm instruments, such as the sticks, cymbals, drums, and triangles.

Quitman Elementary School is pictured above around 1910 or 1920. The teacher is Miss A. Mosley, and there were 22 students in the school.

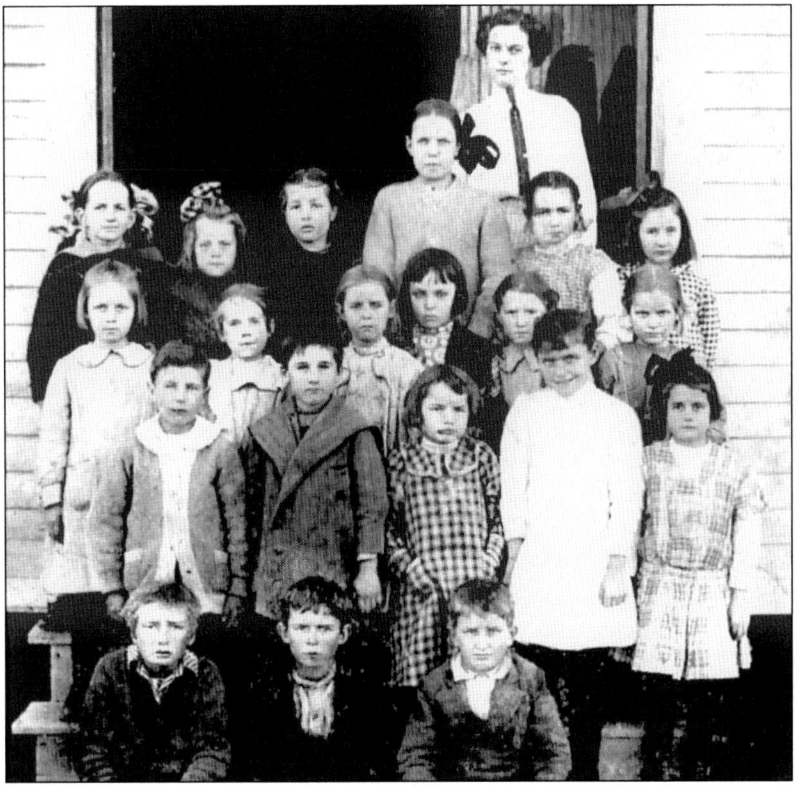

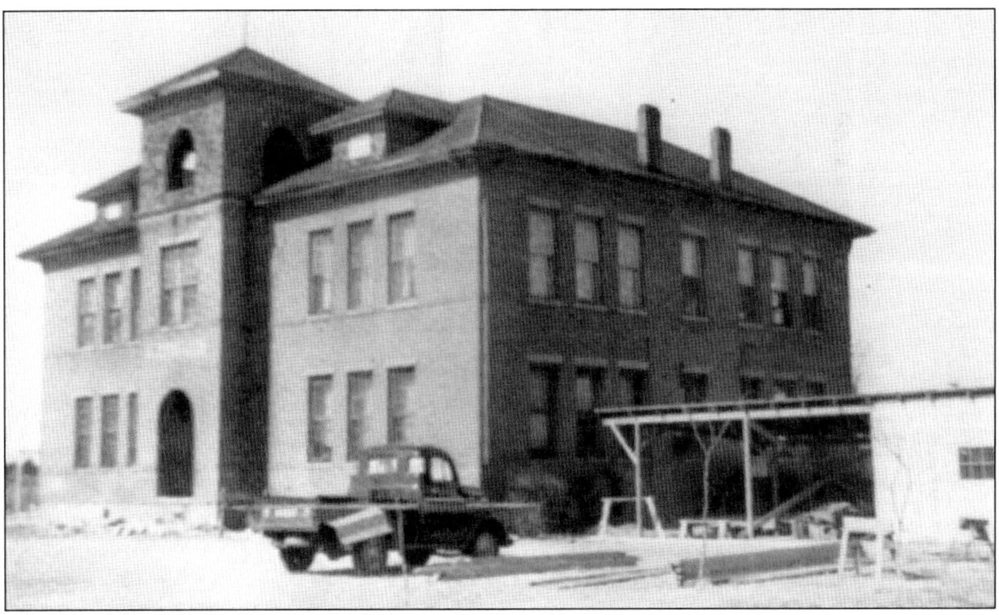

In 1952, students in Alba attended school in this building. Four years later, in 1956, the independent school district merged with nearby Golden ISD to form Alba-Golden ISD. A new building was constructed for the new district between the previous two districts.

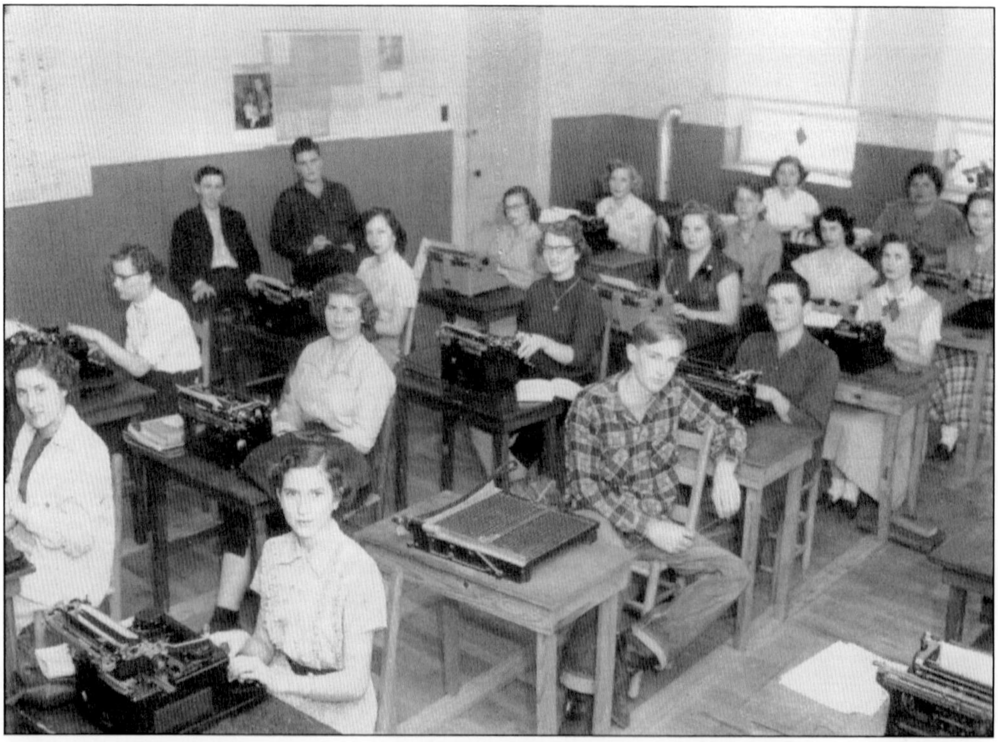

Students from the early 1950s sit at their typewriters in this Alba High School business class. Other subjects taught in the business curriculum included shorthand and bookkeeping.

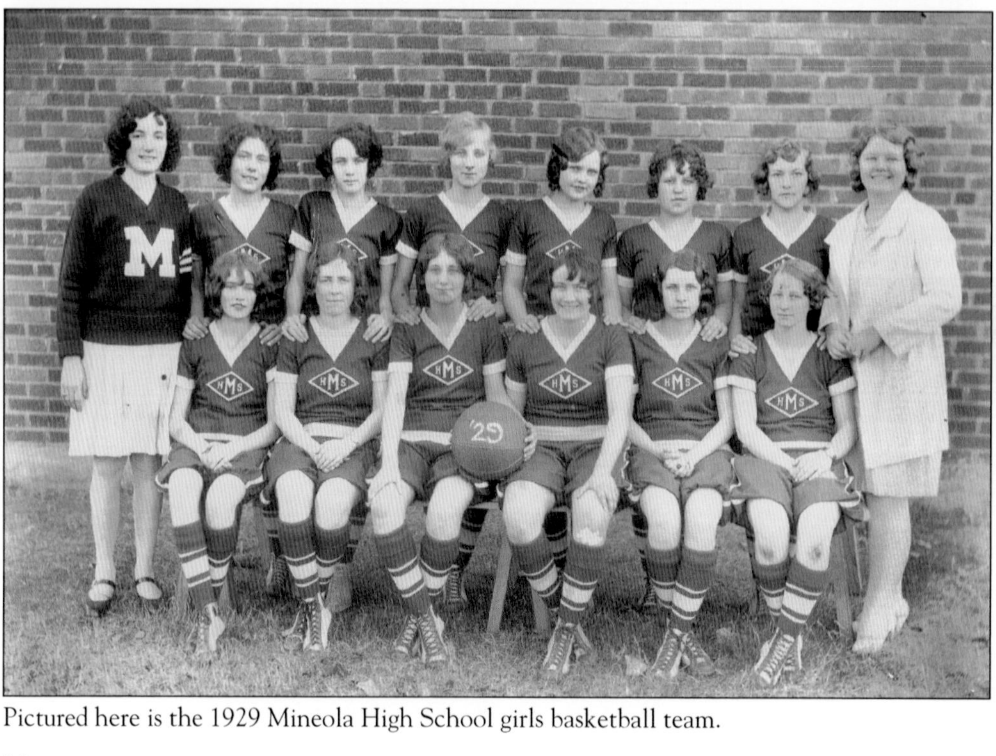

Pictured here is the 1929 Mineola High School girls basketball team.

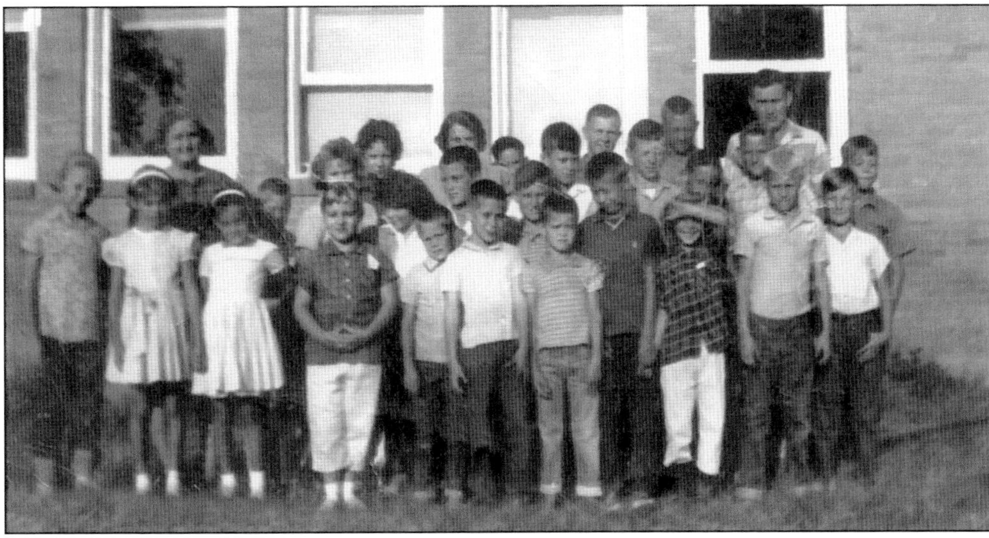

Only four rural schools were still around during the mid-1960s, when this picture was taken. At that time Cartwright was a school consisting of eight grades and was located between Quitman and Winnsboro. Bill McWhorter was the principal. Cartwright, Lone Grove, and New Hope consolidated with Quitman and Mineola in 1964, leaving only one rural school in operation—Lloyd, commonly known as Coke. Coke consolidated with Quitman the following year.

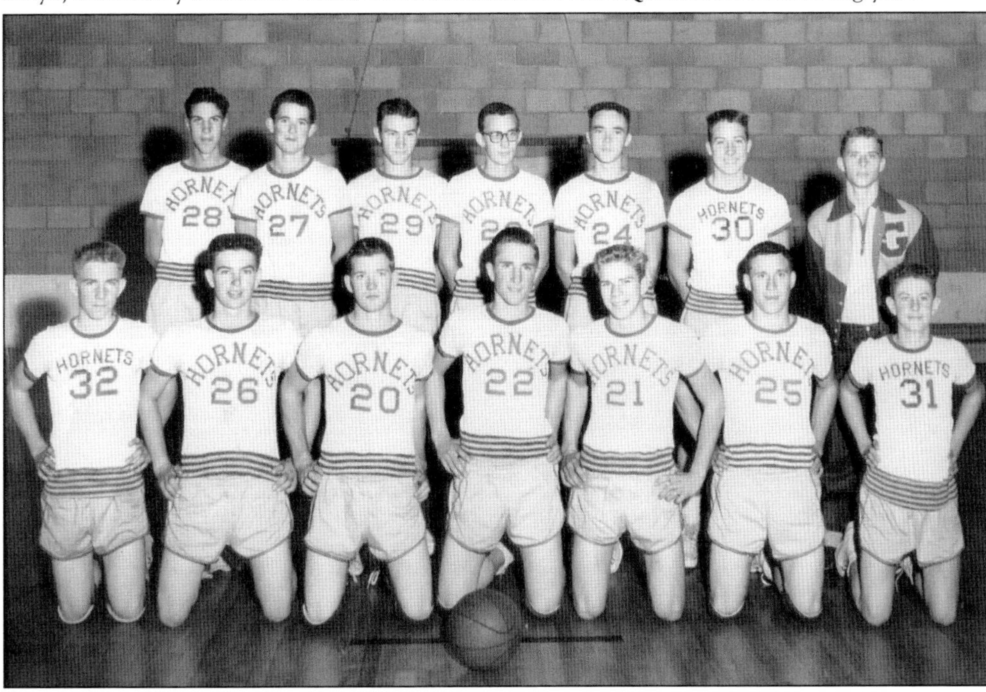

The Golden boys basketball team, which played year-round, won the district championship several years and sometimes advanced to regional competition. The 1955–1956 team is pictured here in the new gym. Team members, are, from left to right, (front row) Dudley Chapman, Billy Earl Madsen, Jerry Ted Brannon, Sam Hughes, George Tom Hayes, Charlie Haisten, and Curtis Brown; (back row) Paul Patrick, Johnny Johnson, Benny Brown, Ronald Weeks, Will Irvin Holland, Taylor Brittain, and Bernice Deuson.

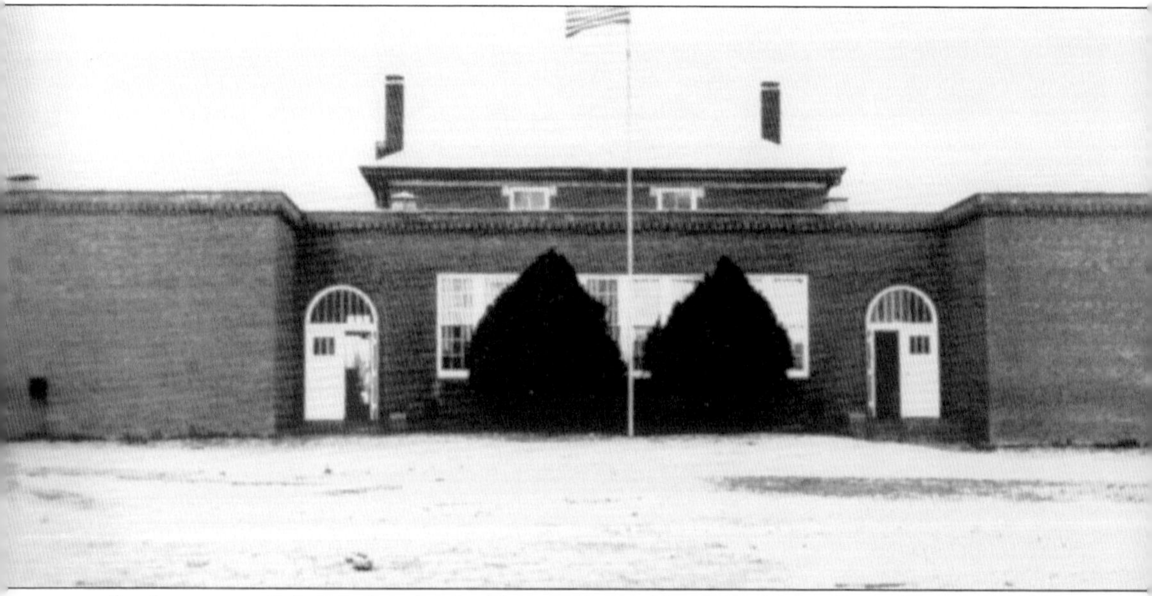

Students attended school in this building in the Golden ISD during the 1950s. It served as the elementary school after Golden and Alba merged their districts.

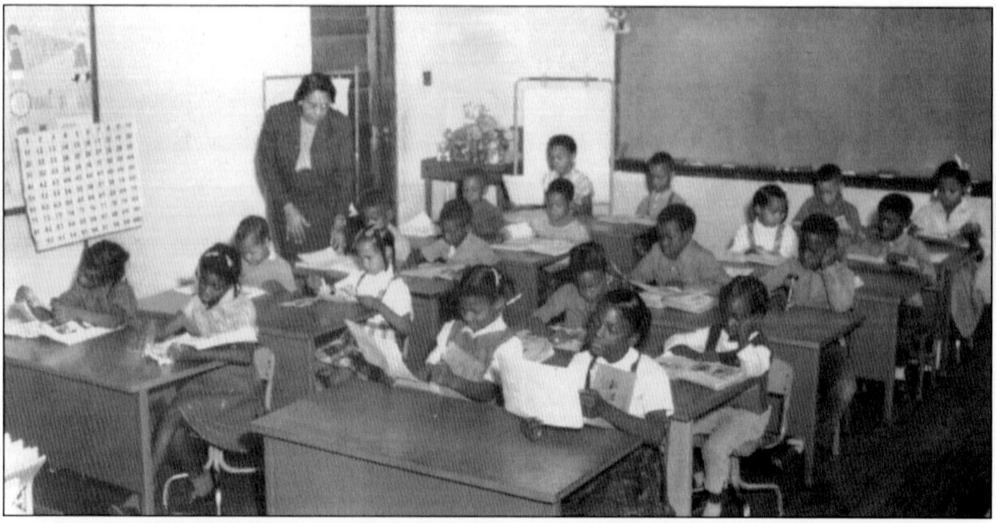

Primary age children are seen in their classroom in the W.B. Clark School in Quitman. The school was named for William Benjamin Clark, a beloved educator in the community. The teacher in the picture is his daughter, Miss Virdie Mae Clark, who was well known for her teaching abilities and love of children.

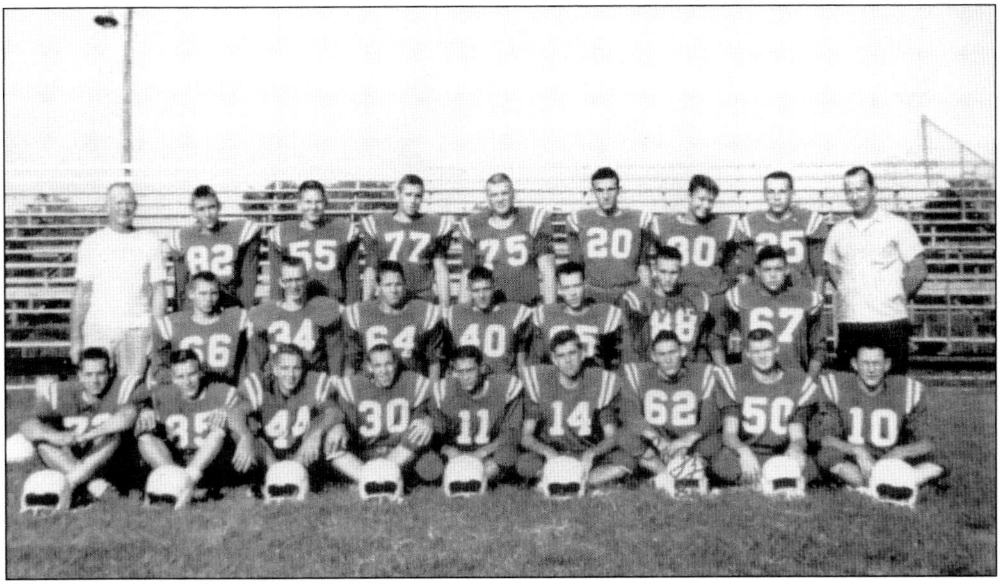

The members of the 1963–1964 Hawkins football team are, from left to right, as follows: (front row) D. Tate, R. Byrd, D. Thornton, D. Wright, R. Dacus, J. Brim, J. Mooney, P. Eubanks, and G. Arnold; (middle row) R. Duncan, J. Broadus, R. Haire, J. Holmes, O. McWilliams, B. Dobbs, and P. Barnett; (back row) Coach Lowrance, J. Wilson, W. Kennedy, T. Little, G. Owen, J. Foster, L. Shipp, J. Hughes, and Coach Horne. Coach Lowrance coached at Hawkins for 27 years and won district 11 years.

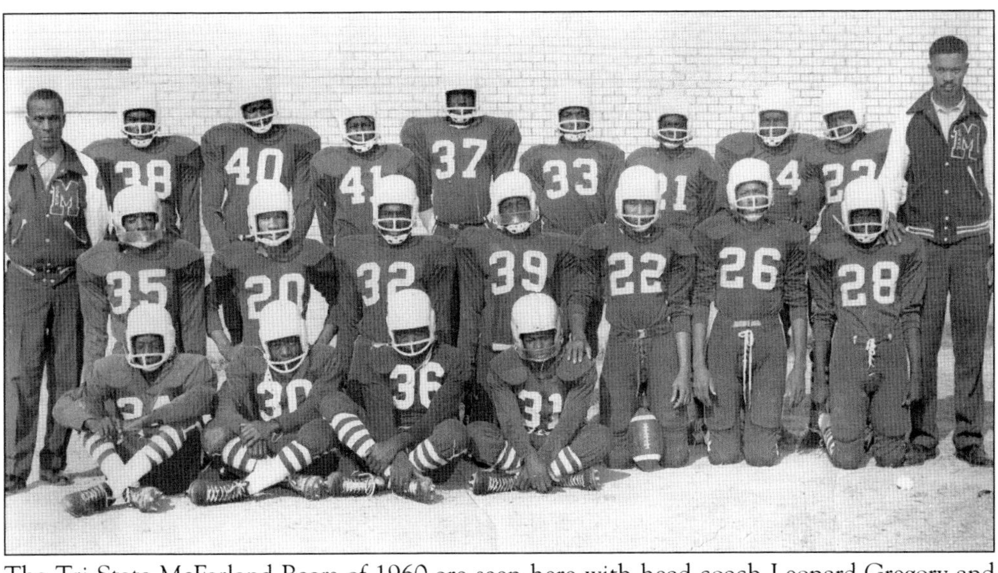

The Tri-State McFarland Bears of 1960 are seen here with head coach Leonard Gregory and assistant coach Elbert Reed.

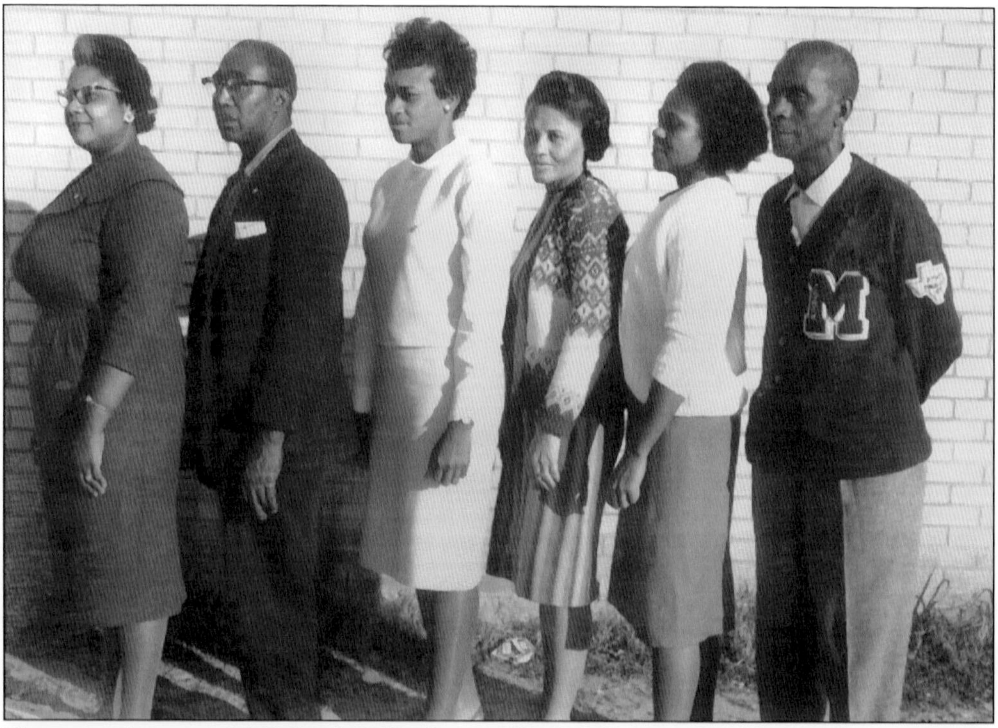

These teachers of McFarland School are, from left to right, Mrs. Johnnie Bendy, Wilbur McWilburn, Earline "Pink" Wynn, Willie Sue Stewart, Jewell White, and Coach Leonard Gregory. The final school year for McFarland High School came in 1965–1966.

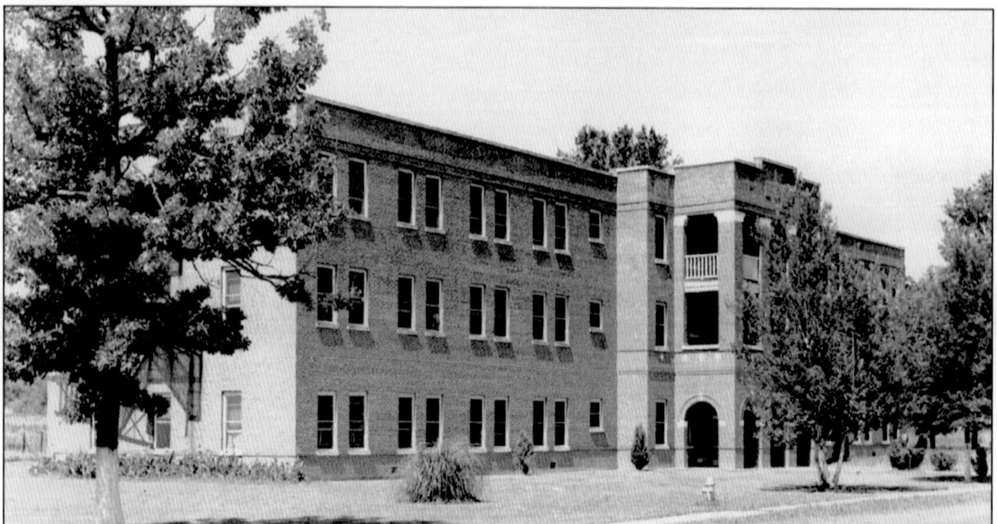

African-American students make up the majority of those attending Jarvis College, near Hawkins, and the school has an average enrollment of approximately 400 students. It has become known as one of the outstanding African-American schools in the South. Jarvis College has owned considerable oil properties and used this income to help construct new facilities and provide its students with the best technology. Pictured here is the Jarvis College Administration Building in the 1940s.

Seven

Notable Sons and Daughters

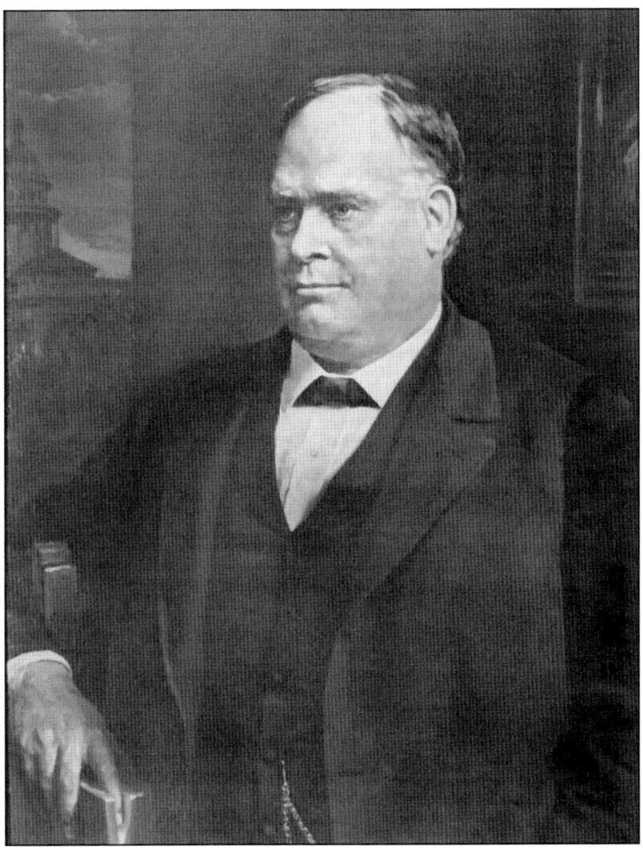

James S. Hogg, later governor, came to Wood County in 1872. Shortly thereafter he married Miss Sallie Stinson, and on July 10, 1882 a daughter, Ima, was born. Ima, together with her brother Will Hogg, took the fortune of the family and set up a foundation for mental health, historic preservation, and the arts. Through the years Wood County has had its share of other famous "sons and daughters." The county may be small geographically but it has produced many people endowed with an abundance of intelligence, talent, and a determination to succeed.

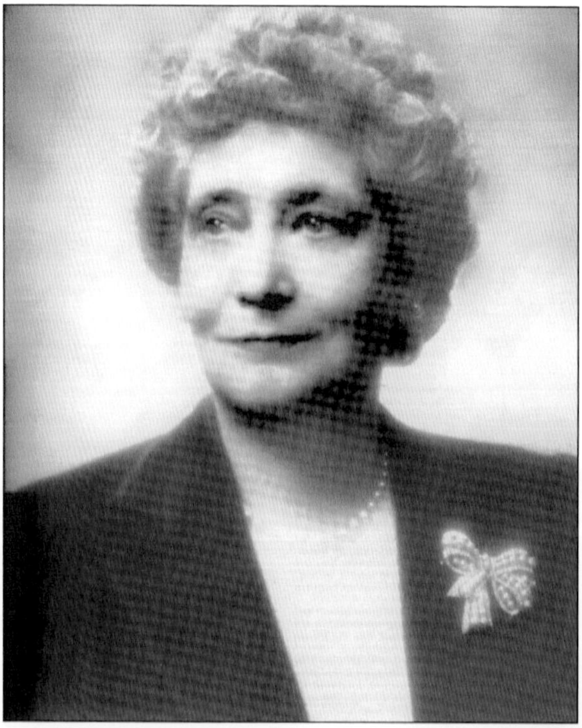

Miss Ima was born in Mineola on July 10, 1882, where her parents, future governor James S. Hogg and Sallie Stinson Hogg, were living. After two years at the University of Texas at Austin, Miss Ima went to New York and Europe for musical training. Miss Ima spent millions restoring Texas historic landmarks including the Honeymoon Cottage and the Stinson House here in Wood County. Upon her death, Miss Ima left her beautiful historic home, "Bayou Bend," to the Houston Museum of Fine Arts.

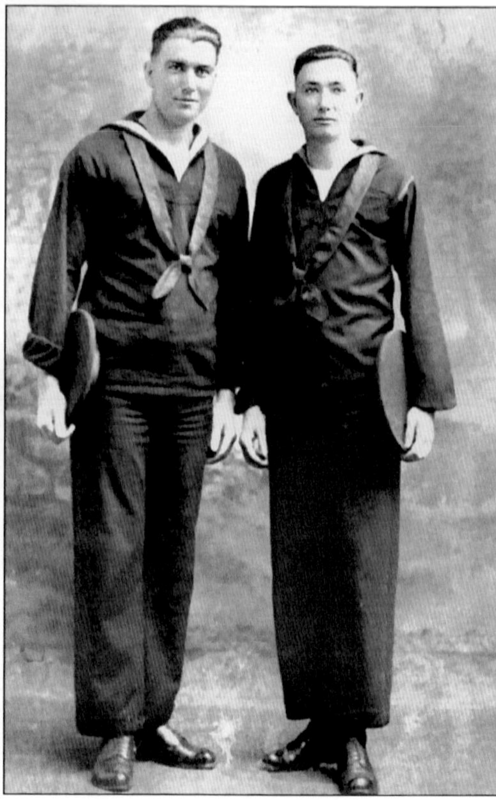

First World War Navy buddies from Wood County are pictured in their uniforms. Both these men returned home after honorable service. They are just a few of the many notable sons and daughters of Wood County who have served their country from the Civil War to the present.

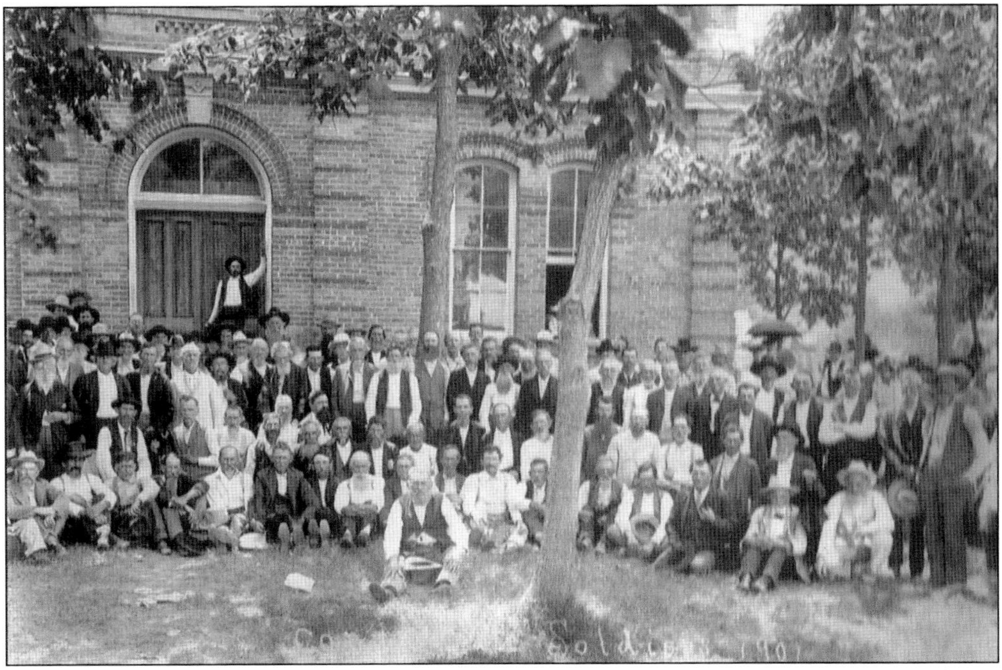

Confederate veterans from Wood County are pictured in front of the old courthouse, which was destroyed by fire in 1924.

John Simmons, a Confederate soldier who served from March 15, 1862 to the end of the Civil War, wrote this letter to his wife, Nancy, who lived in Wood County.

Monroe, Louisiana
July 15, 1863

Dear Companion,

I now seat myself this morning to drop you a few lines to let you know that I am in only tolerable health at this time, hoping these few lines may find you all in good health - when they come to hand - which is a great blessing. I have not received any letter since I last wrote to you. The last one I got was dated the 20th of June. I am getting anxious to hear from you again. I have nothing of importance to write to you at present. I left the company and came out here a few days ago. They were at Delhi when I left them. The whole division will be out of the swamps in a few days. They have destroyed everything from Delhi to the river, such as corn, fodder, mills, cotton, and bridges - anything and everything that might be of benefit to the enemy. Stood but a poor show; it's an awful thing to think of destroying things in such a manner. It looks like destroying the country forever.

Vicksburg has fallen, and no doubt it was surrendered on the 4th of July. There were in the fort, when surrendered, over thirty thousand men. They have been all paroled till changed. I have seen a great many of them. Fort Hudson shared the same fate on the 9th. There they got a right smart of our boys. Harrisburg is said to have went up the spout, too. It's fifty miles below here on this river. It looks as if the Feds are a-going to run over us rough-shod now. I think a few more months will tell the tale. Our brigade will get to this place this evening if nothing happens, but to be in the army is one of the uncertainest places a man ever was, for one minute you have one thing and the next another way, so I can't say anything as to what will be our movements now. I rather think that we will fall back towards the Red River and take a rest, if the Feds will let us. We may have a fight right here in less than a week. I am not surprised at no movement no more; I was at first. So no more at present but to remain your affectionate husband till death,

John Simmons to Nancy Simmons

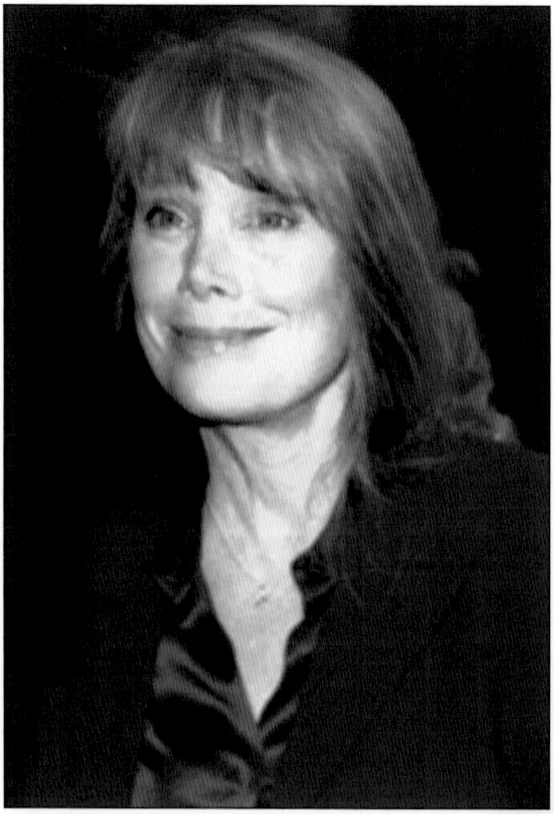

Sissy Spacek, born Mary Elizabeth Spacek on December 25, 1940, moved to New York after her graduation from high school. Although best known for her Academy Award–winning role in *The Coal Miner's Daughter*, Sissy has had many screen roles, and in 1991 won a Golden Globe Award for Best Actress in a Motion Picture Drama for her role as a vengeful mother in Todd Field's gritty dysfunctional family drama *In the Bedroom*.

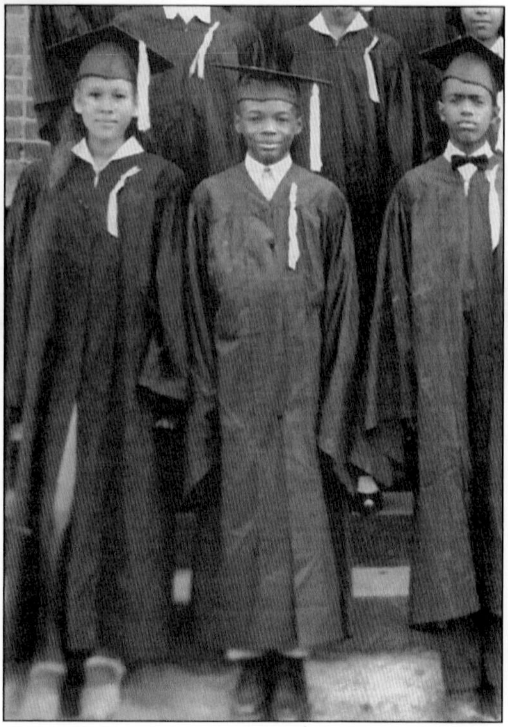

In 1951 a 17-year-old African American man named Willie Brown left his hometown of Mineola, Texas, for San Francisco. He took the oath of office 45 years later as that city's first African-American mayor. He dominated California politics for more than two decades, first as a member and then speaker of the California state assembly. Willie is shown here at his eighth-grade graduation in 1947.

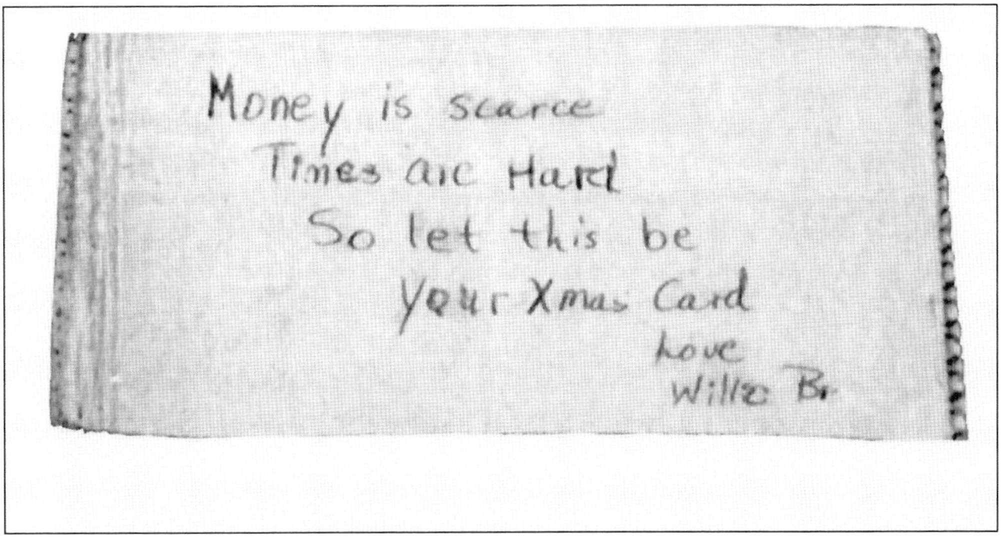

This photograph shows a Christmas card Willie Brown sent his mother in 1954. The message was penned on a piece of corrugated cardboard.

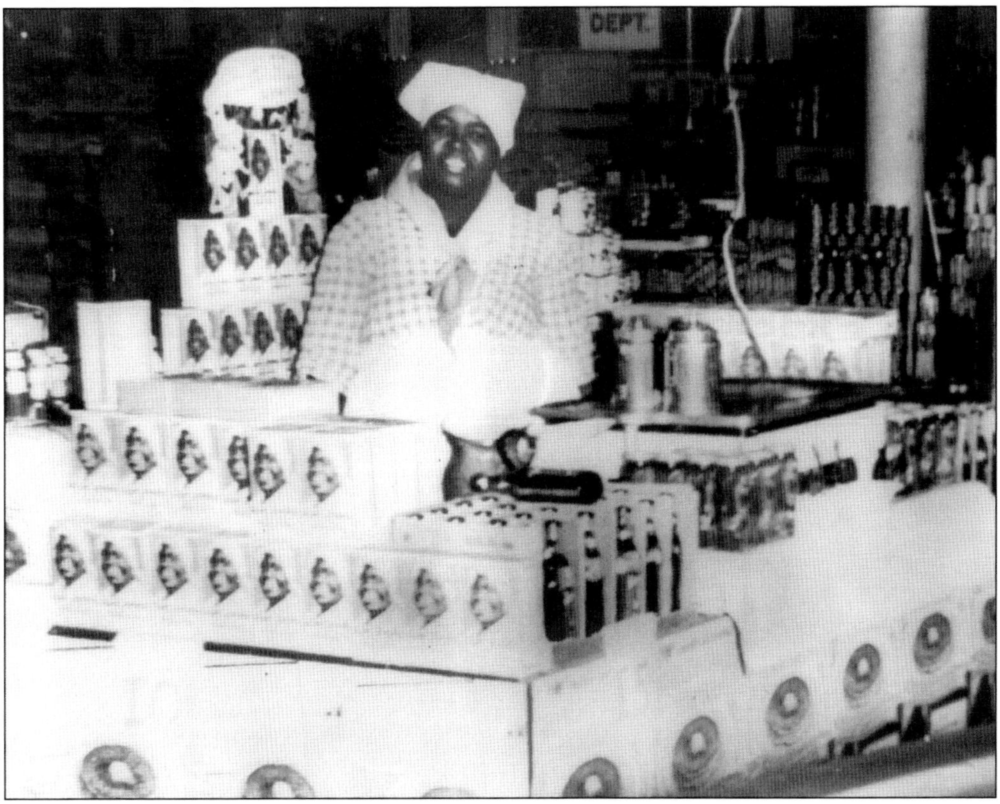

Aunt Jemima was born Lillian Richard on March 23, 1891, in Hawkins. At the age of 20 Lillian went to Dallas looking for work and a short time later was contacted by Quaker Oats Company asking her to go store to store, dressed as Aunt Jemima, to demonstrate Aunt Jemima's pancakes and other products. Her career with Quaker Oats lasted over 37 years. In 1995 The Texas legislature passed a resolution declaring Hawkins "The Pancake Capital of Texas."

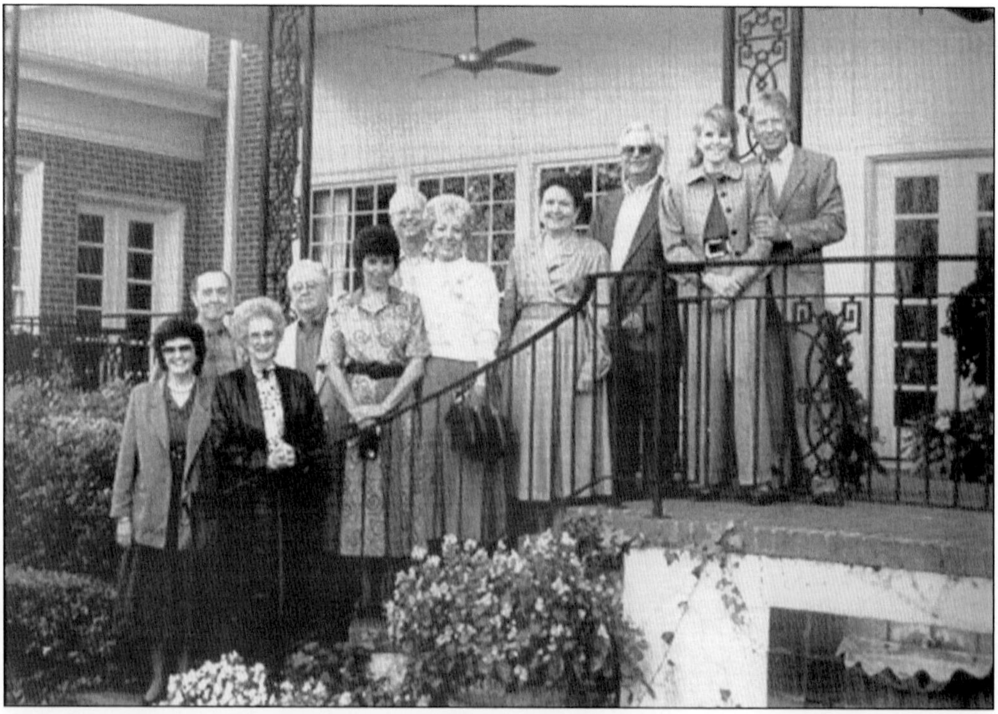

Born in Golden to Reuben L. Simmons, Golden School superintendent, and Fairess Simmons, a well-educated English teacher and pianist, Harold Simmons graduated from the University of Texas at Austin. After graduation he became a bank examiner. Having a knack for locating opportunity, he bought a bank and then one drugstore after another until, in time, his initial $33,000 investment mushroomed into a $1.3 billion trust fund.

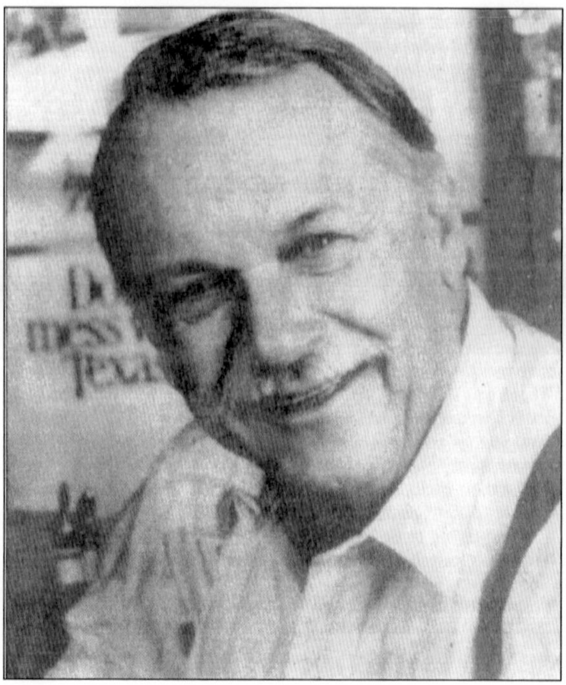

Noble Willingham was born on August 31, 1931, in Mineola, where he grew up. After graduation from high school he attended Baylor University where he received a master's degree and taught school briefly before being one of the local Texans chosen to appear in *The Last Picture Show* (1971). Even though Noble appeared in many movies and television series, he is best known for his portrayal of C.D. Parker, a former Texas Ranger on *Walker, Texas Ranger* from 1993 to 1999. Noble Willingham died in 2004 in California.

Pictured here are Wood County officials in 1907.

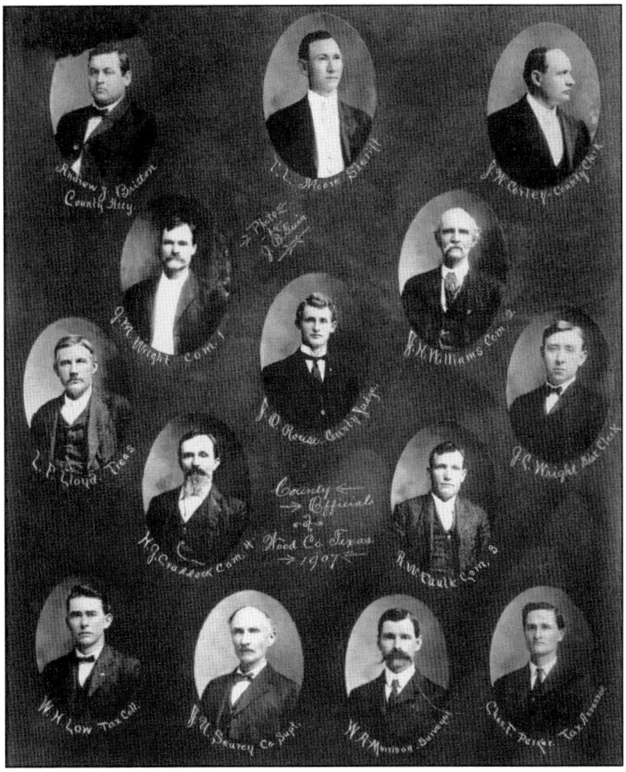

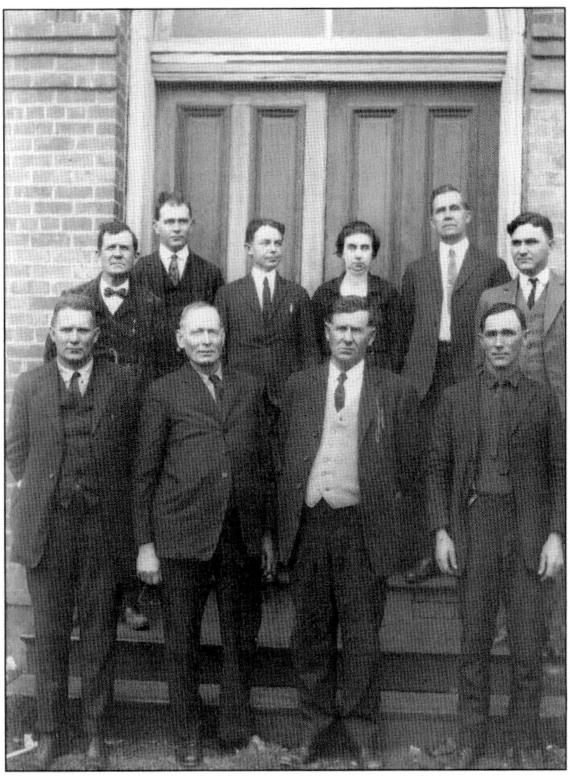

The incoming and retiring officials of Wood County are pictured here in 1922.

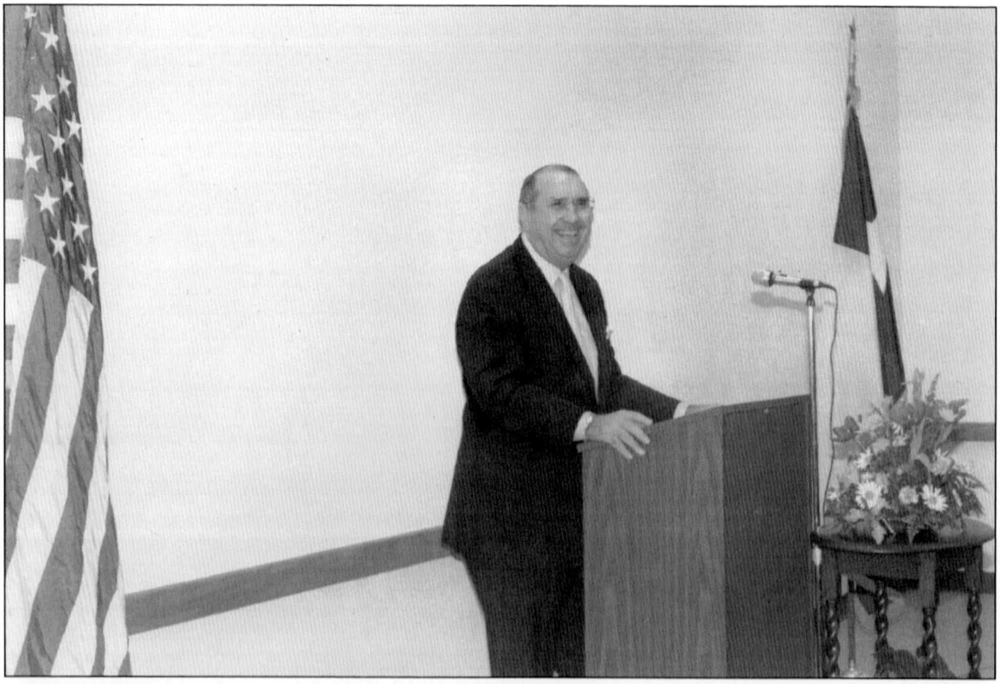

Peyton McKnight was born on December 10, 1924, in Alba. He was elected to the Texas House of Representatives at the age of 25, and in 1953 he was appointed U.S. marshal for the Eastern District of Texas, making him the youngest marshal in history at the age of 28. In 1972 he was elected state senator and served 12 years. While in the legislature he helped create the Sabine River Authority, of which he was a member.

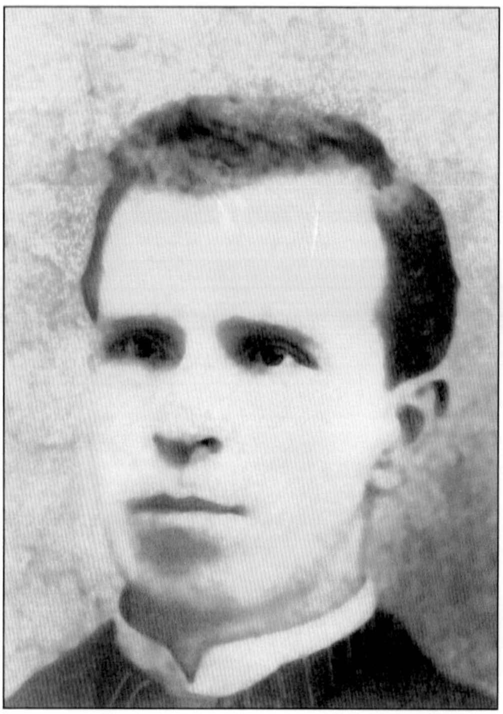

Senator John Creighton Buchanan, who was born in 1850 and died in 1885, practiced law in Quitman. He was elected county attorney in 1876 and to the state senate in 1878 where he served 6 years. While a senator he was the author of a bill to establish normal schools in Texas; Mineola and Galveston were two of three cities in the state to have normal schools. Senator Buchanan also drafted the bill that created the University of Texas at Austin.

Sarah was the wife of Senator Buchanan. She had been in the wedding party when (later governor) Jim Hogg and Sallie Stinson were married. When Senator Buchanan died at the age of 35 leaving her with three small children and a debt of $1100, Governor Hogg appointed her to teach English at Sam Houston State Normal College in Huntsville where she taught for 24 years. She became the first woman in Texas to be named a full professor.

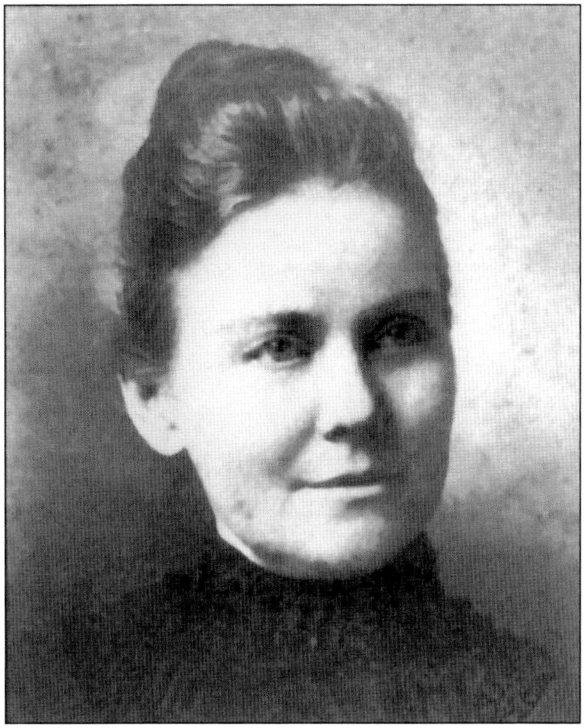

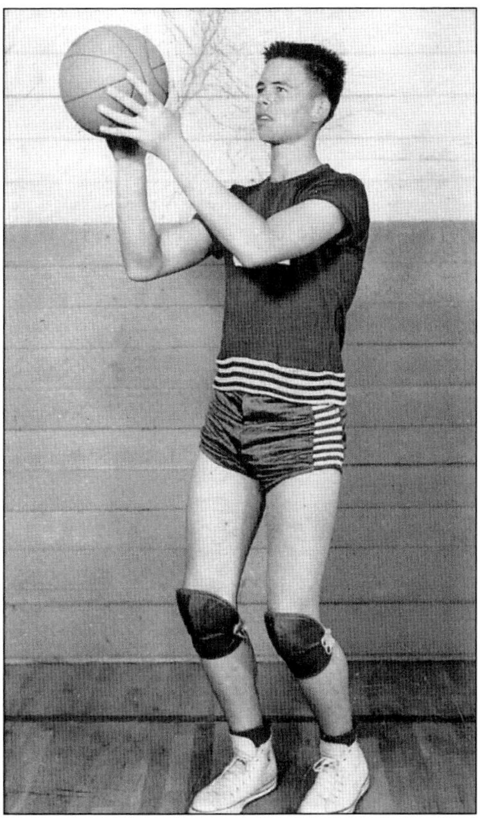

Carroll Dawson grew up in Alba, played basketball in high school, and attended Paris Junior College where he was named an All-American. He went on to play at Baylor where he made the Southwest Conference team in 1960. Later, Dawson was the head basketball coach at Baylor University from 1973 to 1977. In 1980 he began coaching with the Houston Rockets and, in 1996, was named general manager. On February 12, 2004, Dawson was inducted into the Texas Sports Hall of Fame.

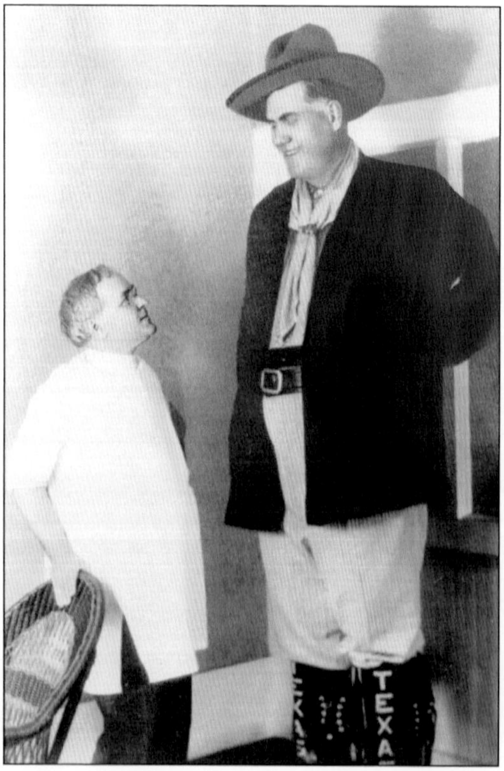

Jim Tarver was born in the Cottonwood community near Golden. "Big Jim Tarver" was 8 feet, 4 inches tall and weighed 460 pounds.

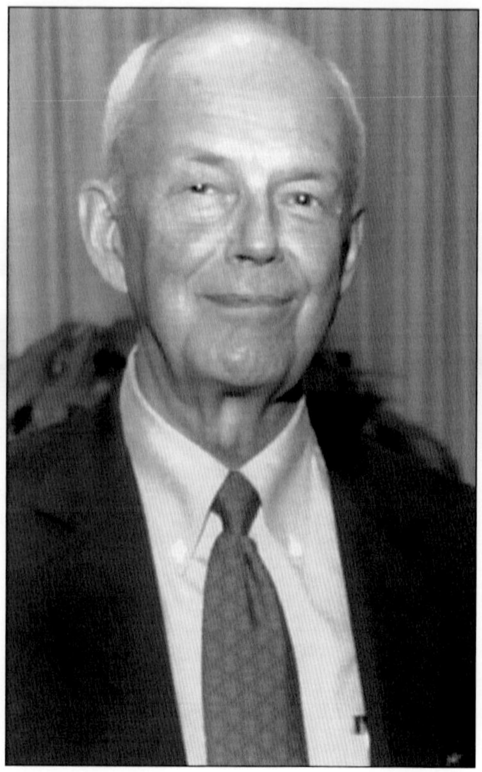

Bobby Inman was born in Rhonesboro, attended school in Mineola, and graduated from the University of Texas at Austin at the age of 19. He joined the Naval Reserves, commissioned as an ensign, and spent the next 19 years as an analyst for Naval Intelligence. He was named the director of National Security in 1977 and in 1981 he became the deputy director of Central Intelligence.

Eight

Business and Industries

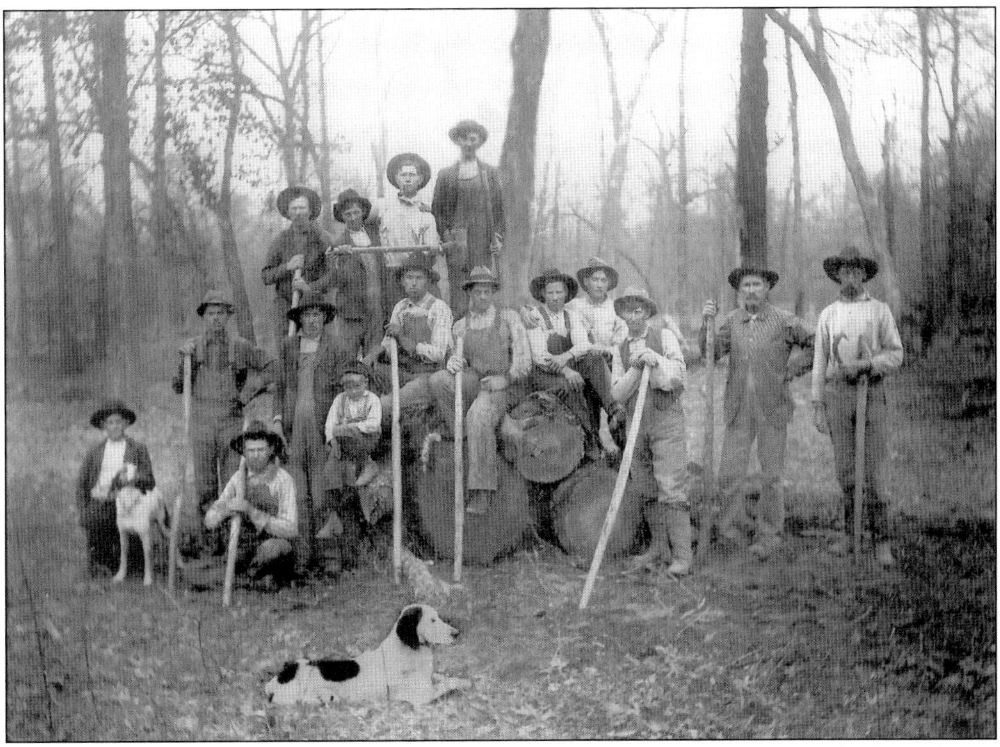

Wood County was a virgin forest, heavily timbered, when it was first settled. These forests provided not only material to construct their homes and barns but also provided a local industry and a means of livelihood for the newly arrived settlers. Through the years, Wood County has depended largely on its agriculture and when agriculture began to decline the beef cattle and dairy cattle industries became a principal source of income. Today, however, the non-agricultural economy has become much stronger and includes a wide range of business activity such as a water plant, oil refinery, manufacturing, retail trade, and service-related jobs.

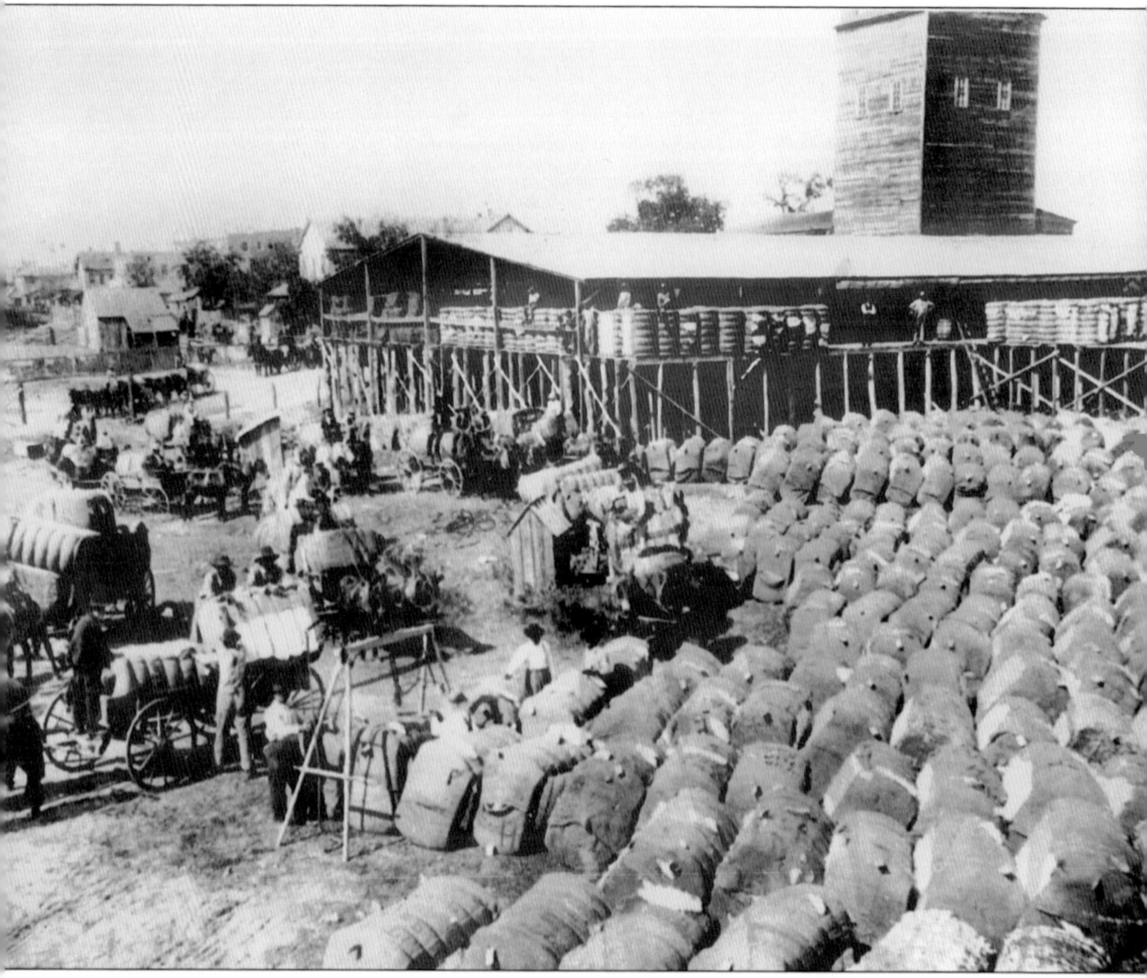

Cotton was a very important "cash" crop for farmers, pictured above on their way to the gin, *c.* 1915.

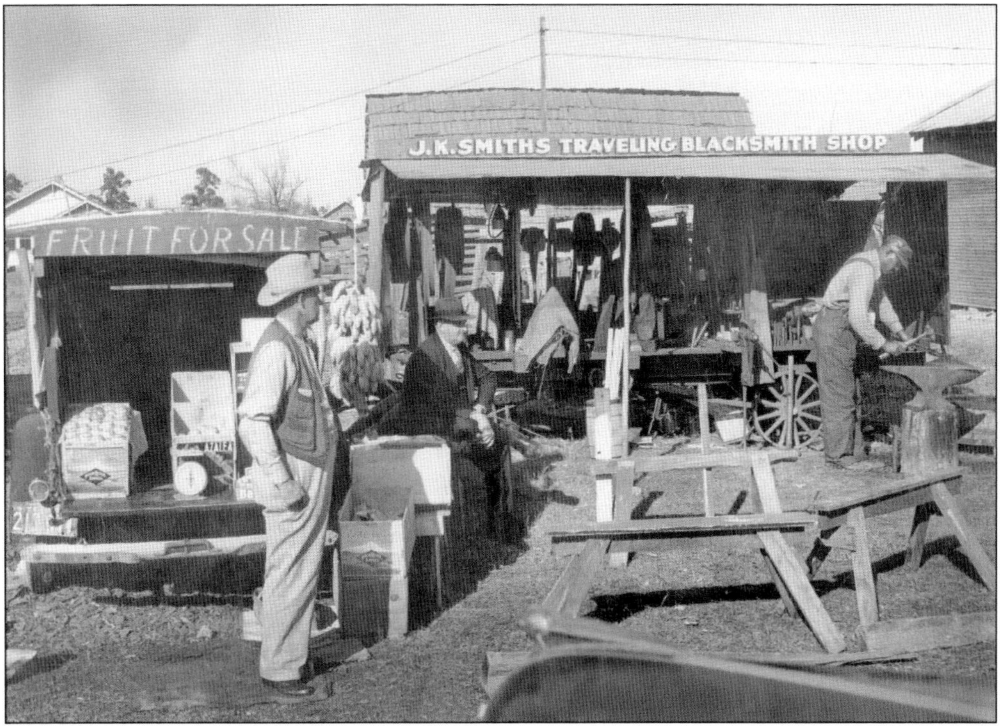

J.K. Smith, owner, and his family lived in Mineola and later moved to Hoard, a small community about six miles east of Mineola. On the left of this late 1930s scene in Hawkins, fruit is offered for sale.

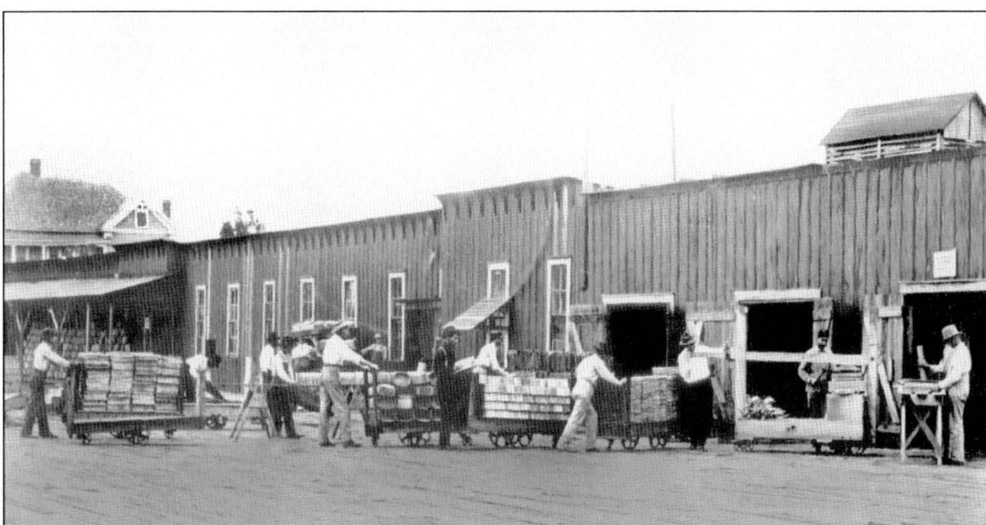

The R.J. Smith Chair Factory was located in the 400 block of East Broad Street in Mineola. In 1897, the Tilley Bros. set up Mineola's first electric plant, and the engines and generators for the system were housed in the Chair Factory. The Chair Factory operated during the day and the electric plant operated at night since the customers only used electricity for lighting purposes.

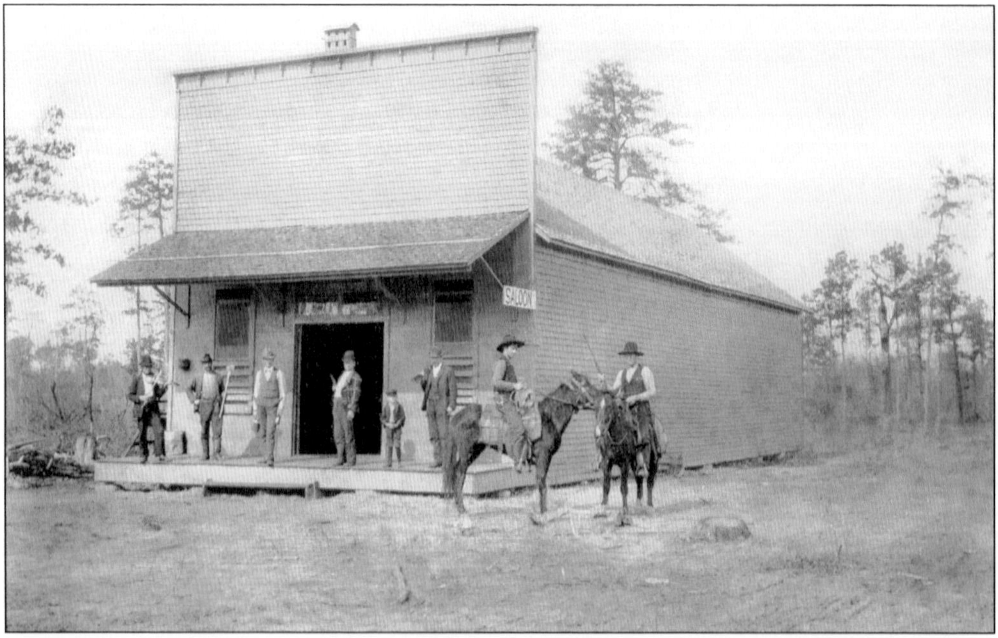

The Peach community in east Wood County was settled in the 1850s, though there was no village until the Texas Southern Railway built through the area in 1897. When the fruit industry became active locally, the community was named Peach. Saloons existed in all parts of the county. Sitting atop the saloon in the photograph is a birdhouse.

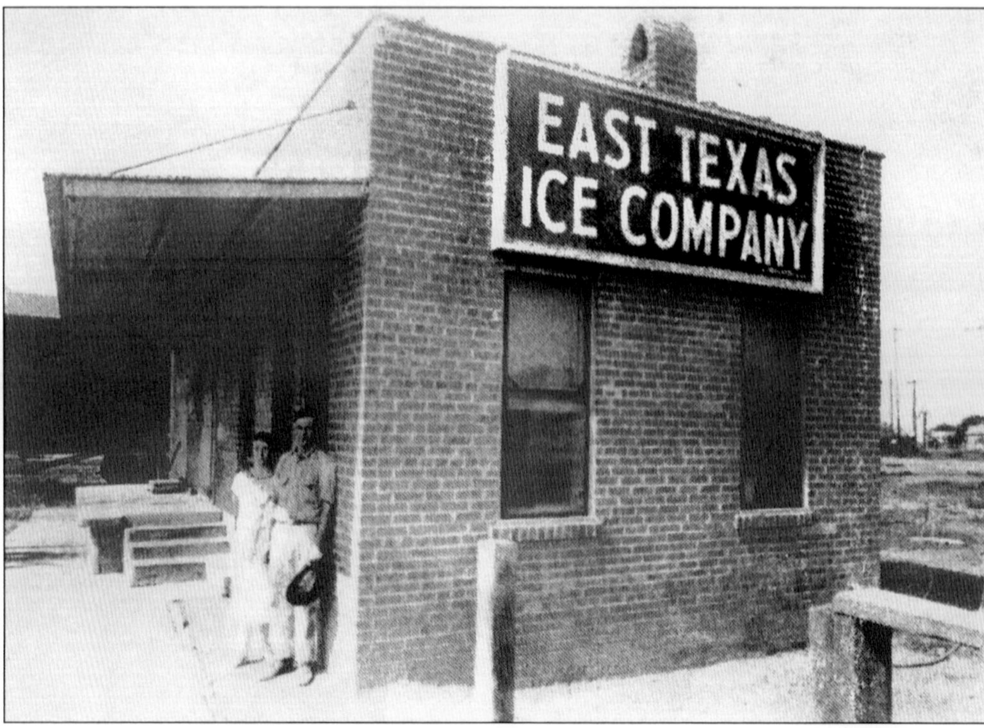

The Ice House in Alba was located in the south part of town directly across from the water tower. Mrs. Grady Barnett was the manager.

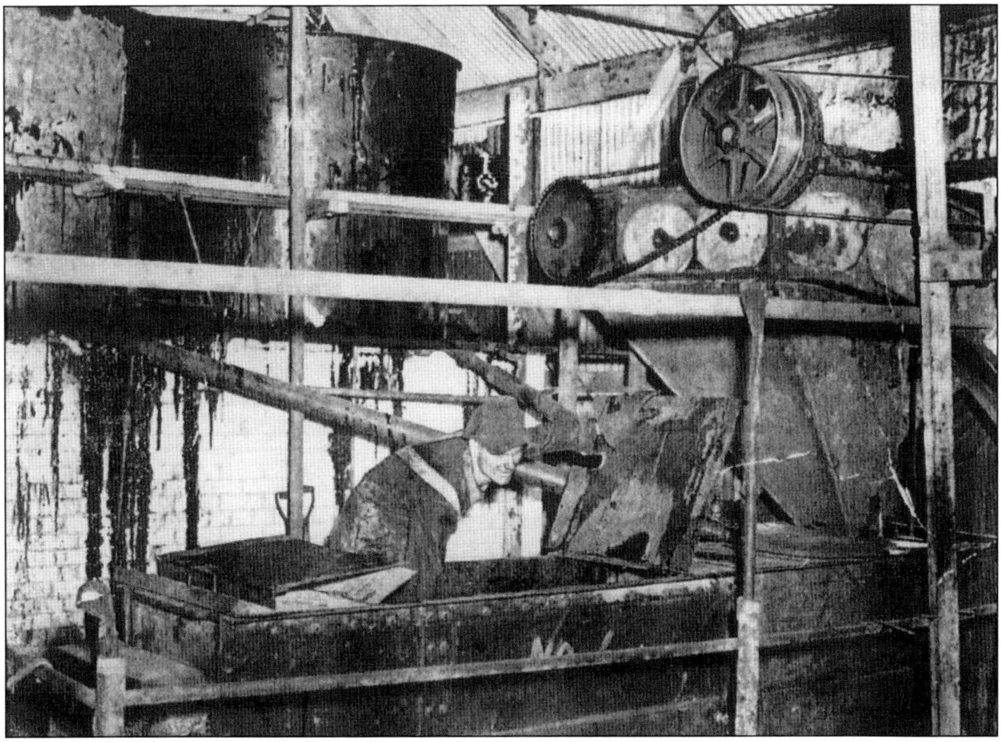

Consumers Lignite, who owned one of the coal mines in the Alba area, operated this plant that made charcoal briquettes. The date of this picture is unknown.

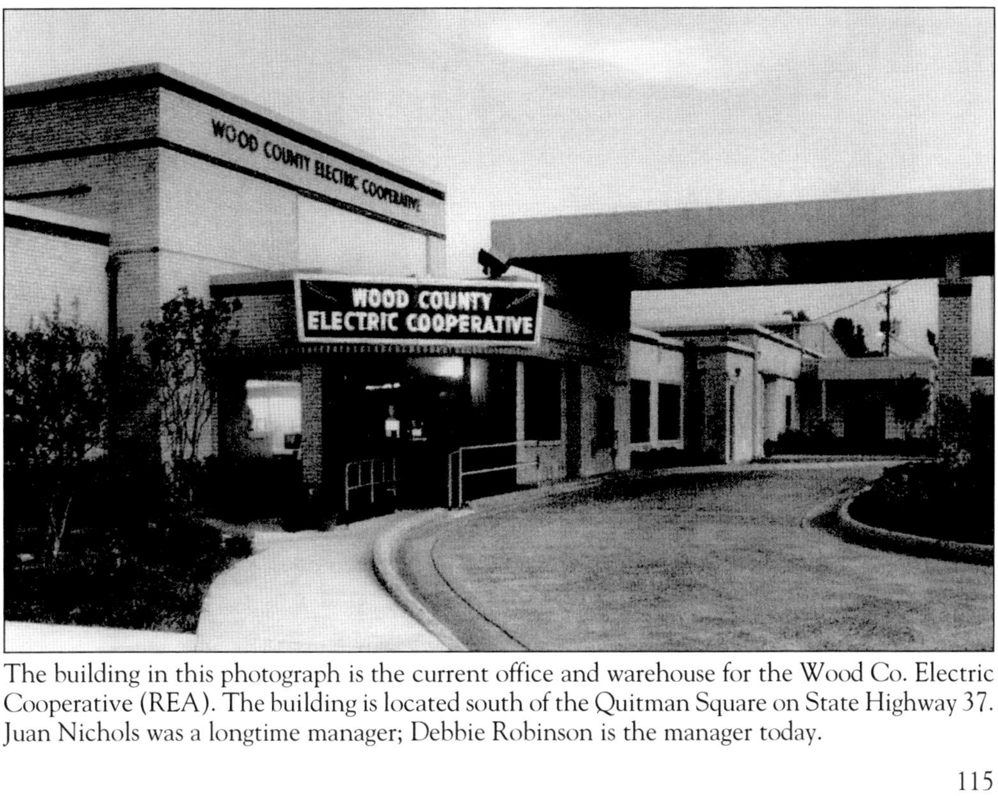

The building in this photograph is the current office and warehouse for the Wood Co. Electric Cooperative (REA). The building is located south of the Quitman Square on State Highway 37. Juan Nichols was a longtime manager; Debbie Robinson is the manager today.

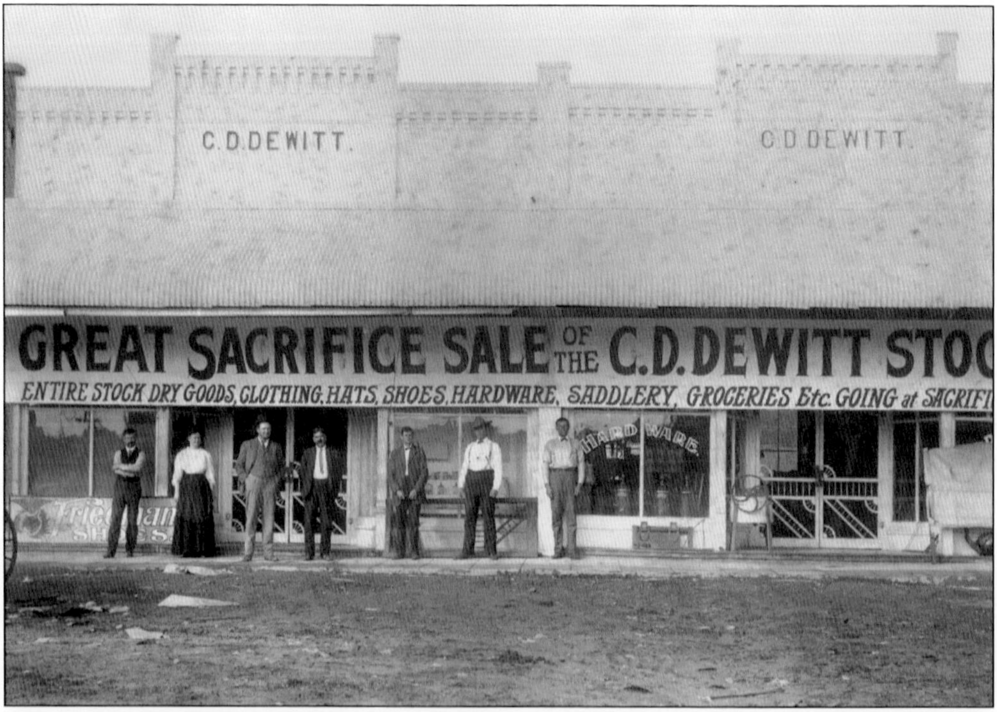

This general merchandise store, located in Alba, carried nearly every item a family might need. The exact date of this photograph is not known.

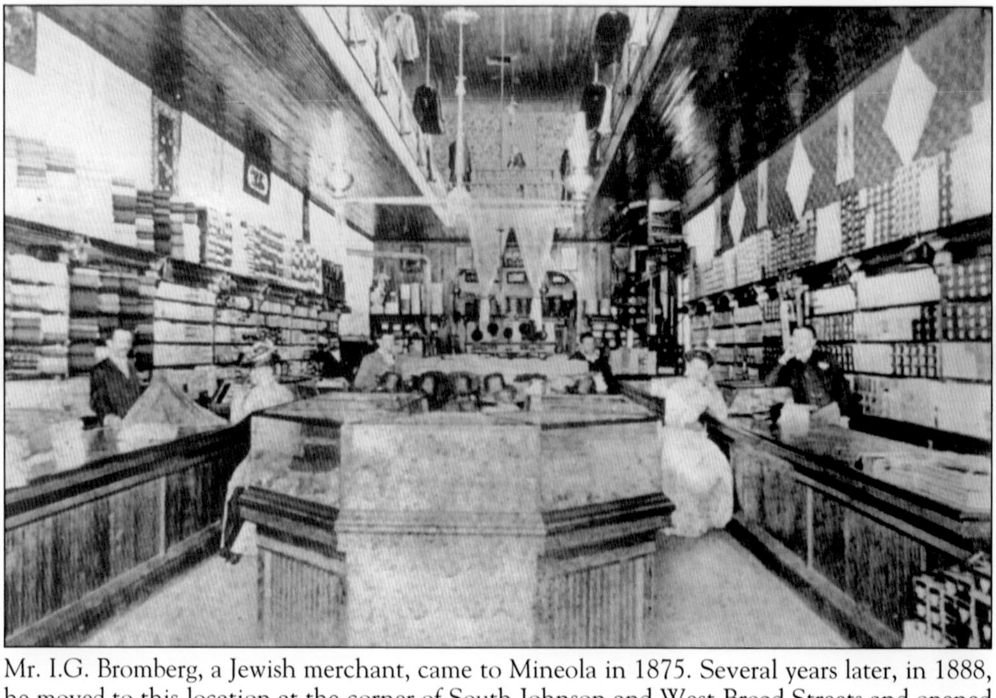

Mr. I.G. Bromberg, a Jewish merchant, came to Mineola in 1875. Several years later, in 1888, he moved to this location at the corner of South Johnson and West Broad Streets and opened his store with a varied assortment of merchandise. In the 1920s the Bromberg family moved to Dallas and bought an interest in E.M. Kahn Department Store.

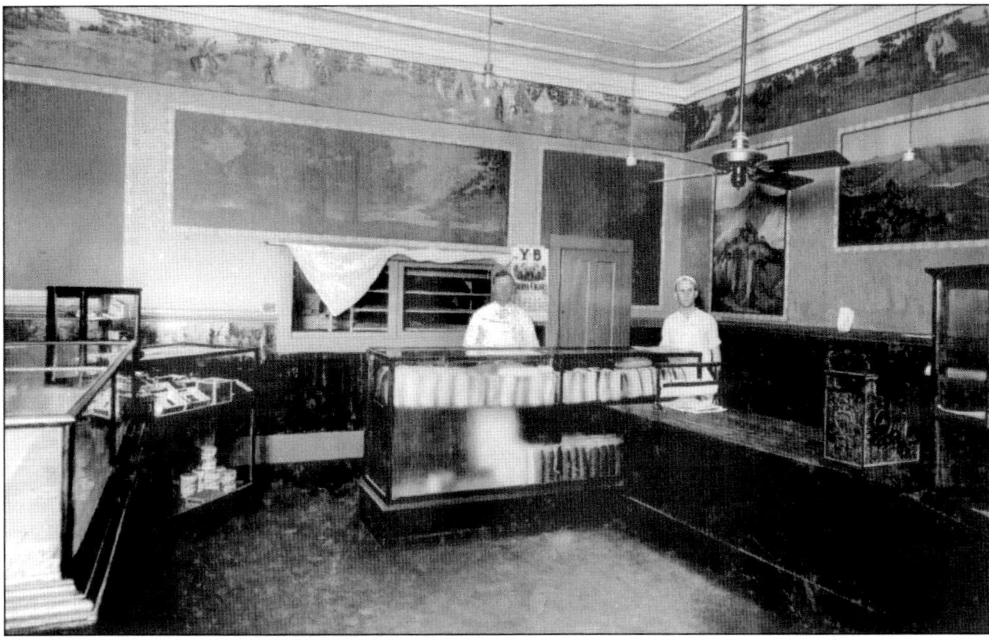

Mike Nuss owned and operated a bakery on South Johnson Street in Mineola for many years. The photograph shows the bakery as it appeared in the early 1930s. Its first location was on East Broad Street. The Nuss family farm was located north of the downtown area and was in the country at that time. Today, it has been sold and a residential area developed in its place.

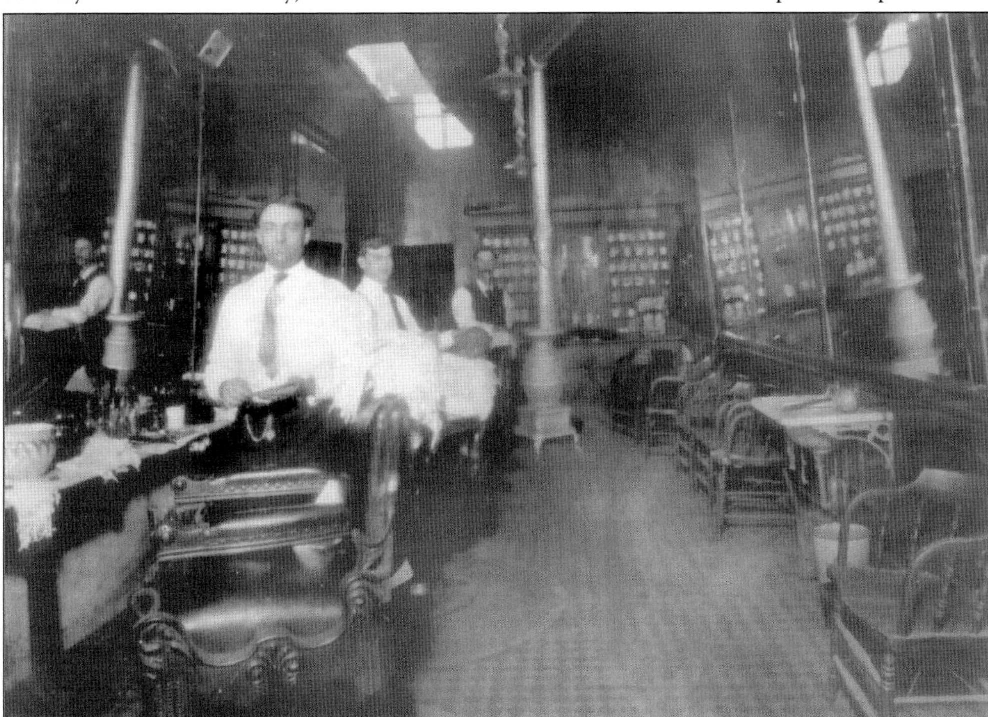

Mr. E.Q. Hearn is shown in his barbershop in downtown Mineola about 1920 with his employees and customers.

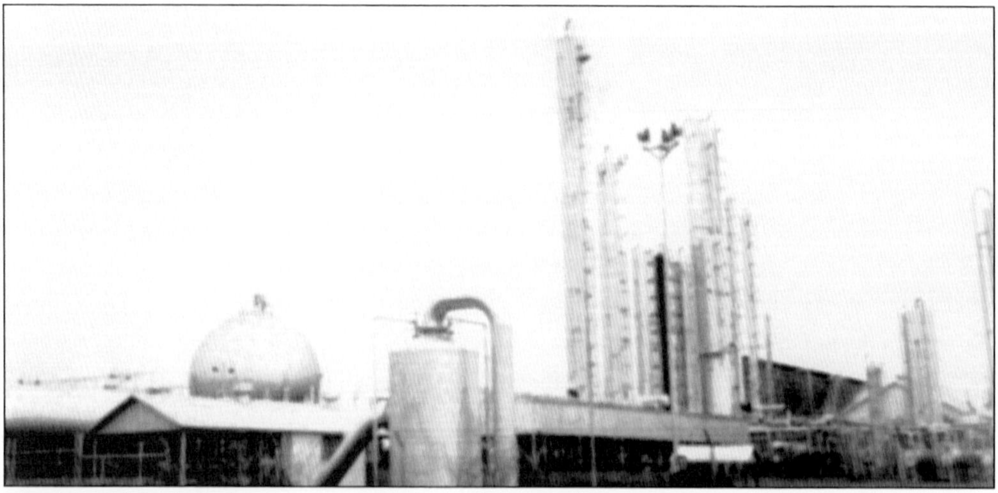

Humble Oil and Refining Company built this gas plant in Hawkins that employs several hundred people. When the oil boom hit in 1940, Humble Oil, now Exxon, built a residential section north of Hawkins for the use of its permanent employees.

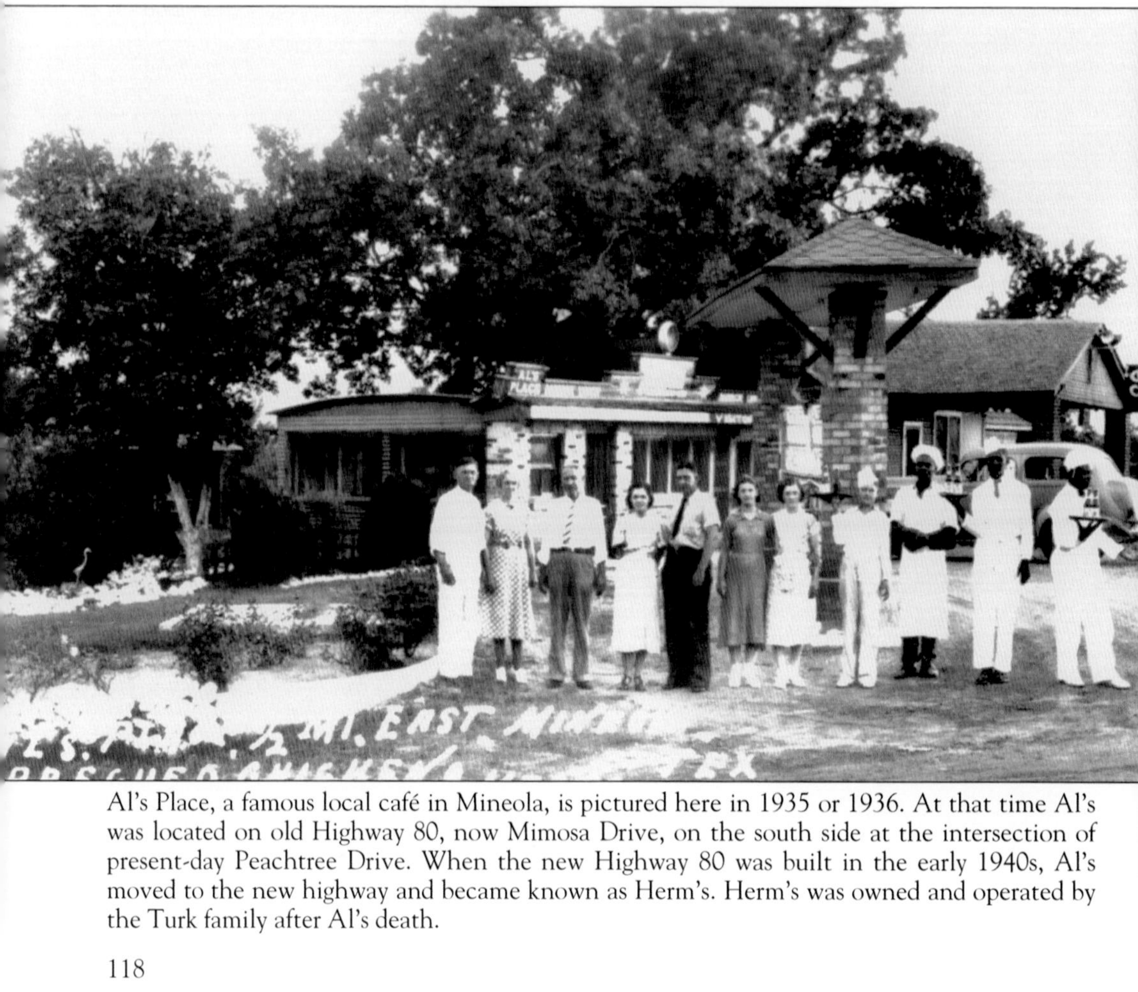

Al's Place, a famous local café in Mineola, is pictured here in 1935 or 1936. At that time Al's was located on old Highway 80, now Mimosa Drive, on the south side at the intersection of present-day Peachtree Drive. When the new Highway 80 was built in the early 1940s, Al's moved to the new highway and became known as Herm's. Herm's was owned and operated by the Turk family after Al's death.

Washing clothes became "easy" with the new modern washing machines shown in this photograph. This washateria in Quitman, c. 1940, was located on the south side of the square across from the courthouse. Local residents are using this new equipment to do their laundry. The washateria was owned and operated by Hiram Gill from the mid-1940s to the mid-1950s.

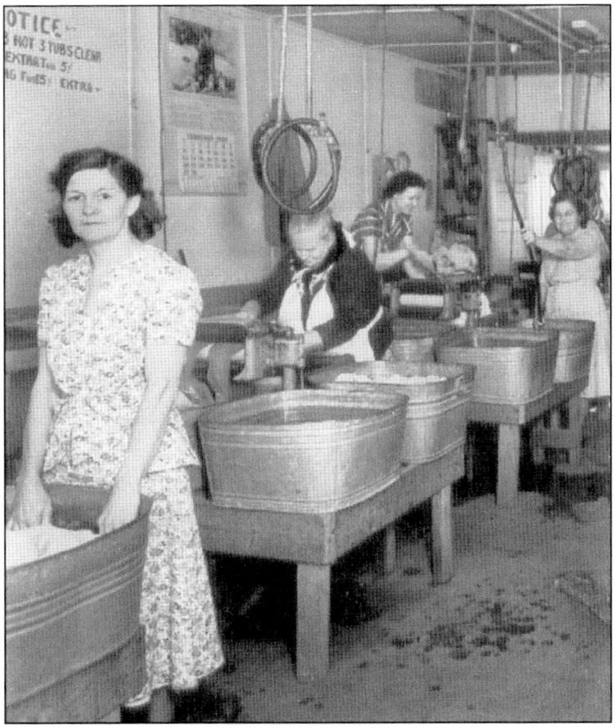

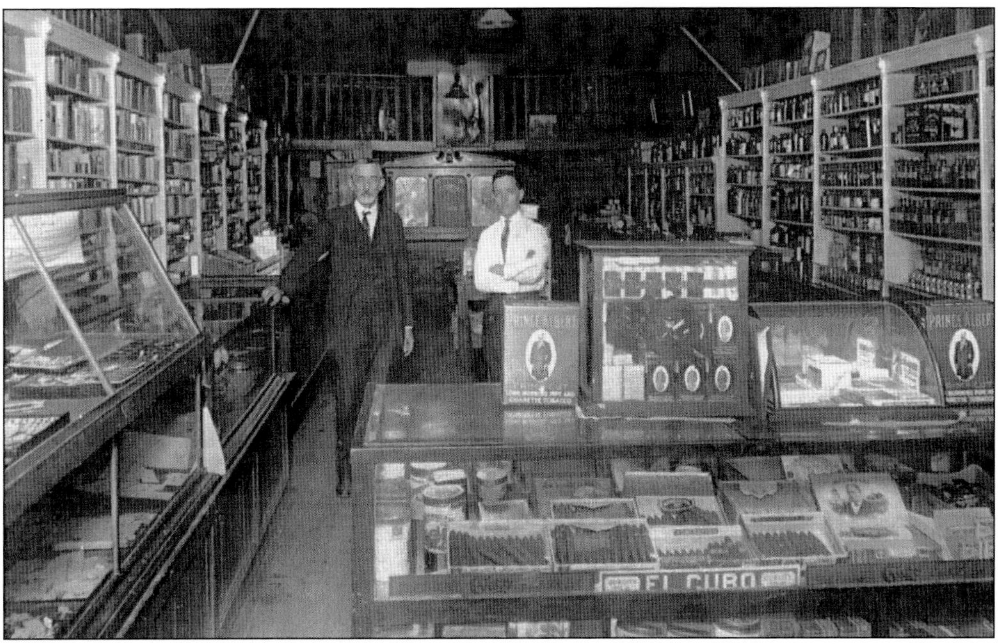

This drugstore, owned and operated by the Coleman family, was on South Johnson Street in Mineola. It was established in 1902 by Dr. W.J. Coleman and his son Charles D. Coleman, a pharmacist. In approximately 1933 a clinic was opened in the back of the story and the operating room was on the first floor. Upstairs were patients' rooms and nurses' offices. The clinic closed when World War II began, and the drugstore closed in 1964 due to the declining health of Charles D. Coleman.

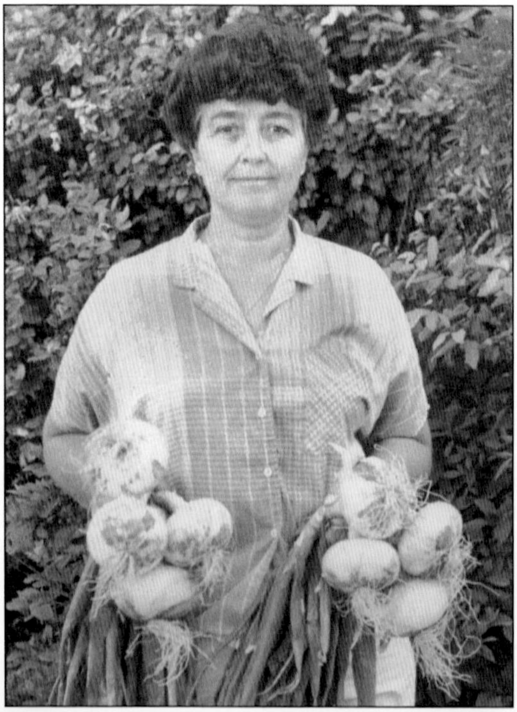

Farming and agriculture crops have always been the backbone of the economy of Wood County. Not only are agriculture products grown and sold, but many families even today have gardens and orchards for their personal use. These prize onions were grown in the county and were shown in the *Wood County Democrat*.

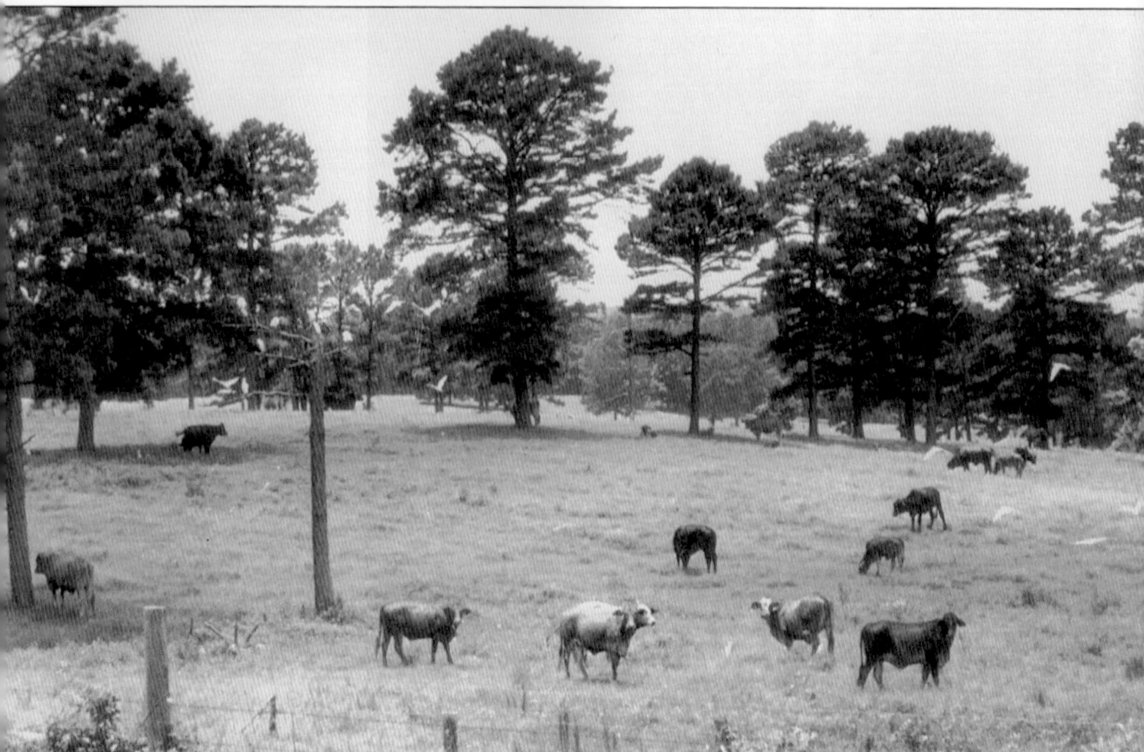

Cattle graze in Wood County pasture. Even today, cattle raising is still a vital part of the agricultural economy.

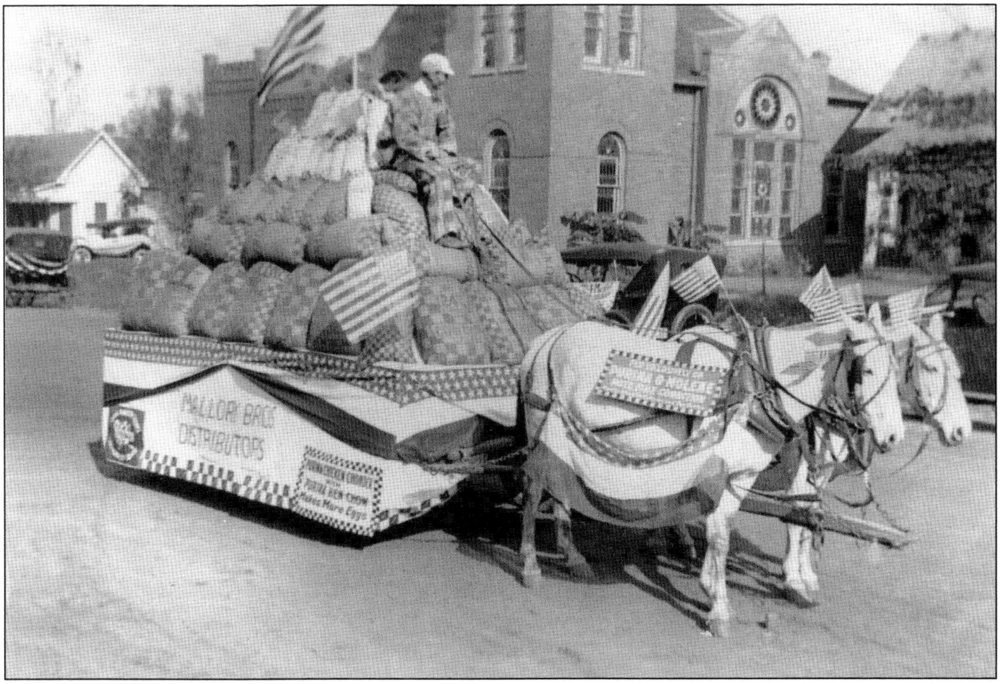

Wood County citizens were very patriotic and always celebrated national holidays such as July 4th and Armistice Day. This *c.* 1930 scene shows a parade entry from local Mineola business Mallory Bros. Distributors with sacks of Purina Feed, mules, and an American flag prominently displayed on the float.

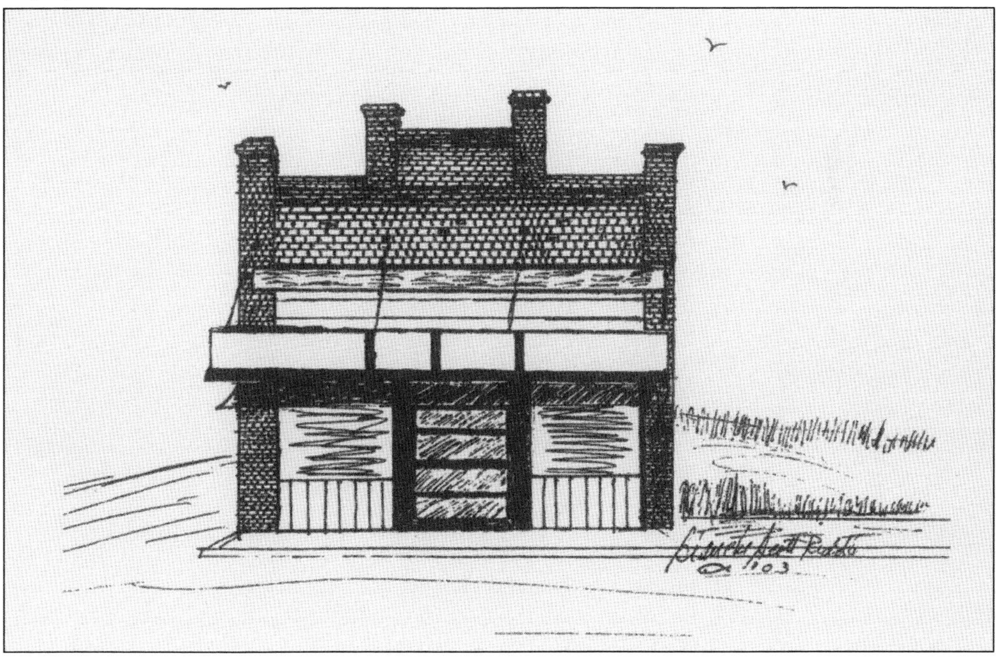

The building in this photograph was constructed in 1888 by German merchant John Grimm on Franklin Street (Smokey Row) in Winnsboro. The building was used as a grocery store and café. The tale goes that the infamous Bonnie and Clyde ate here. The building was torn down in 2003.

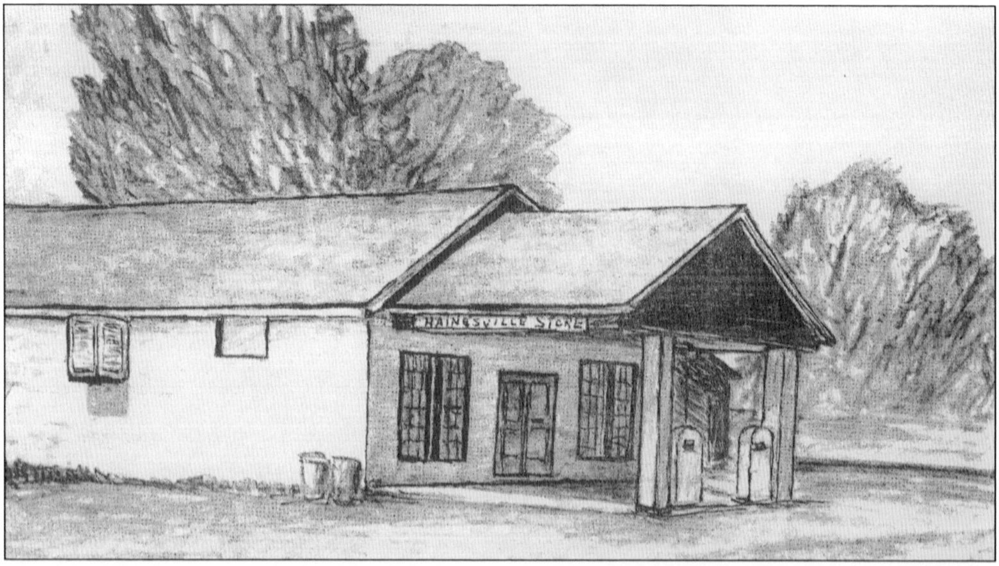

The Hainesville Store is located at the intersection of Farm to Market Roads 49 and 778 and was, for many years, a local landmark in the community. Buddy Tucker, a longtime resident, owned and operated the store for several years. Today, it has been bought by the Hainesville Baptist Church and is used for church youth activities.

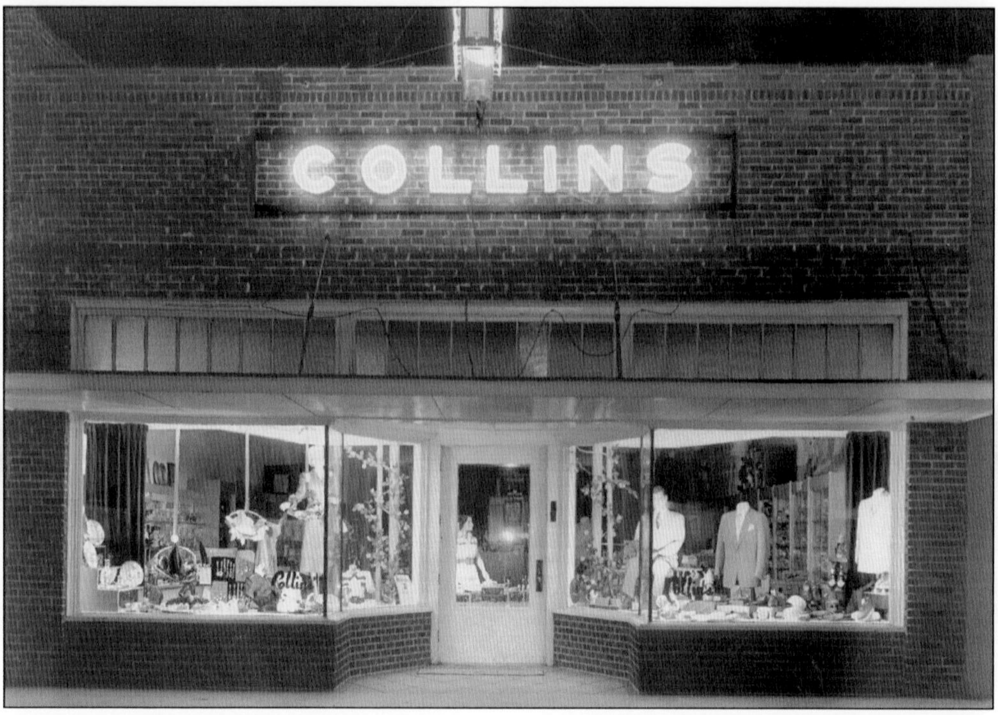

The T.A. Collins family opened its new store on Broad Street in downtown Mineola in 1950, having just purchased the Brooks Shop. Prior to that the family had sold men's clothing in its dry cleaning shop. Wayne Collins, the son of Mr. and Mrs. T.A. Collins, returned to Mineola after completing college and serving in the Navy during World War II to help run the business. In the 1990s Wayne closed the Mineola and Tyler stores.

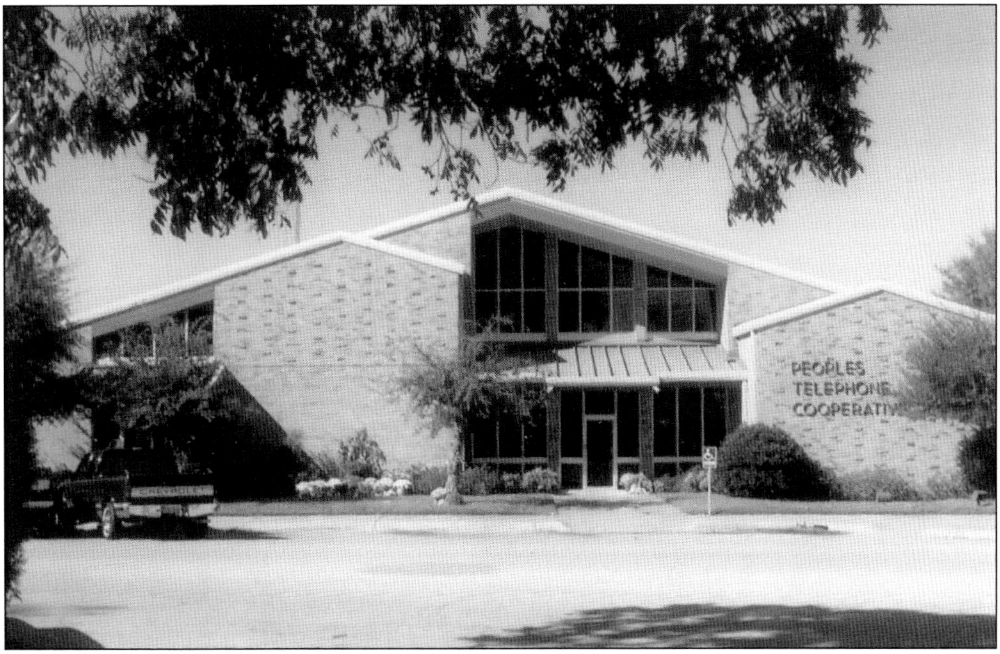

The first pole for Peoples Telephone Cooperative was set at the Golden Exchange on August 13, 1954, marking the beginning of a telephone system built in Wood, Hopkins, and Franklin Counties. The Cooperative is on the west side of the square in Quitman and has grown from 263 members to 13,500 members today. It includes 2 subsidiaries, Peoples Communication and Peoples Wireless, and 13 exchanges.

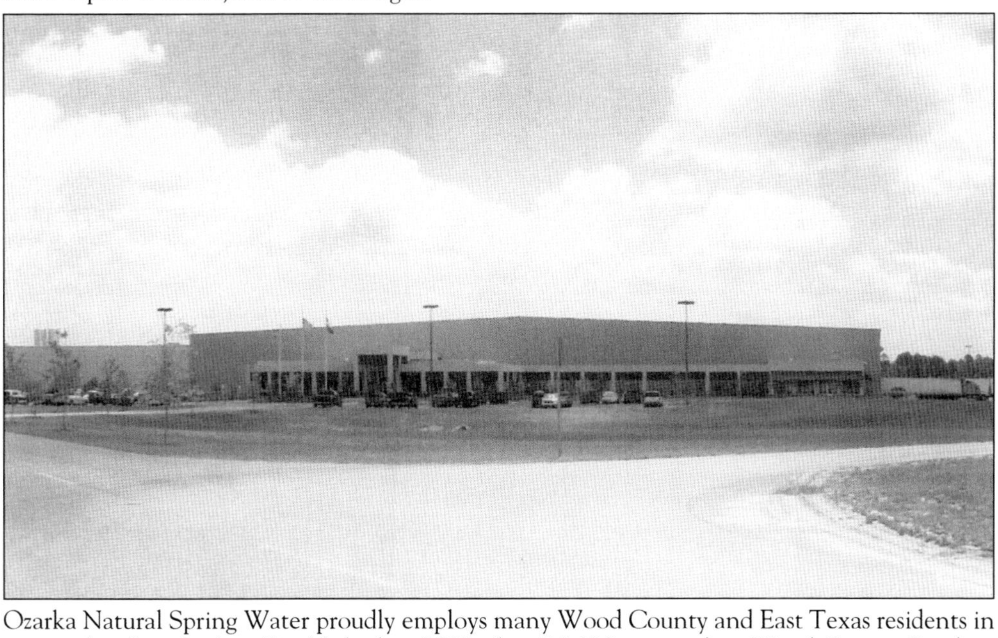

Ozarka Natural Spring Water proudly employs many Wood County and East Texas residents in its new bottling facility. Established in 2001, the 415,000-square-foot Wood County Bottling Facility employs 105 people. As an involved corporate citizen and a responsible manufacturer producing a healthy product, Ozarka works hard to ensure that it has a positive impact in the community and on the environment surrounding its springs and facilities.

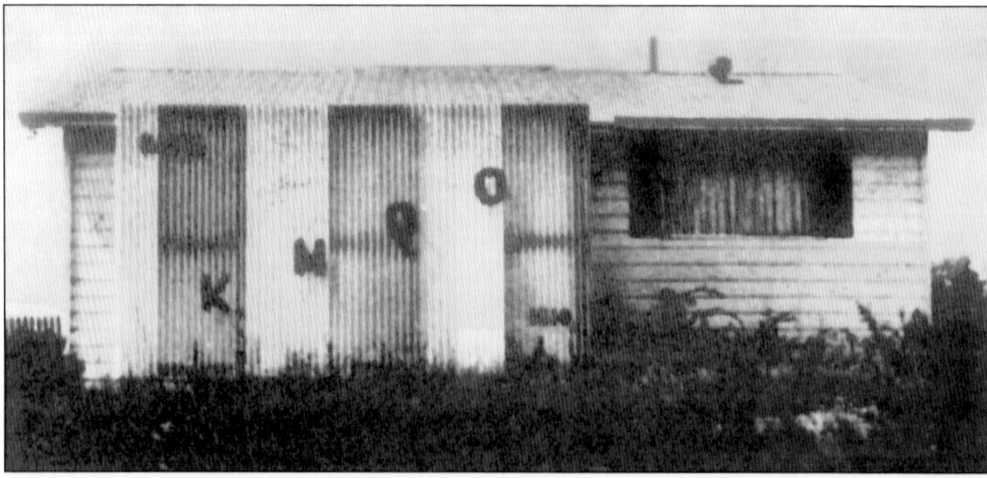

Shown in this photograph is the first building for the Radio Station KMOO, which began operation in September 1963. This was the first local station in the county and made Mineola and the whole county very proud. It was owned and operated by Sam Curry for many years and today is owned and operated by Jason Hightower.

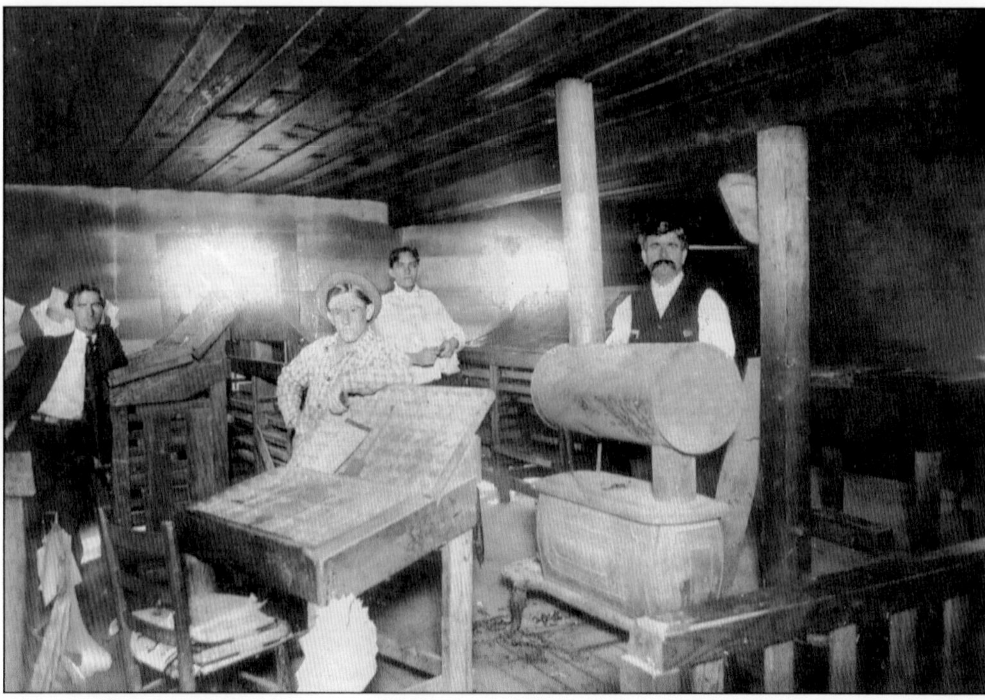

The *Wood County Democrat* was established in 1893, and this picture is believed to have been taken around the turn of the century. The Quitman area has had six different newspapers. The *Wood County Democrat* is still in operation and located on the north side of the square across from the courthouse in Quitman.

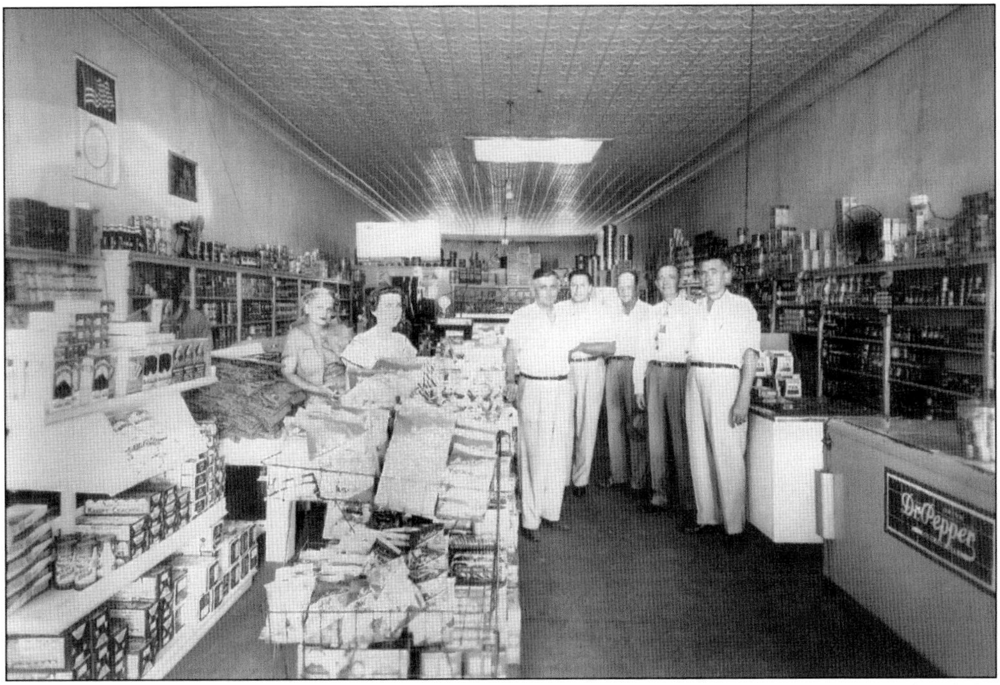

The Cathey Grocery Store, owned by the Cathey family, was located on the north side of the square in Quitman. This photograph was taken in the 1940s.

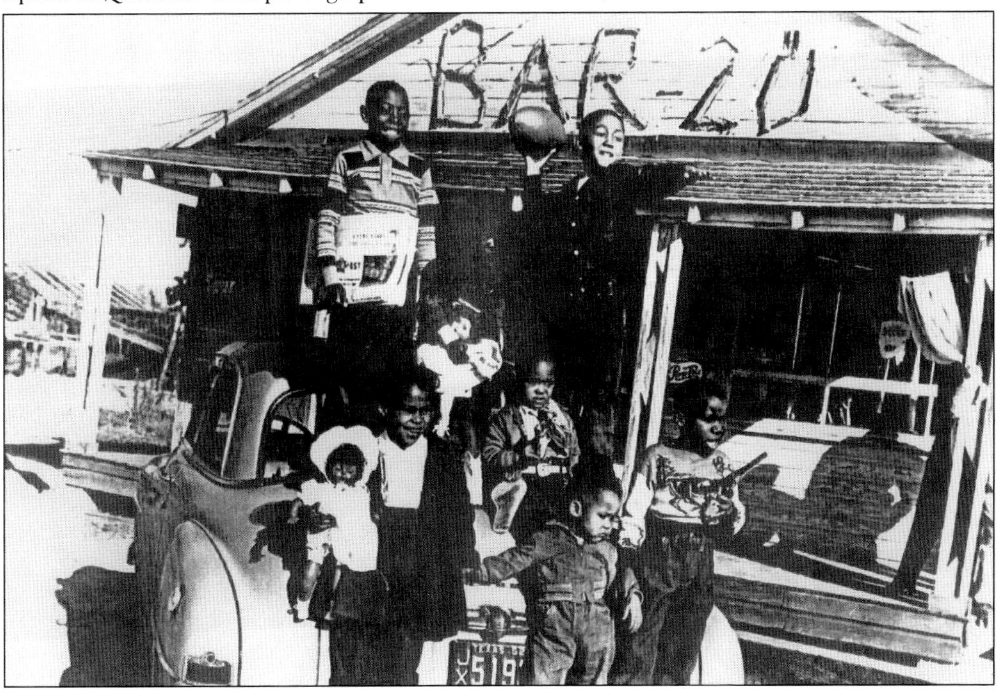

The Bar 20 Store in south Mineola was owned and operated by the Hickman family. The first store was built in 1937, but that store burned and was rebuilt by R.C. Hickman in 1945 after his discharge from the U.S. Army. R.C. is quoted as saying "when I was in the Service, I sent all my money home to my Mother."

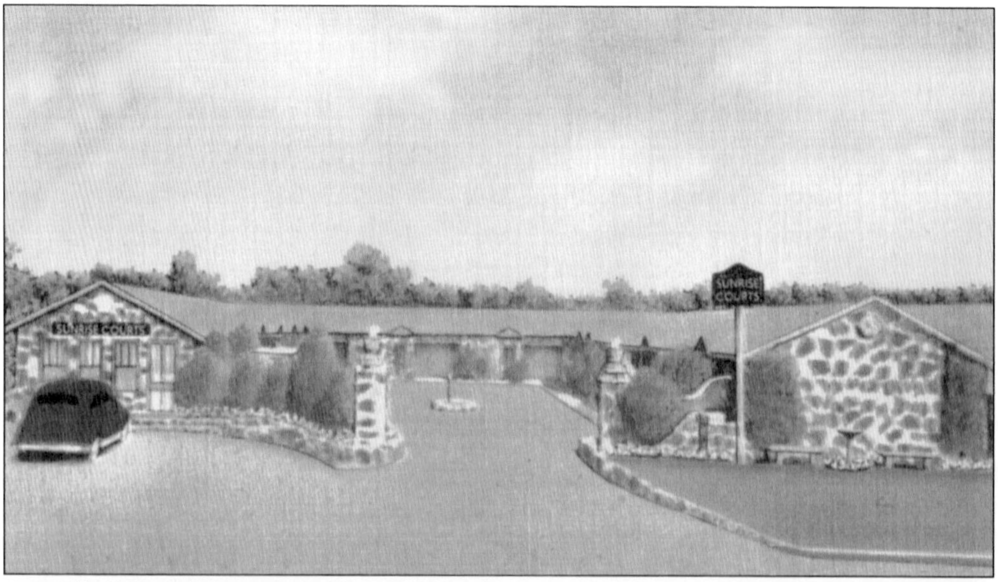

Owned by Mr. and Mrs. H.R. White, the Sunrise Courts in Mineola pictured here represented the early motels for travelers. This postcard shows a postmark of January 25, 1951 and is addressed to Dr. Dorothy Darling in Gary, Indiana.

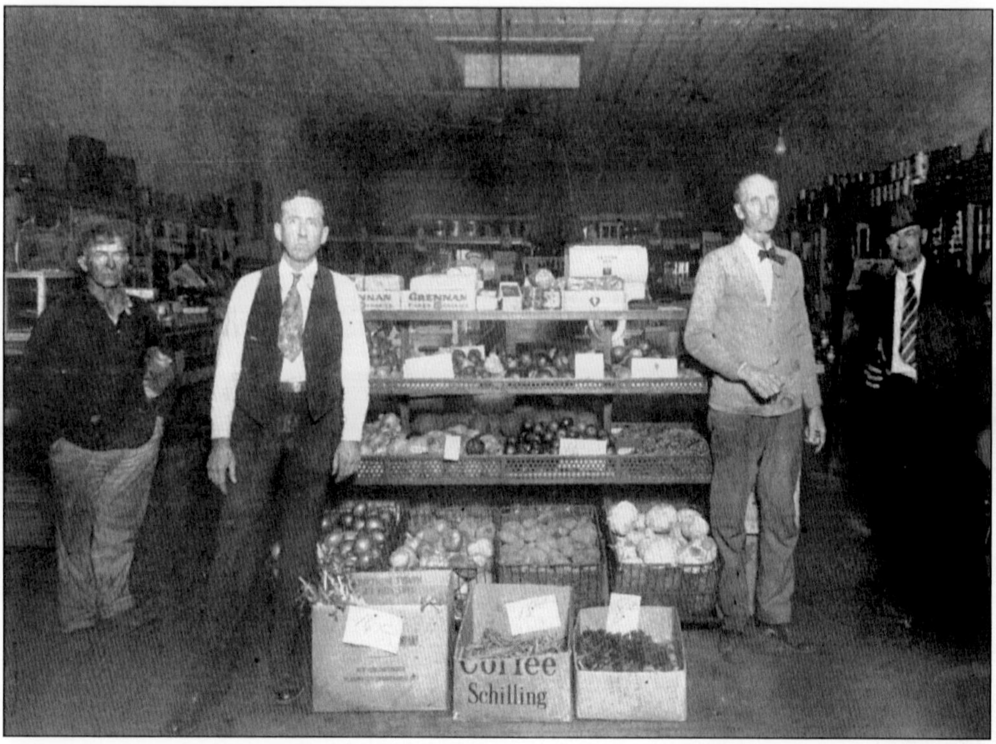

The W.D. Williams Grocery Store was located on the north side of West Broad Street in downtown Mineola. Mr. Williams provided home delivery for his customers and it was an expected service. His daughter Vivian delivered the grocery orders.

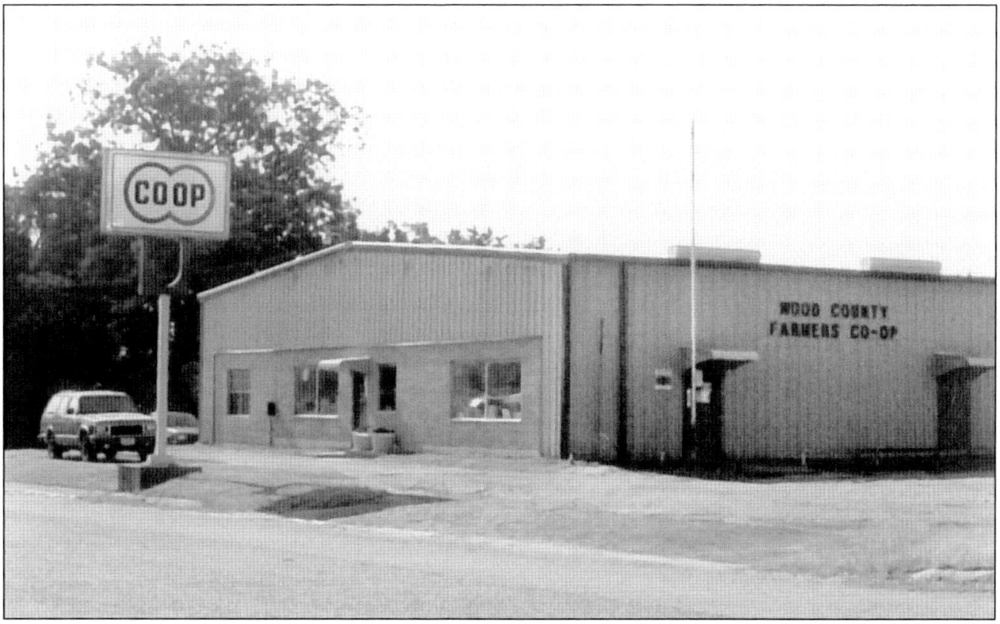

The Wood County Farmers Cooperative was organized on August 9, 1935. Over 100 farmers joined their efforts to purchase the Wadell Conley and Co. The first directors of the Co-op were J.A. Blalock, J.B. Ziegler, J.W. Reich, H.D. Ingram, W.A. Shurley, M.P. Matheson, H.S. Cathey, J.W. Weems, and J.H. Gilbreath. The co-op sells fertilizers, poison, feed, seed, farm supplies, veterinarian supplies, and horse tack.

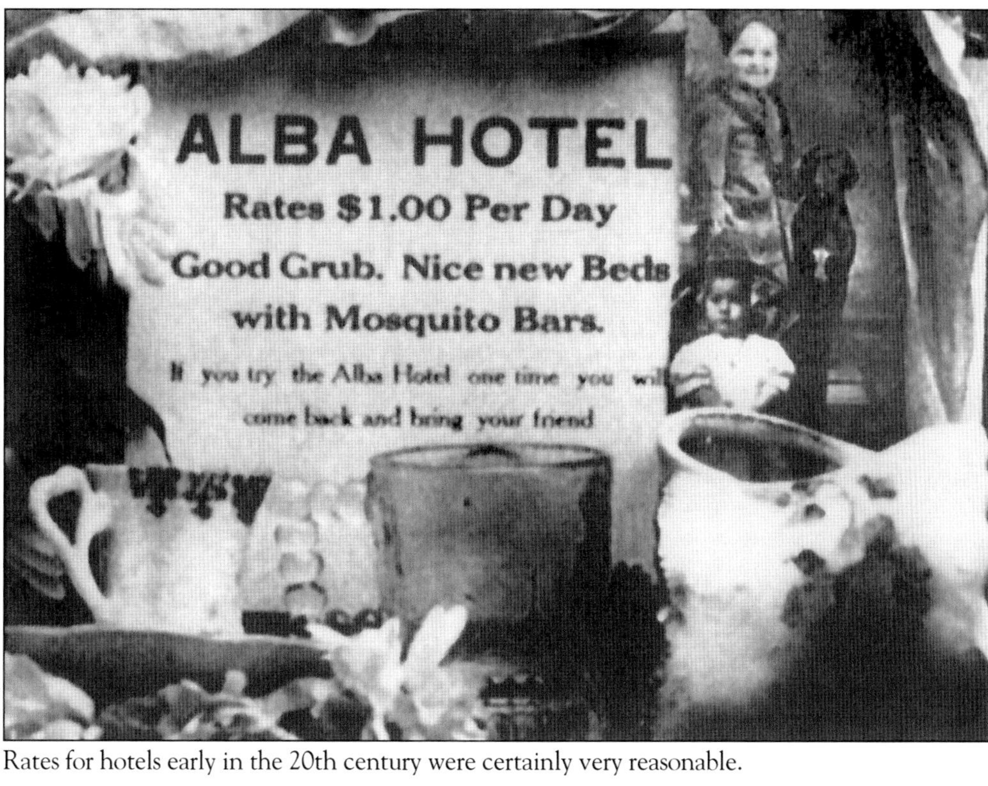

Rates for hotels early in the 20th century were certainly very reasonable.

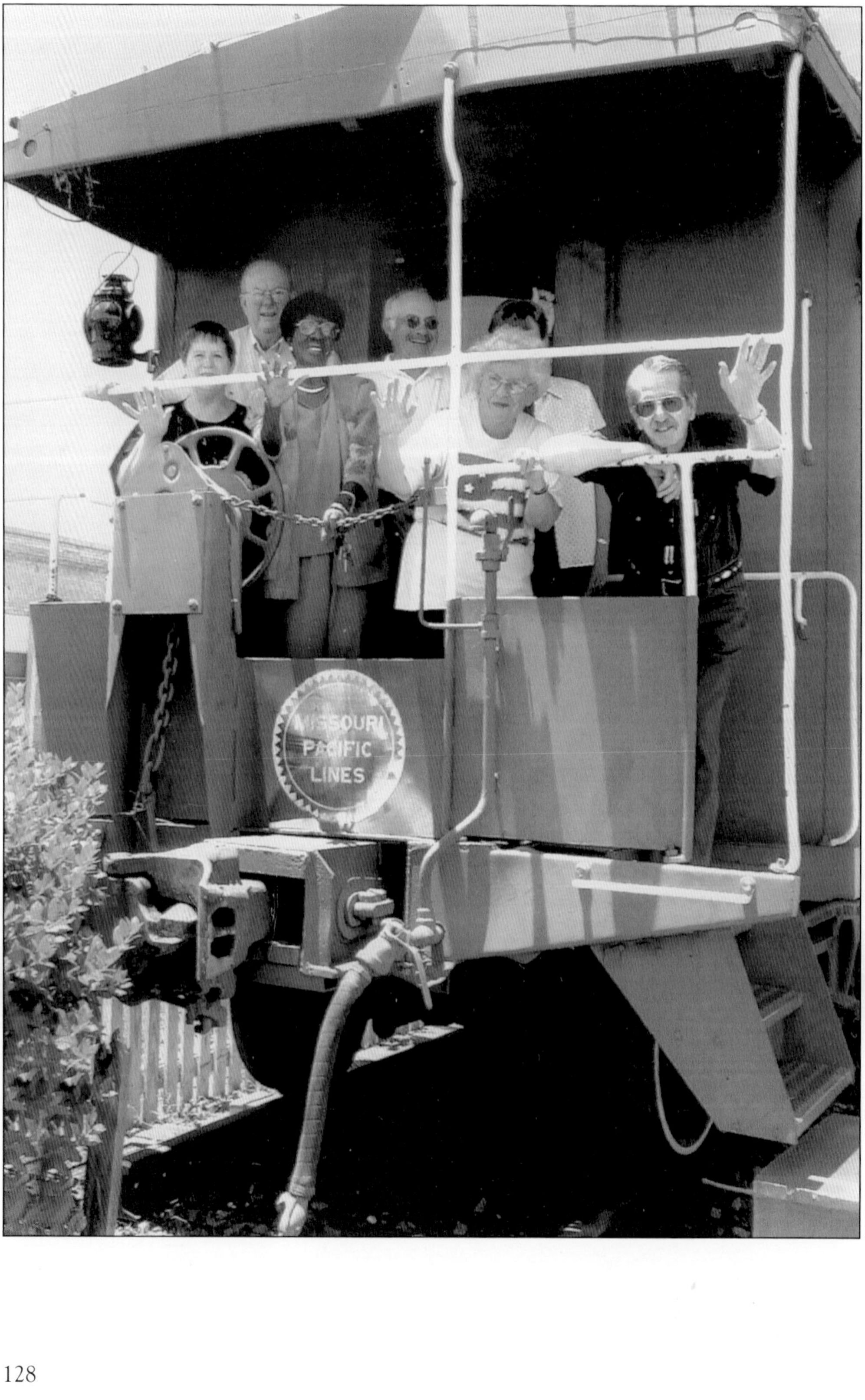
MISSOURI
PACIFIC
LINES